A Photographic Field Guide to

BIRDS OF SOUTH INDIA

Om Books International

First published in 2024 by

Om Books International

Corporate & Editorial Office
A-12, Sector 64, Noida 201 301
Uttar Pradesh, India
Phone: +91 120 477 4100
Email: editorial@ombooks.com
Website: www.ombooksinternational.com

Sales Office
107, Ansari Road, Darya Ganj,
New Delhi 110 002, India
Phone: +91 11 4000 9000
Email: sales@ombooks.com
Website: www.ombooks.com

ISBN: 978-81-19750-58-0

Printed in India

10 9 8 7 6 5 4 3 2 1

A Photographic Field Guide to

BIRDS OF SOUTH INDIA

CONTENTS

The external boundary as shown in this map, may not be authentic or exact.

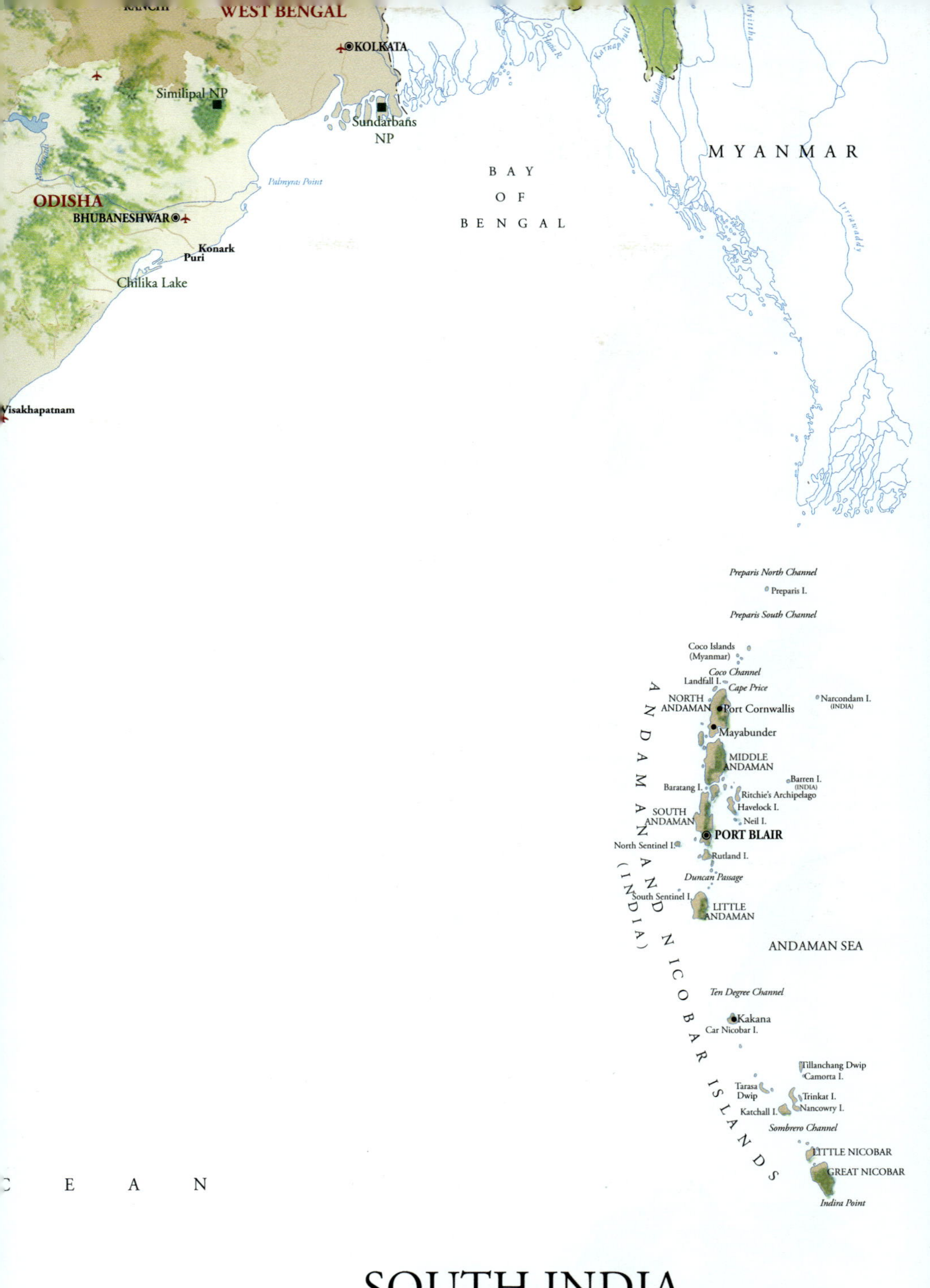

SOUTH INDIA

Scale:- 1 : 7,200,000 (1 Centimetre = 72 Kilometre)

Km. 100 50 0 100 200 300 400 500 Km.

INTRODUCTION

Great Eared Nightjar

Historically, the Vindhyas were regarded as the boundary between North and South India. As per legend, the Vindhyas were so much higher than the Himalayas that they obstructed the sun. The great sage Agastya on his journey south, asked Vindhya to lie prostrate till he returned in order to facilitate his passage. Agastya settled in the south, and Vindhya, true to its word, never grew further – an allegory to the actual crossing of the Vindhyas by Agastya, a prominent sage of North India, for the first time in history.

Geographically, the inverted triangle at the base of the subcontinent capped with the Vindhya and Satpura Ranges and the Tapti and Mahananda Rivers form the peninsula of Southern India. Within it lie the states of Andhra Pradesh, Telangana, Karnataka, Tamil Nadu and Kerala, and the Union territories of Lakshadweep, and Puducherry. To the west is the Arabian Sea, and on the east is the Bay of Bengal. On the south lies the boundless Indian Ocean.

Yellow-throated Bulbul

At its heart is the Deccan Plateau (a colonial distortion of dakshina or dakkhin, meaning south), said to have been formed by massive volcanic eruptions 90 million years ago during the Cretaceous Period. More than 25 million years later, the basalt beds of the Deccan were laid that separated the subcontinent from the ancient continent of Gondwanaland.

Parallel to the western coast and the Arabian Sea are the Sahyadri Mountains, also referred to as the Western Ghats. The range runs 1,600 km north to south from the Dang region of Southern Gujarat, almost reaching the southern tip of India – Kanyakumari. Designated as a UNESCO World Heritage site, this ecological 'hot-bed' has an overwhelming diversity of plants, butterflies, reptiles and mammals. Its bird list alone crosses 600 species and over 350 globally threatened species occur in the region.

Blue-cheeked Bee-eater

Mirroring this, along the eastern coast, lies a lower and discontinuous mountain range referred to as the Eastern Ghats. Starting from Northern Odisha, it runs through Andhra Pradesh and on to Tamil Nadu, and taking in parts of Karnataka and the Wayanad region of Kerala.

The Nilgiri Mountains run in a crescent almost corresponding to the borders of Tamil Nadu, Northern Kerala and Karnataka, and are an eastern arm of Western Ghats that extend to the low-lying hills of the Eastern Ghats – the Tirupati and Anaimalai Hills.

The Deccan Plateau slopes gently to the east allowing its four major rivers – Godavari, Mahanadi, Krishna and Kaveri – to empty into the Bay of Bengal. The three major river deltas of South India, Kaveri, Godavari and Krishna, are the most fertile regions and called the rice bowls of South India.

Painted Bush-quail

Climate

The climate of South India (except for the hilly regions) is mostly tropical with little difference between summer and winter temperatures. April and May are the hottest months of the year.

Northern Shoveler

Black-winged Stilt

The monsoons play an important role in the climate of this region with heavy rainfall between June and October. The monsoon rises from the Arabian Sea and hits the subcontinent along the Western Ghats and Kerala. It then moves north to the Konkan Coast and areas lying west of the Western Ghats. The Coromandel Coast on the east however lies in a 'rain shadow' and does not receive rains from the southwest monsoons but instead has rainfall from November to early March caused by the northeast monsoons.

The months from March to June are hot and dry with the temperatures rising to 40°C. Minimum temperatures rarely drop below 10°C.

Blue-tailed Bee-eater

Forest types

The Arabian Sea Coast and the Western Ghats consist of tropical forests. Moist forests are found along the coast. Moist deciduous forests are found in the eastern and northeastern parts of the plateau. The southern Western Ghats comprise deciduous forests that are situated at intermediate heights. These dry forests stretch over an area of 240,200 sq km which are home to *Hardwickia binate* and *Albizia amara* trees that are different from the teak and sal found in other parts of the Deccan. Apart from teak in the north, other trees include *Boswellia serrata, Lannea coromandelica, Albizia lebbeck* and *Anogeissus*. The west, south and southeast parts mainly have thorn scrub forests, which are drier and depend on the rainfall of the Western Ghats. Scrub has also taken over where forests have been denuded.

Asian Fairy-Bluebird

Wetlands are abundant in the region, including freshwater, saline and brackish. These include lakes, backwaters, saline flats, mangroves and local water tanks which provide staging points to migratory birds and breeding grounds for the resident population. Grasslands are fast disappearing but a few still exist, mostly in the eastern part. The seas on both the coasts are excellent for gulls and terns and more and more pelagic species are being sighted.

The region also boasts of some of the famous national parks, sanctuaries and protected areas in India. These include Periyar National Park, Kalakkad-Mundanthurai and Nagarjunsagar-Srisailam Tiger reserves. The Nilgiri Biosphere Reserve is spread over the states of Karnataka, Kerala and Tamil Nadu. Parks in the vicinity of the Nilgiris include Mudumalai National Park, Bandipur National Park, Nagarhole National Park, Silent Valley National Park, Wayanad Wildlife Sanctuary and Sathyamangalam Wildlife Sanctuary. The Anaimalai Ranges have the Eravikulam National Park, Chinnar Wildlife

Asian Koel

Pheasant-tailed Jacana

Sanctuary and the Parambikulam Wildlife Sanctuary. The main wetlands include Ranganathittu Bird Sanctuary, Kumarakom Bird Sanctuary, Nelapattu and Pulicat bird sanctuaries. The Pulicat Lake in Andhra Pradesh and Pichavaram in Tamil Nadu are other protected sites. The Vembanad Lake, Ashtamudi Lake and the Kayamkulam Lake are part of the famed backwaters of Kerala.

Birdwatching in South India

Bay Owl

Andhra Pradesh and Telangana

Sri Lankamalleswara Wildlife Sanctuary is located in the Kadapa District and is best known for being the only habitat to India's rarest bird, Jerdon's Courser. This nocturnal bird is extremely difficult to find.

Uppalapadu Bird Sanctuary is located near the city of Guntur, and is famous for waterbirds that use village tanks for nesting. One can see hundreds of Spot-billed pelicans which nest in artificial trees constructed to provide them with nesting sites.

Rollapadu Wildlife Sanctuary, near the city of Kurnool, was set up to protect the highly endangered Great Indian Bustard, which might have disappeared from the area.

Pulicat Sanctuary in the Nellore District is best known for sighting the Greater Flamingo and is one of the largest brackish water ecosystems. Several waterbirds can be seen here.

Kolleru Bird Sanctuary is a Ramsar site well known for its migratory waterbirds.

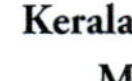

Magpie Robin

Kerala

Munnar is a picturesque hill station located 125 km from the nearest airport of Kochi. Its short grasslands make it a fecund hunting ground for many endemic species like the Nilgiri Wood Pigeon, Nilgiri Pipit, Grey-headed Bulbul, Black-and-orange Flycatcher, Broad-tailed Grassbird, Crimson-backed Sunbird and the Kerala Laughingthrush.

Eravikulam National Park, near Munnar, is primarily famous for the endangered Nilgiri Tahr. Spread over 97 sq km, this park is famous for the Jungle Bush Quail, Fairy Bluebird and a host of raptors.

Chinnar Wildlife Sanctuary is mostly scrub forest and a great place to see the endangered Giant Grizzled Squirrel.

Thattekad Bird Sanctuary is a small 25 sq km sanctuary, close to Kochi. Officially known as Dr Salim Ali Sanctuary, it is becoming increasingly popular as a birding hotspot. Highlights include Crimson-throated Barbet, Bay Owl, Red Spurfowl, Sri

Lanka Frogmouth, Great Eared Nightjar, Eastern Grass Owl and Great Hornbill. It boasts of a huge checklist of over 400 birds.

Kumarakom Bird Sanctuary is a large wetland close to the Vembanad backwater labyrinth, and is a good place to see wetland birds like bitterns.

Malabar Trogon

Tamil Nadu

Anamalai Tiger Reserve, earlier known as the Indira Gandhi National Park, consists of the Anamalai Hills of Tamil Nadu as well as the Nelliyampathy Ranges of Kerala. The best birding spot is around the Topslip area (also called Valparai) and is a good place to see Black Baza, Blue-faced Malkoha and Indian Swiftlet.

Mudumalai National Park, was the first to be designated as a national park in South India. Located near Coimbatore, its habitat consists of tropical dry deciduous, tropical moist deciduous and southern tropical thorn, and this makes it amongst the most exciting birding destinations. It's known for the Grey Junglefowl, Green Imperial Pigeon and Alpine Swift.

Kerala Laughingthrush

Karnataka

Ootacamund or Ooty is a popular hill station and is the capital of the Nilgiris District, located at an altitude of 2,240 m. The soothing climate of the city attracts tourists all around the year. It is an excellent place to see the Nilgiri Laughingthrush, White-bellied Shortwing, Black-and-orange Flycatcher, Rusty-tailed Flycatcher as well as the Nilgiri Flycatcher.

Brahmagiri Wildlife Sanctuary is located in the Kodagu District of the Western Ghats. This sanctuary of 180 sq km has several rivers and streams that drain out into the Bay of Bengal or the Arabian Sea. It's well known for its vultures, the Nilgiri Wood Pigeon, Blue-winged Parakeet and the Small Sunbird.

Bannerghatta National Park is within striking distance of the bustling city of Bengaluru. This 104 sq km park has both dense forests as well as scrubland. It is an excellent place to see the endemic Yellow-throated Bulbul.

Ranganathittu Bird Sanctuary is located near the historical town of Srirangapatna. While it occupies only 69 sq km, it also plays host to an incredible number of waterbirds, both migratory as well as resident. It is the best place to observe pelicans.

Nagarhole National Park is located at a distance of 94 km from Mysore and has a checklist of over 350 birds. The critically endangered Grey-headed Fish Eagle, Malabar Grey Hornbill and the White-bellied Treepie are easily seen here.

Kali Tiger Reserve was recently formed by amalgamating the Anshi National Park and Dandeli Wildlife Sanctuary. Its excellent

Peregrine Falcon

Loten's Sunbird

Grey Junglefowl

Jacobin Cuckoo

forest cover along with heavy rainfall results in high density of birds and its checklist covers over 360 species. These include Malabar Grey Hornbill, Flame-throated Bulbul, Malabar Pied Hornbill and Black-naped Monarch. The area around Ganeshgudi is most favourable for birding.

Kudremukh National Park covers the thick hilly forested and shola areas of the Western Ghats near the coastal plains, spread over three districts. It is a good place to spot Jerdon's Nightjar.

Agumbe Rainforest is located in the Shimoga District and is known for its very heavy rainfall. It is a good place to spot the King Cobra and the Lion-tailed Macaque. Birds include Malabar Trogon, White-rumped Needletail and the Chestnut-headed Bee-eater.

Goa

Carambolim Lake is located near the Karmali Railway Station in North Goa. It is a good place to see Lesser Whistling ducks, Purple swamphens and Migratory Waterfowl.

Bhagwan Mahavir Wildlife Sanctuary is located next to the Dudhsagar Falls. It is haven for Western Ghat birds like the Malabar Trogon, Sri Lanka Frogmouth and the Flame-throated Bulbul.

Cotigao Wildlife Sanctuary, situated in south Goa, is known for its tall forests, which are home to the Heart-spotted Woodpecker, Malayan Heron and Velvet-fronted Nuthatch.

The maps in the book give the range of the species in the subcontinent. The red areas indicate resident birds. The blue areas denote non-breeding winter visitors.

Nilgiri Flycatcher

Green Bee-eater

PAINTED FRANCOLIN

Francolinus pictus Phasianidae

Size 31 cm

Voice Noisy when breeding (SW monsoon). Call a high-pitched, harsh grating 4- or 5-noted *khik…kheek…khee…khheeki*, quite similar to that of Black Francolin; may call every 20–30 seconds, for upto 40 minutes; often in duet

Range Most of India; south of range of Black Partridge; south of line from C Gujarat, N Madhya Pradesh, S Uttar Pradesh

Habitat Grasslands; scrubs; cultivation

Medium-sized, profusely marked bird. Distinguished from the female Black by lack of rufous hind-collar and white spots on underside. Rufous face; chestnut head and throat. Upperparts blackish-brown; neck and underparts densely spotted white; white rump and tail finely barred with black; yellowish orange legs. Female similar to male, but paler head and buff-white throat and no spurs on legs. Pairs or adults with young. Skulking, shy and secretive; not easily flushed. Rarely flies. Roosts in trees. Feeds on grain, grass and insects.

GREY FRANCOLIN

Francolinus pondicerianus Phasianidae

Size 34 cm

Voice Noisy. Call a very loud, high-pitched 2- to 3-noted *pat…ee…la*

Range Resident; all subcontinent, south of the Himalayan foothills

Habitat Open scrubs; grass; cultivation

Medium-sized, greyish-brown francolin with spear-shaped buff streaks. Pale face bordered with fine black gular-band; orange cheeks, throat and forehead. Upperparts grey-brown and rufous; buffy-rufous below; breast and abdomen greyish-buff with dark barring; mantle and wings chestnut with lighter streaking; fine cross-bars on throat and upper breast; fine black markings on abdomen and flanks.

COMMON QUAIL

Coturnix coturnix Phasianidae

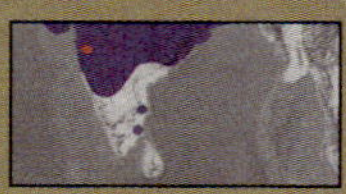

Size 20 cm

Voice Fluid, whistling *wet…me…lips* of male is common and familiar call

Range Resident; local migrant; breeds in Kashmir and parts of N and NE India; common in winter over the country

Habitat Cultivation; standing crop; grasslands

Smallish roundish bird, overall streaked brown with distinct white eye-stripe. Upperparts pale buff-brown, boldly marked; black to russet throat with stripe down throat centre and narrow stripe curving towards ear-coverts; black-and-white striped head. Rufous-buff breast with white shaft streaks; streaked flanks; long wings. Female has pale underparts, whitish belly, buffy throat; breast heavily streaked with black. Seen in pairs or small groups on ground, feeds on seeds, grain and small insects. Secretive; can only be seen when flushed. Usually located by its distinct call. Reluctant to fly. Nests in grass.

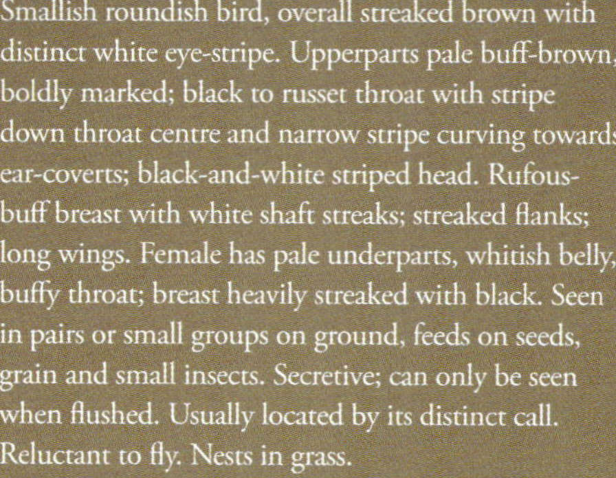

RAIN QUAIL

Coturnix coromandelica Phasianidae

Size 18 cm

Voice Call a loud, high-pitched, repeated, *whit…whit*

Range Subcontinent

Habitat Grasslands; crops

Small quail with distinct black-and-white head pattern similar to European but bolder. The male has buff breast with black 'anchor' breast-patch; diagnostic stripe on the crown and supercilium; white neck bordered with black; flanks streaked with black. Female very similar to the female Common, minus barring on primaries. Found in small groups. Nervous and jumpy. Feeds on grass and weed seeds, small insects and insect larvae. Nests in standing crops. Cultivated as a table bird.

♀

KING QUAIL

Coturnix chinensis Phasianidae

Size 14 cm

Voice High-pitched call of three descending notes

Range Widespread. Not found in the NW

Habitat Grasslands and scrubs

Overall dark brown bird with diagnostic slaty-blue breast and black throat-patch bordered with white band and black stripe; black eye-stripe; chestnut-red belly and undertail-coverts, black-and-white patterning on head, white lores, moustachial-patch and crescent-shaped gorget, bordered in black, and bright yellow legs. Female smaller and more evenly brown with a rusty-brown belly and breast barred black, narrower crown-stripe; slaty-grey breast-patch absent. Black beak and orangish-yellow legs. Shy, elusive and difficult to spot. Generally found in small coveys; flushes easily, but difficult to flush again. Nests on ground in sparsely-lined nests. Rarely seen.

♀

JUNGLE BUSH QUAIL

Perdicula asiatica Phasianidae

Size 17 cm

Voice Call a trilling, musical *tirri…tirri…*

Range All over India, to about 1,200 m in the outer Himalayas

Habitat Dense grass; scrubs; edges of forests

Very small, heavily barred back with whitish underparts, slightly barred with brown, rufous head; crown slightly mottled with brown-and-white; white supercilium and moustache; dark eyebrow-stripe bordered in white, coming down to nape; variegated wings. Upperparts mottled black, brown-and-yellow. Brown beak, black tip; orangish-yellow legs and feet. Small spurs also present.

♀

ROCK BUSH QUAIL

Perdicula argoondah Phasianidae

Size 17 cm

Voice Call a musical, ascending trill

Range W India from Haryana to S Kerala, Gujarat to Madhya Pradesh

Habitat Dry semi-desert; thorny scrubs

♀

Male similar to Jungle but with white underparts barred with black; rufous stripe above pale eyebrows; vermiculated beige and black underparts; pale undertail-coverts. Female has plain rufous face, whitish chin and pale supercilium. Small coveys feed under vegetation. Nests under rock cover. Feeds on grain, seeds and leaves, sometimes insects.

PAINTED BUSH QUAIL

Perdicula erythrorhyncha Phasianidae

Size 17 cm

Voice Calls *kirikee...kirikee*

Range Endemic resident: Eastern and Western Ghats, hills of C India

Habitat Low, hilly scrubs along forest margins

♀

Distinct-looking bird, easily recognised by big bold spots on brown upperparts, black face and white throat; rufous underparts and flanks, white scapular line and wing-coverts; black around eyes, forehead and chin; bright red bill and legs. Female not as bright-coloured and no black-and-white markings on head and brick-red below. Seen feeding in small groups on grass, seeds, weeds, grains and insects in the open, early mornings or late afternoons. Subspecies *P. e. erythrorhyncha* occurs in the Western Ghats in Maharashtra, Kerala and Tamil Nadu. Subspecies *P. e. blewitti* occurs in Maharashtra, Madhya Pradesh, Bihar, West Bengal and Odisha.

RED SPURFOWL

Galloperdix spadicea Phasianidae

Size 36 cm

Voice Loud cackling notes. Calls when flushed

Range From Uttar Pradesh terai south across Gangetic plains through the peninsula

Habitat Scrubs in forested, broken hilly country

stewarti

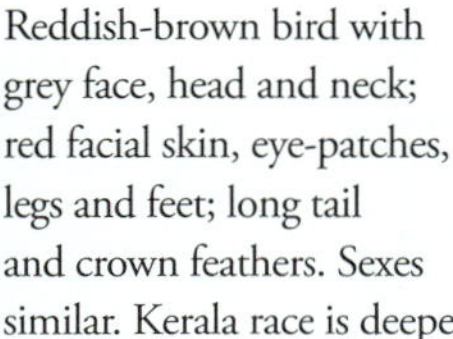

stewarti

Reddish-brown bird with grey face, head and neck; red facial skin, eye-patches, legs and feet; long tail and crown feathers. Sexes similar. Kerala race is deeper chestnut red. Male larger and darker with darker markings with one or two spurs. Shy; runs rapidly if disturbed, rarely taking to flight. Forages in small groups of two to five birds in open patches.

spadicea

PAINTED SPURFOWL

Galloperdix lunulata Phasianidae

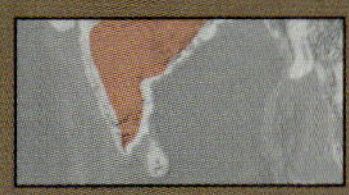

Size 32 cm

Voice Loud call of male reported

Range South of a line from Gwalior to Bengal; absent in Gujarat and Konkan; also Rajasthan

Habitat Dense thorn and bamboo jungles in broken hilly, rocky country

Colourful, medium-sized bird with dark brown upperparts, dark bill and grey legs. Black head and neck have luminous green sheen. Black tail. Male has finely white-barred black head and neck, white-spotted chestnut upperparts; underparts ochre with black flecks; mantle, rump and wing-coverts chestnut. Female uniform brown with paler throat and belly and sparse spotting. Extremely shy and timid, runs swiftly to hide in cover when disturbed. Seen in the shade of fruiting trees. Nests on ground.

RED JUNGLEFOWL

Gallus gallus Phasianidae

Size Male 65 cm; Female 42 cm

Voice Characteristic crow of male, shriller version of domestic. Other cackling sounds

Range The Himalayas, E Kashmir; E and C India, south to Narmada

Habitat *Sal* forests mixed with bamboo and cultivation patches

Both sexes resemble domestic bantam breeds. Male vibrant red-orange with combination of glossy blue-green, rich dark red, maroon-red, fiery orange, rufous and blackish brown feathers; deep red crown and neck; metallic green tail with long, drooping central feathers distinctive. Female has bright chestnut forehead, supercilium continuing to foreneck; reddish-brown plumage, vermiculated with fine black and buff. Seen in small parties, often several hens accompanying a cock; shy and skulking; emerges in clearings and on forest roads; flies up noisily when flushed.

GREY JUNGLEFOWL

Gallus sonneratii Phasianidae

Size Male 80 cm; Female 40 cm

Voice Loud crow of male distinctive. Calls *kuk…kuk…kkura…kuk*; noisy in early mornings, but intermittently calls during day. Rather vocal when breeding

Range Peninsula and S India, range coinciding with teak country

Habitat Mixed deciduous forests; forest clearings

Silvery game bird with pink legs, long tail and elongated neck. Male larger but similar in shape to Red, with gold streaks restricted to neck and wing-coverts, silver belly and black flight feathers. Female overall brown above and black with bold white streaks below. Wings not barred like Red. Feeds in pairs; often seen on roads in morning and evening. Shy, but confiding.

INDIAN PEAFOWL

Pavo cristatus Phasianidae

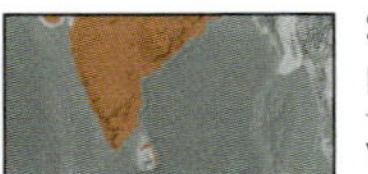

Size Male 110 cm (plus train); Female 95 cm

Voice Loud *may…yow* calls at dawn and dusk; also loud nasal calls and cackles. Very noisy during rains, when breeding

Range All subcontinent except Pakistan, upto about 2,000 m in the Himalayas

Habitat Forests; neighbourhood of villages and cultivated country

Best known for its exquisite train and plumage. Glistening blue neck and breast; wire-like crest and very long distinctive train an iridescent arrangement of multiple colours with ocelli; golden feathers on sides and back. When displayed, male's train spreads out in wide fan, showing off gold, brown, green, and black feathers. Female lacks blue neck and breast; more brown plumage; lacks long train. Familiar bird of India. Solitary or in small parties, several females with one or more males; wary in forested parts, rather tame and confiding.

FULVOUS WHISTLING-DUCK

Dendrocygna bicolor Dendrocygnidae

Tawny-coloured duck with long neck, blue-grey legs and bill. Dark brown wings edged with pale grey; dark cinnamon crown; dark rear neck-stripe; white flank feathers. Larger in size than Lesser, but otherwise similar. Sexes similar, male slightly larger. Feeds at night, on seeds of aquatic plants and grasses, grain; particularly fond of rice. Forages both on land and in water. Swims on the surface, sometimes tipping downward and sticking its head underwater. Extremely wary. Nests high in trees.

Size 51 cm

Voice Call a high-pitched *pe…wheeah*, usually when in flight

Range Scarce and declining breeding resident: NE India, Bangladesh. Rare elsewhere

Habitat Shallow freshwater or brackish marshes; flooded fields and pastures; irrigated rice fields

LESSER WHISTLING-DUCK

Dendrocygna javanica Dendrocygnidae

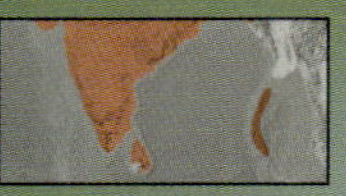

Size 35–45 cm

Voice Call a wheezy, whistling *seasick, seasick*, uttered in flight. Roosts can be quite noisy

Range Largely resident species distributed unevenly from the Pakistan lower river valleys eastwards across most of peninsular India, Nepal terai, Sri Lanka, Bangladesh

Habitat Still freshwater lakes, with plentiful vegetation. Occasionally seeks refuge in the ocean just outside surf area

juvenile

Smallish overall pale buff duck, with maroon-chestnut upperparts; crown darker grey-brown with golden-orange feather margins; chestnut uppertail-coverts; scaly pattern on back, large head, thin neck and long legs, inconspicuous yellow eye-ring. Dark brown, rounded wings with chestnut lesser wing-coverts. Sexes alike. Juvenile duller and paler. Nests in treeholes, abandoned bird nests and platforms of sticks. Gregarious bird, seen perching on tree branches near waterbodies. Feeds on seeds and other vegetation.

BAR-HEADED GOOSE

Anser indicus Anatidae

Size 75 cm

Voice Nasal, quite musical honking

Range Breeds only in Ladakh within Indian limits; winter visitor, commoner from Kashmir, S to C India and east across Gangetic plains to Assam; less common in south of Deccan

Habitat Rivers; large jheels

Silvery-grey and white bird with two horseshoe-shaped, brownish-black bars on back of white head. Body overall grey; dark hindneck and lower flanks; yellow legs, black-tipped yellow bill, white neck-stripe along back of neck, white tail-coverts and grey tail. Juvenile has black cap and lacks head stripes. In flight, the silvery-grey forewings contrast with the dark flight feathers. Feeds on grasses, roots, stems and other plant matter. Very gregarious.

COMMON SHELDUCK

Tadorna tadorna Anatidae

Size 61 cm

Voice Loud honks

Range Local, irregular winter visitor: Pakistan, NW, NE India

Habitat Rivers; lakes; salt pans and the coast

Large duck with white and chestnut body and glossy dark green head and neck. Broad chestnut breast-band that wraps around upper back; black flight feathers, back and belly-stripes; chestnut vent; green speculum; dark pink legs and bright red bill. Male and female look alike, but, female generally duller and smaller. Breeding male has swollen red bill knob. Generally feeds on larvae as well as aquatic animals, plant material, seeds, small fish, snails and crabs.

KNOB-BILLED DUCK

Sarkidiornis melanotos Anatidae

♀

juvenile

Size 55–75 cm

Voice Usually silent, but may occasionally utter some low croaking sounds

Range Almost all over India; mostly resident, but moves considerably with onset of monsoons; uncommon in extreme S and NW India

Habitat Frequents wet areas such as swamps, rivers and lakes with scattered trees

Unmistakable because of fleshy knob (comb) on top of beak. White head and neck, speckled black; purple-green glossy back; bluish and greenish iridescence, especially prominent on the secondaries; white lower neck-collar and underbody; short black bars extend to upper breast sides and flanks. Female duller, smaller; lacks comb. Juvenile has dull buff underparts, face and neck, dull brown upperparts, crown and eye-stripe. Small parties, either on water or in trees over water. Nests in trees.

RUDDY SHELDUCK

Tadorna ferruginea Anatidae

Size 66 cm

Voice Call a loud, goose-like honking, on ground and in flight

Range Breeds in Ladakh; winter visitor, all over India; less common in the south

Habitat Around freshwater, salty and brackish lakes and rivers in open country, avoiding areas with dense, tall vegetation

♀

breeding

Distinct rusty orange coloured bird with lighter head and white face. Stubby black bill; buff neck; rump, tail, primary and secondary feathers black. White wing-coverts conspicuous in flight; legs and feet black. Black collar on neck present in breeding bird. Female similar to male, but smaller, with more white on the face, no collar and buff wash on upperwing-coverts. Juvenile similar to female but duller and with more brown back. Pairs or small parties; nocturnal feeder; rather wary; rests on riverbanks, sandbars, edges of jheels during day; prefers clear, open water.

COTTON PYGMY-GOOSE

Nettapus coromandelianus Anatidae

Size 32 cm

Voice Clucking noises, uttered in flight

Range Almost all over India; not common. Possibly absent over arid NW regions

Habitat Still freshwater lakes (jheels); rain-filled ditches; inundated paddy fields; irrigation tanks, etc.

Small duck with round head and short blackish bill. White head, neck and underparts; glossy dark green above; narrow dark breast-band. Breeding male has green-black upperparts and white underparts; black cap and breast-band; pale grey flanks. Striking white wing-bars visible in flight. Non-breeding plumage similar to female; drabber, more brown; dark stripe through eye and white eyebrow. Feeds in flocks on seeds and other vegetation, crustaceans, insects and vegetation.

♀

GADWALL

Anas strepera Anatidae

Size 50 cm

Voice Single-noted, low call of male; loud quacking of female

Range Winter visitor, fairly abundant; all over India, but decreasing in numbers towards S India

Habitat Prefers marshes, sloughs, ponds, and small lakes with grasslands in both fresh and brackish water during breeding

Medium-sized dull, grey-brown duck. Male has distinct vermiculations on scapular and back feathers; grey and brown upperparts; grey bill and orange legs. Brown head; upper and lower tail-coverts black. Long, pointed, silver-grey tertials; white secondaries with black greater secondary coverts distinctive and obvious in flight. Female lacks vermiculation, very similar to male with plumage but more brownish on back and buffy tan on breast.

♀

EURASIAN WIGEON

Anas penelope Anatidae

Size 50 cm

Voice Male has a haunting *wheeo* whistle; female a gruff bark

Range Common winter visitor throughout. Most numerous in N India

Habitat Jheels, marshes and large rivers where there is access to short grass or cereals for grazing

Medium-sized, plump, large-headed and short-necked duck. Breeding male has grey back, white belly and pink chest, rusty red head with buff forehead, tail predominantly black. White shoulder patch; stubby, greyish-blue bill with black tip. Male in eclipse resembles female. Female dull, mottled greyish-brown. Juvenile very similar to female. Both sexes show white belly, long, pointed wings and pointed tail in flight. Very gregarious, often mixing with other ducks.

♀

♀

MALLARD

Anas platyrhynchos Anatidae

Size 60 cm

Voice Call a loud, wheezy *yheeep* of drake; female quacks loud, loudest when alarmed

Range Very small numbers breed in some of Kashmir's lakes. Winter visitor: N, C India. Rare in Deccan and further south

Habitat Marshes; lakes; swamps; rivers; streams; ponds

Large heavy-looking duck said to be the ancestor of most domestic ducks. Male has long, grey body and black stern. Head and neck are glossy deep green; white neck-ring and dark purplish-brown breast; whitish underparts; yellow bill. Diagnostic blue patch on top of wings bordered white; two curly feathers on tail. Female and eclipse male mottled brown; orange bill. Both sexes have orange feet and bluish-purple speculum, edged with white.

INDIAN SPOT-BILLED DUCK

Anas poecilorhyncha Anatidae

Size 65 cm

Voice Call a loud, duck-like *quack*

Range Resident; all over India, to about 1,800 m in Kashmir; local migrant in some areas

Habitat Wetlands; freshwater vegetation; covered jheels; reservoirs

Overall grey bird with paler head and neck; black bill with bright yellow tip. Whitish wings with black flight feathers below; whitish head; upperparts blackish-brown, feathers edged paler; black cap, dark, broad eye-stripe; green-blue speculum bordered above with white; coral-red legs and feet. Male has black bill tipped yellow; red spot on base of bill. Sexes alike. Juvenile more brown and duller than adult. Pairs or small parties seen on marshy land, wet cultivation, or upending in shallow water.

NORTHERN SHOVELER

Anas clypeata Anatidae

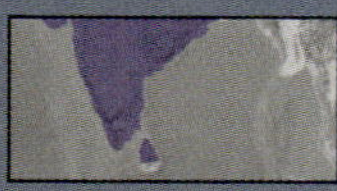

Size 50 cm

Voice Call a loud, 2-noted quacking of male

Range Abundant winter visitor across the subcontinent

Habitat Vegetation-covered jheels, lagoons

Broad, long beak diagnostic. Male has metallic-green head and neck; in flight, dark head, back-centre, rump and uppertail-coverts contrast with white of back and tail; also, dull blue upperwing-coverts against dark flight feathers; metallic-green speculum and white wing bar; in overhead flight, dark head, thick white neck, dark chestnut belly and flanks. Female mottled brown with blue-grey shoulders (wing-coverts) and dull green speculum distinctive. Pairs or small flocks.

NORTHERN PINTAIL

Anas acuta Anatidae

Size 60 cm (excluding tailpins)

Voice Usually quiet

Range Common winter visitor across the subcontinent

Habitat Shallow ponds and marshes in open areas

Elegant, slim and long-necked duck with dark brown head and white breast and throat. White line extends till the neck; light grey body with black-edged feathers; white belly; black, long rump. Female mottled brown-and-black with pointed tail and dark bronze speculum on wings. Both sexes have grey legs and dark grey bill, although bill of the male lined with blue on sides. Male in eclipse plumage similar to female, but with more white patches on neck sides. Wary and secretive when flightless. Forages on land.

♀

GARGANEY

Anas querquedula Anatidae

♀

Size 40 cm

Voice Male's mating call a distinctive crackle

Range Abundant winter visitor

Habitat Narrow or well-sheltered, and shallow standing freshwaters, merging into grasslands, floodlands, or other wetlands

Small duck with large grey bill and flat crown. Dramatic broad, white supercilium crossing to the back of mottled brown head and curving downwards to neck; grey flanks; brown breast and spotted brown stern; white underparts; silvery-blue forewings seen in flight. Female similar to Common Teal, but paler, more patterned head, mottled brownish and distinct eye-stripe; pale supercilium; loral and chin spots and larger bill. Gregarious and social, seen often with other species.

♀

COMMON TEAL

Anas crecca Anatidae

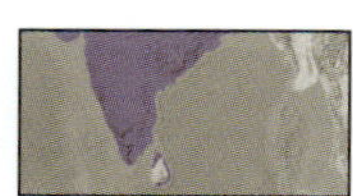

Size 34 cm

Voice Call a *krit...krit...*. Also, wheezy *quack*

Range Entire subcontinent in winter

Habitat Jheels; marshes; village ponds. Often hunted

Small pale-grey duck with chestnut head. Underparts finely streaked dark grey; creamy patch on chest has fine black spots. Dark russet-red head with bottle green eye-stripe bordered white. Both sexes display dark green, black-and-white wing-bars in flight. Female mottled dark and light brown; pale belly; black and green wing speculum. Most common migratory duck. Swift flier.

PINK-HEADED DUCK

Rhodonessa caryophyllacea Anatidae

Unmistakable. Long-bodied and long-necked, with slightly tufted head in the male, and peculiar stiff-necked posture. Adult male has chocolate-coloured body; deep pink head and hindneck. Female and juvenile duller, appearing much like dark female Red-crested Pochard with pinkish tinge to the head. Presumed extinct.

RED-CRESTED POCHARD

Netta rufina Anatidae

Size 55 cm

Voice Silent

Range Rather scarce winter visitor throughout lowlands

Habitat Well-vegetated large rivers and lakes

♀

Large duck with deep orange-crested head and red bill. Black neck and breast; pale flanks; brown back and black stern. Female lighter brown with pale cheeks and darker crown, dark bill. Juvenile darker with multicoloured belly. In flight, both sexes display broad white wing-bars. Nests near slow-moving rivers and clearings of open water with shrubs. Feeds actively early morning and late evening. Feeds on aquatic plants and animals by diving and upending.

FERRUGINOUS DUCK

Aythya nyroca Anatidae

Size 40 cm

Voice Usually silent, although female sometimes makes burring sound in flight

Range Scarce and local winter visitor throughout lowlands. Commonest in NW India. Rarely in large numbers

Habitat Well-vegetated jheels, rivers, canals and ponds

♀

Small diving duck with peaked head. Both sexes are mahogany brown, darker on back and head. Large triangular patches of white under the tail. Male brighter, russet-brown; sharp white iris. Long white wing-bars and belly visible in flight. Not as gregarious as other diving ducks. Usually keeping in small groups. Cautious and wary.

TUFTED DUCK

Aythya fuligula Anatidae

♀

Size 45 cm

Voice Rather quiet. Male has high bubbling note; female croaks

Range Fairly common winter visitor throughout lowlands. Less common in E and S India

Habitat All kinds of open water including reservoirs

♀

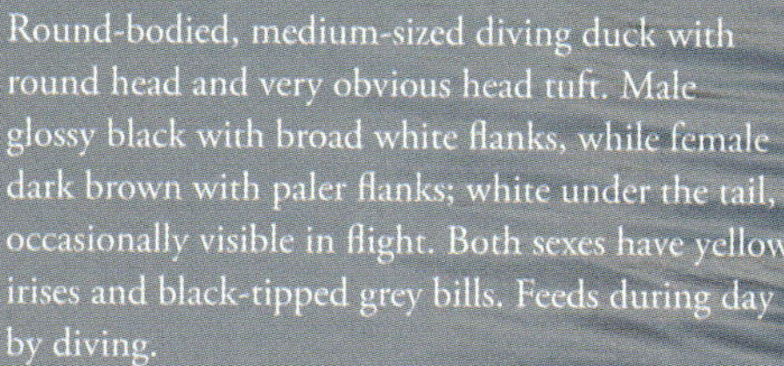

Round-bodied, medium-sized diving duck with round head and very obvious head tuft. Male glossy black with broad white flanks, while female dark brown with paler flanks; white under the tail, occasionally visible in flight. Both sexes have yellow irises and black-tipped grey bills. Feeds during day by diving.

WEDGE-TAILED SHEARWATER

Puffinus pacificus

Big, broad-winged bird with long tail occurring in two colour morphs. The tail's wedge shape not usually visible in flight, as the shearwater folds its tail so that it appears long and pointed. Long dark bill. Flight action slow with lazy flapping followed by short glides. Can often be seen tagging behind fishing boats. Vagrant off the coast of Goa; also Lakshadweep.

SHORT-TAILED SHEARWATER

Puffinus tenuirostris

Brownish shearwater with steeply rising forehead; short bill; relatively short tail. Strong, deliberate flight action with comparatively fast, skip-winged flapping, followed by long glides. Vagrant in the region. Feeds mainly underwater, diving deep below the surface in pursuit of prey.

FLESH-FOOTED SHEARWATER

Puffinus carneipes

Large, dark brown bird. Flight action elegant and relaxed with slow, powerful flapping interspersed with leisurely stiff-winged glides. Catches prey by plunge diving underwater to follow its quarry. Vagrant off the southern Indian coast; Lakshadweep.

AUDUBON'S SHEARWATER

Puffinus lherminieri

Small shearwater with white underparts and head. Distinguished from other shearwaters by blackish-brown upperparts, rectrices, undertail-coverts and distal undersides of remiges and sometimes entire feathers. Dark, dull pink feet; grey bill, darker towards tip.

WILSON'S STORM-PETREL

Oceanites oceanicus

White rump and dark underparts. Tail square-ended with yellow webbed feet projecting much beyond tail. Found in the southern Indian coast; commonest along the coast of Mumbai.

LITTLE GREBE

Tachybaptus ruficollis Podicipedidae

non-breeding

breeding

Size 23–29 cm

Voice Shrill trilling notes. Occasional *click*

Range Subcontinent, upto 2,000m in Kashmir. Resident in most areas

Habitat Reasonably large waterbodies in lowlands, with plenty of vegetation

Very small grebe, with short neck; short, straight beak; plump, rounded body. Black head, nape, breast and back; dark reddish-brown cheeks, throat and neck; dark brown flanks. Diagnostic small yellow patch at base of pale-tipped, black beak. Dark green legs; reddish-brown iris. Juvenile paler than adult, with dark cap, nape and back; yellowish-brown cheeks, neck sides and flanks, and reddish-brown lower neck and chest. Feeds on small fish, insects, crustaceans, shellfish and molluscs by diving or dabbling. Hard to spot as mostly concealed in vegetation. Floating nest built near shoreline, attached to aquatic plants or branches of waterside bushes; territorial, solitary nester. Performs a variety of elaborate courtship display.

GREATER FLAMINGO

Phoenicopterus roseus Phoenicopteridae

Size 120-145 cm

Voice Assortment of cackles. Also, goose-like honking *ka-haunk*

Range Breeds in Kutch. Wanders widely throughout the region particularly to E coast and NW India. Sporadic in appearance

Habitat Breeds on saline or brackish lagoons

Easily recognisable bird with long, thin curved neck, long pink legs, and distinctive downward-bending pale pink beak with black tip. Rose-white plumage; red shoulders and black tips to wings; yellow eyes. Female smaller than male. Juvenile grey-brown with some pink in underparts, wings and tail, and brown legs and beak. Distinguished from Lesser by larger size, paler plumage, lighter beak, and pink rather than dark red legs. Characteristic flight with legs and neck stretched to full length. Feeds in any shallow water including estuaries, lakes, rivers and flooded fields. Feeds with head immersed; often rests on one leg, neck coiled and head tucked in feathers.

juvenile

LESSER FLAMINGO

Phoenicopterus minor Phoenicopteridae

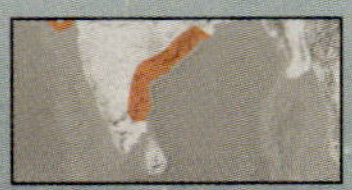

Size 80–90 cm

Voice Call a *murr-err, murr-err*. Feeding flocks may make goose-like honking sound, higher-pitched than Greater.

Range Breeds in Kutch. Some wander particularly to the E coast

Habitat Prefers salt and brackish lagoons and salt pans

ASIAN OPENBILL

Anastomus oscitans Ciconiidae

Size 76–81 cm

Voice Call a mournful *hoo-hoo*. Very noisy while flying in flocks

Range Locally common breeding resident throughout lowlands. Rare in Pakistan

Habitat Large wetlands. Rare on the coast

juvenile

breeding

Smallest stork in the region. Breeding adult has white plumage, lightly washed with smoky grey; glistening purplish-greenish black on wings and tail. Non-breeding adult grey; black scapulars, flight feathers and tail; white or grey head; characteristic open bill formed by hollow in lower mandible; pinkish-grey bill; greyish-pink lores; pink to red legs. Sexes similar. Juvenile has brownish tinge on plumage with dark grey bill and straighter lower mandible. Feeds in rice fields and marshes in freshwater.

Shorter and darker rose-pink bird than Greater, with light pink bill, tipped with black. Pale pink feathers with black primaries and secondaries, deep crimson legs; yellow-orange eyes with maroon ring. Male slightly taller than female. Juvenile has brown feathers and dark grey beak. Feeds with long neck bent over and bill upside down in water. Spectacular courtship takes place throughout the year. Very sociable.

juvenile

PAINTED STORK

Mycteria leucocephala Ciconiidae

Size 95 cm

Voice Characteristic mandible clattering of storks

Range Resident and local migrant, from Terai south through the region's well-watered areas

Habitat Inland marshes; jheels; occasionally riversides

juvenile

Fabulously coloured waterbird with long neck and striking wing pattern. White plumage; blackish-green and white wings; blackish-green breast-band and black tail; rich rosy-pink wash on greater wing-coverts; large, slightly curved orangish-yellow bill. Juvenile pale dirty brown, with neck feathers edged darker and lacks breast-band. Common and gregarious; feeds with beak partly submerged. When not feeding, settles hunched up outside water; regularly soars high on thermals.

BLACK STORK

Ciconia nigra Ciconiidae

Size 95–100 cm

Voice Voiceless

Range Scarce winter visitor mainly to N India

Habitat Prefers undisturbed, open forests and woodlands, upto 2,000 to 2,500 m

Similar to White, but sturdier with wider wings. Long neck, bill, and legs; short tail; black upperparts with varying green and purple gloss; white breast and belly; scarlet red bill and legs, brighter in breeding and more brownish in non-breeding. Flies with neck and legs extended; white triangles on underwings visible in flight. Sexes alike, though male larger. Juvenile, less brightly-coloured. Secretive.

juvenile

WOOLLY-NECKED STORK

Ciconia episcopus Ciconiidae

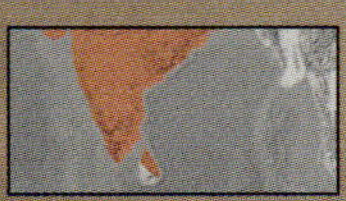

Size 86–95 cm

Voice Usually silent, but may give some croaking *honks*. Seldom heard

Range Locally common breeding resident; subcontinent, upto about 1,400 m in the Himalayas

Habitat Wetlands such as rivers, marshes, lakes, rice fields, flood plains and pastures; swamp forests

Large, glossy black-and-white stork with huge wingspan. Bare grey face; red legs and deep red eyes; well-defined, glossy black forecrown and crown, back and breast (black parts have distinct purplish-green sheen); white lower back and rump; black forked-tail, concealed by long white undertail-coverts; white neck and lower abdomen, with pale purplish wash; long, stout, black bill, occasionally tinged crimson. Sexes alike. In juvenile, glossy black replaced by dark brown. Usually seen alone, walking slowly along water; sometimes, in pairs or small scattered parties, feeding along with other storks, ibises and egrets; stalks on dry land too; settles on trees.

WHITE STORK

Ciconia ciconia Ciconiidae

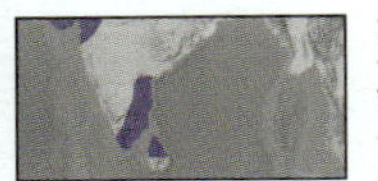

Size 100–115 cm

Voice Voiceless. Claps its bill

Range Scarce winter visitor mainly to S India

Habitat Cultivation and open, grassy marshes

Large long-necked wading bird with slender orangish-red legs and long, sharp, red bill. Upperparts mainly white, with black wing feathers. Dark iris; shadow around eye. Sexes alike, male little larger. Black parts replaced by brown in juvenile; brown bill and legs. Long, broad wings, suitable for soaring. Flies with outstretched neck. Feeds on amphibians, reptiles and insects, particularly grasshoppers. Sociable and not shy. Flocks often seen soaring high on thermals. Red bill and legs tell it apart from Openbill. Long feathers on lower neck and upper breast form ruff that extends during courtship display.

juvenile

BLACK-NECKED STORK

Ephippiorhynchus asiaticus Ciconiidae

juvenile

♀

Size 140 cm

Voice Voiceless, but clatters mandibles

Range Increasingly rare breeding resident throughout Indian lowlands

Habitat Wetlands

Largest stork in the region. Unmistakable, massive black bill. Overall white with glossy greenish-black head, wing-bar and tail. Iridescent purple tinted green-blue neck; coral-red legs. White wings with broad band along length, conspicuous in flight. Sexes identical except for iris, which is yellow in female, brown in male. Singly, or in pairs; sometimes family group. Shy and wary.

juvenile

LESSER ADJUTANT

Leptoptilos javanicus Ciconiidae

Size 110–120 cm

Voice Usually silent

Range Globally threatened, rare, but widespread breeding resident throughout lowlands. Most frequent in Nepal and NE India. Recently undergone rapid decline in number, rare throughout its range

Habitat Wet areas such as mangroves, mudflats, marshes, flooded grasslands, coastal swamps, lakes and rice fields

Adult has dark slaty blue-black upperparts and white underparts; white neck base spotted black. Black underwing and undertail; bare yellow head in non-breeding and red in breeding male; bare pinkish-orange neck, with sparse grey feathers; bony plate on top of head; long, thick beak greyish to horn-coloured; pale blue-grey eyes and legs. Juvenile has more feathering on neck and duller upperparts. Characteristic hunched posture. Solitary and shy. Feeds on aquatic animals and grasshoppers by walking slowly on ground or through shallow water. Small colonies or individual pairs. Breeds in wet habitats.

GREATER ADJUTANT

Leptoptilos dubius Ciconiidae

Size 150 cm

Voice Silent, apart from croaks and bill-clattering

Range Globally threatened and now very rare except in Assam, where locally common

Habitat Marshes; jheels; cultivation and urban garbage dumps

Tall, greyish-white stork with almost prehistoric appearance. Breeding male has bare red head and neck (yellowish-brown in non-breeding). Long, thick yellow bill; pendulous gular pouch; large pale pink bill. Silvery-grey wing-band and thick white neck ruff; white underparts. Dark legs. Juvenile similar to adult, but duller plumage and more feathery neck. Slow, measured gait, gives it its name. Heron-like flight with retracted neck. Nests of sticks in canopy of large trees. Sometimes eats injured ducks and carrion.

BLACK-HEADED IBIS

Threskiornis melanocephalus Threskiornithidae

Size 75 cm

Voice Loud, booming call; nasal grunts reported during breeding

Range Resident; local migrant; subcontinent, from south of Terai

Habitat Marshes; riversides

Large, white bird with prominent bare black head and neck, and long, down-curved bill. Grey ornamental tail feathers. Breeding adult has blood red patches on underwings, blue tinge on head, glossy black legs and loose ruff of white feathers on lower neck and sometimes yellowish wash on breast and back. Sexes alike. Juvenile has grey feathers on head and white neck. Feeds actively in water; probing mud with partly open bill; can submerge entire head and neck while wading when necessary. Feeds and nests communally.

juvenile

RED-NAPED IBIS

Pseudibis papillosa Threskiornithidae

Size 70 cm

Voice Calls include loud 2- to 3-note nasal screams, uttered in flight

Range Scarce breeding resident; NW India, east through Gangetic plains; south to Karnataka

Habitat Lakes; marshes; riverbeds and irrigated farmlands

juvenile

Medium-sized bird with diagnostic triangular-patch of red warts on head and long downcurved bill. Glossy dark brownish-black plumage glazed blue; scapulars and back feathers, bronze green. Brown neck, mantle, lower back and rump; bright orange-red eye; black tail, richly glazed with blue green; short legs hidden beneath steel blue tail and lesser wing-coverts with white shoulder-patch, visible in flight. Red or fleshy pink legs. Re-uses nest year upon year. Feeds in shallow water.

GLOSSY IBIS

Plegadis falcinellus Threskiornithidae

Size 60 cm

Voice Usually silent

Range Fairly common, but local breeding resident subject to wandering. Most frequent in N and W India

Habitat All types of shallow freshwater, particularly with floating vegetation

Dark wading bird with long legs and decurved bill. Breeding adult chestnut with green and purple gloss; naked, grey, facial skin; pale blue lines bordering the front part of face; brown eyes and bill; grey legs with red knee joints. Flies with neck and legs outstretched. Nests on ground, in reeds or low shrubs. Feeds in shallow water or marshy wetlands on small fish, aquatic insects, molluscs, frogs, and food sifted from water surface.

juvenile

EURASIAN SPOONBILL

Platalea leucorodia Threskiornithidae

when breeding

Size 80-93 cm

Voice Mandible clattering, short grunts when breeding

Range Locally common breeding resident, winter visitor: NW, W, S India and Sri Lanka

Habitat Shallow wetlands, marshes, rivers, large waterbodies with muddy, clay or fine sandy beds

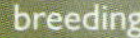

breeding

breeding

non-breeding

Snowy-white bird, with long, spoon-shaped black bill and long, blackish legs. Breeding adult has orangish-yellow tip on bill, crest and yellow breast-patch. Sexes alike. Immature has paler bill and black wing-tips. Flies with neck and legs outstretched, with flapping movements interspersed with gliding. Spends much of day sleeping on one leg. Feeds on aquatic animals by sweeping bill from side to side through water.

GREAT BITTERN

Botaurus stellaris Ardeidae

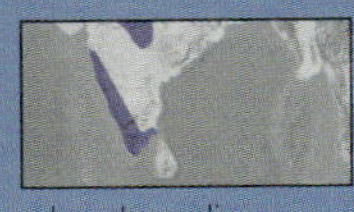

when breeding

Size 75 cm

Voice Call a deep croak in flight. Far-carrying booming when breeding

Range Rare, but widespread winter visitor throughout lowlands of Pakistan, India and Nepal

Habitat Reeds in marshes

Overall golden brown with black crown and moustache; mottled above and dusky stripes below; thick neck; green legs; yellowish bill; brown cheeks and white throat. Upperparts intricately patterned with black; black stripes run down foreneck. Heavy owl-like flight with retracted neck. When startled, adopts camouflage by pointing bill upwards and stretching neck vertically. Secretive.

YELLOW BITTERN

Ixobrychus sinensis Ardeidae

Size 35–38 cm

Voice Occasionally a sharp *kark*. Male's breeding call a quiet *uu…uu*

Range Rather local breeding resident mainly in NE India, Bangladesh, Sri Lanka and Indo-Gangetic Plains. Monsoon breeding visitor to NW India

Habitat Reed beds and wet scrubs near rivers, jheels and wet paddy

Small bittern with dull yellowish-brown upperparts and whitish underparts streaked darker from chin to belly. Short neck; longish bill. Crown, short crest and nape black marked with buff; orangish-brown on side of face, head and neck; deeper rufous on hindneck, greyer on forehead and supercilium; white undertail- and underwing-coverts; black tail. Female has brown streaking on crown, neck, and breast. Juvenile similar, but heavily streaked brown below, and mottled buff above. Solitary; hunts quietly in reed beds and undergrowth. Solitary but breeding densities can be quite high. Usually seen in feeding flights.

juvenile

CINNAMON BITTERN

Ixobrychus cinnamomeus Ardeidae

Size 36–38 cm

Voice Male's breeding call a loud *kok…kok*

Range Rather local breeding resident mainly to eastern coast, NE India, parts of the Indo-Gangetic Plains, Bangladesh and Sri Lanka

Habitat Reeds in marshes

juvenile

Solitary and crepuscular bittern, overall cinnamon in colour with darker crown. Sides of face, mantle, back and tail paler and tinged with pink; underparts rich buffy-brown with dark reddish-black central streaks down the middle from chin to belly. Chin and throat whitish. Flanks pale cinnamon; vent and undertail-coverts pale buffy-brown. Female has more brown crown and mantle, more streaked neck, while immature darker and more boldly streaked.

BLACK BITTERN

Dupetor flavicollis Ardeidae

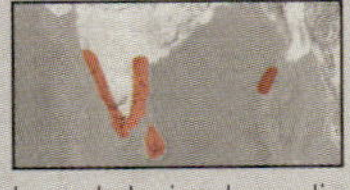

Size 58 cm

Voice Characteristic booming call mainly heard during breeding season, at day or night

Range Scarce breeding resident

Habitat Reed beds with bushes and bushy margins of canals, rivers and jheels

Medium-sized bittern with diagnostic yellow neck-stripe. Male has dull black upperparts; buff streaks on throat; rufous-streaked, black and grey belly. Female paler than male, with more yellowish wash on underparts. Immature more streaked; upperpart feathers have buff fringes. Nests on bed of sticks on branch overhanging water. Feeds on frogs, reptiles, fish and invertebrates. Crepuscular, solitary and extremely secretive. May fly quite high to feeding sites.

MALAYAN NIGHT HERON

Gorsachius melanolophus Ardeidae

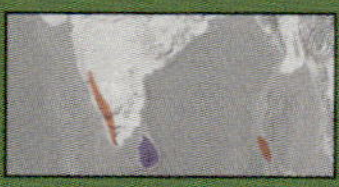

Size 47 cm

Voice Usually silent

Range NE India; S Western Ghats; Nicobar Islands. Winter visitor to Sri Lanka

Habitat Subtropical and tropical swamps, streams, marshes; especially regions with high rainfall

Reddish-brown heron with streaked underparts, black underwings, black crown and variable bluish lores; reddish-brown sides to head and neck; stout dark bill. Sexes similar, but male may have dark crest. Juvenile greyish-brown with black-and-white spots and streaked underparts. Immature greyish-brown above with black-and-white spots; underparts buff with brown spots and bars. Rarely seen. Nests in forest trees and bamboos.

BLACK-CROWNED NIGHT HERON

Nycticorax nycticorax Ardeidae

Size 58-72 cm

Voice Call a harsh raucous *quak quak*, mostly in flight

Range Locally common breeding resident throughout lowlands

Habitat All wetland types including paddy and mangroves

Stocky heron with short neck and legs. Black cap, upper back and scapulars; grey wings, rump and tail; stout, black bill; blood-red iris; pink legs in breeding; creamy-white underparts. Sexes alike. Juvenile buff-spotted and streaked brown. Social; nests colonially on trunks or forks of branches.

juvenile

juvenile

INDIAN POND HERON

Ardeola greyii Ardeidae

Size 45 cm

Voice Call a harsh croak, usually when flushed

Range Common resident throughout subcontinent

Habitat Marshes; jheels; riversides; roadside ditches; tidal creeks

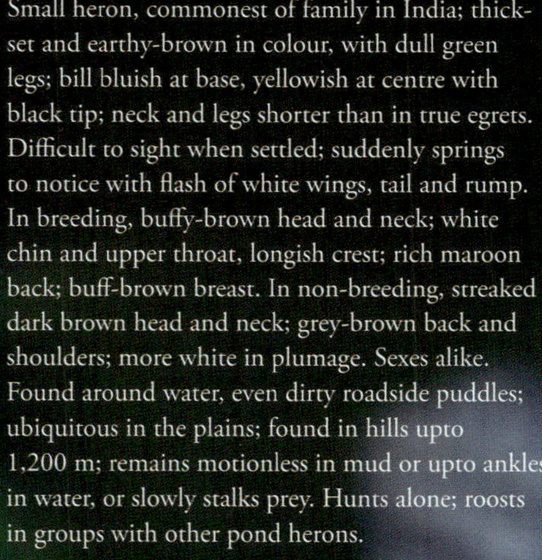

Small heron, commonest of family in India; thickset and earthy-brown in colour, with dull green legs; bill bluish at base, yellowish at centre with black tip; neck and legs shorter than in true egrets. Difficult to sight when settled; suddenly springs to notice with flash of white wings, tail and rump. In breeding, buffy-brown head and neck; white chin and upper throat, longish crest; rich maroon back; buff-brown breast. In non-breeding, streaked dark brown head and neck; grey-brown back and shoulders; more white in plumage. Sexes alike. Found around water, even dirty roadside puddles; ubiquitous in the plains; found in hills upto 1,200 m; remains motionless in mud or upto ankles in water, or slowly stalks prey. Hunts alone; roosts in groups with other pond herons.

breeding

non-breeding

GREY HERON

Ardea cinerea Ardeidae

Size 100 cm

Voice Call a loud *quaak* in flight

Range Mostly resident; subcontinent; breeds upto 1,750 m in Kashmir

Habitat Marshes; tidal creeks; fresh waterbodies

Long-legged, long-necked bird of open marshes. Ash-grey above; white crown, neck and underparts; black stripe after eye continues as long, black crest; black-dotted band down centre of foreneck; dark blue-black flight feathers; golden-yellow iris at close range. Sexes alike. Mostly solitary except when breeding; occasionally enters shallow water; usually stands motionless, head pulled in between shoulders, waiting for prey to come close; characteristic flight, with head pulled back and long legs trailing.

STRIATED HERON

Butorides striata Ardeidae

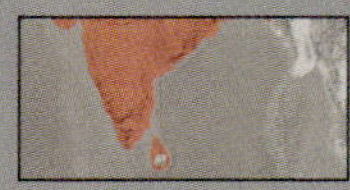

Size 45 cm

Voice Call a Redshank-like *tewn… tewn*

Range Uncommon resident, south of the Himalayas

Habitat Secluded pools. Found in mangroves, intertidal flats

Small, squat heron with longish drooping crest. Upperparts slaty-grey, washed green; underparts grey with pinkish tint; green wing feathers outlined with yellow; yellow eye has deep grey surround; deep green forehead; short legs, grey head and black crown. Orange feet in breeding. Juvenile darker, more heavily streaked and mottled. Characteristic hunched posture with head tucked into body.

PURPLE HERON

Ardea purpurea Ardeidae

Size 78–90 cm

Voice Usually silent. Occasionally, a harsh croak

Range Mostly resident

Habitat Marshes and lakes with extensive reed beds. Prefers more open wetlands with fringing vegetation outside breeding season

juvenile

Slender-necked, lanky bird with slaty-purple upperparts, black crown with long, drooping black crest; rufous rear neck with prominent black stripe along length; white chin and throat; deep slaty-grey and chestnut below breast; almost black on wings and tail; pale yellow eyes; yellow bill; orange-yellow legs and feet. Crest and breast plumes less developed in female. Juvenile more brown and lacks crest; duller in colour and narrow streaks in neck and underparts. Solitary; crepuscular; extremely shy but master of patience; freezes and hides.

CATTLE EGRET

Bubulcus ibis Ardeidae

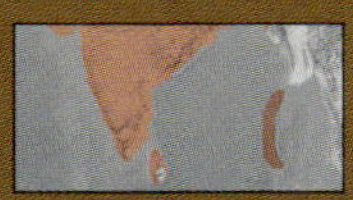

Size 50 cm

Voice Mostly silent except for some croaking sounds when breeding

Range Resident; subcontinent, upto 1,800 m in outer Himalayas. Rare in NW and NE India

Habitat Marshes; lakes; forest clearings; also, fields

Non breeding

breeding

Small snowy-white heron with characteristic hunch and relatively short legs and thick neck. Breeding adult white with orange-buff feathers on crown, neck and back; bright red bill, lores and legs; yellow eyes. Non-breeding adult very similar to Little, but told by yellow beak and from other egrets by size. White plumage, sometimes with pale reddish-buff wash. Sexes alike. Juvenile resembles non-breeding adult, has blackish bill, legs and feet. Eyes pale yellowish. Immature has black leg and bill. Very social. In large flocks; follows livestock, also farm equipments like tractors to catch insects that are disturbed. Nest of sticks in bushes or trees.

GREAT EGRET

Casmerodius albus Ardeidae

Size 94-104 cm

Voice Occasional croak

Range Resident, local migrant; not common but widespread across country

Habitat Marshes; jheels; rivers; tidal estuaries

Large, almost entirely white heron with contrasting black feet and long, black legs. Black tip to bright yellow bill; greenish-yellow patch between bill and eye; long S-shaped neck prominent in flight. Breeding adult displays beautiful plumes extending from back to beyond tail. In courtship display, bird spreads plumes into a fan shape. Juvenile similar but without plumes. Feeds actively at dawn and dusk, waiting motionlessly to catch prey.

INTERMEDIATE EGRET

Mesophoyx intermedia Ardeidae

Size 80 cm

Voice Usually silent

Range Locally common breeding resident throughout lowlands and the coast

Habitat Wetlands; the coast

As its name implies, intermediate in size between Great Egret and smaller white egrets. Overall striking white bird with dark legs and thickish, yellow bill. Breeding adult may have reddish or black bill, greenish-yellow gape skin, loose filamentous breast trails and back plumes, and dull yellow or pink upperparts. Sexes similar. Stalks prey in shallow water, including flooded fields. Feeds on fish, frogs, crustaceans, and insects. Nests in colonies with other herons, normally on platforms of sticks, trees, or shrubs.

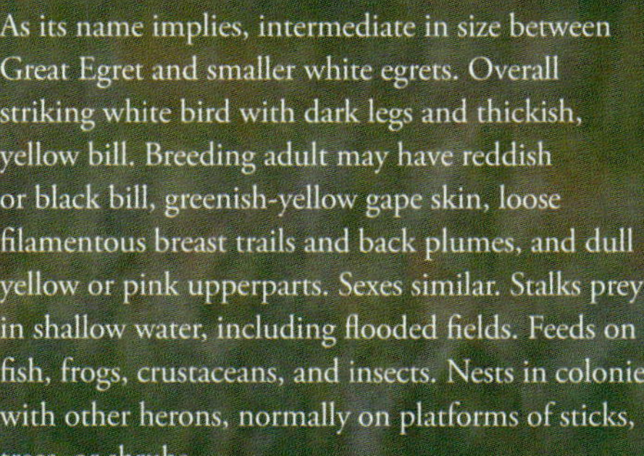

breeding

LITTLE EGRET

Egretta garzetta Ardeidae

Size 65 cm

Voice Occasional croak

Range Fairly common breeding resident; subcontinent, upto 1,600 m in the outer Himalayas

Habitat Margins of coastal and inland water habitats, preferring open areas with shallow freshwater

Striking and elegant heron distinguished by pure white feathers, long sinuous neck, long, black legs and dark, pointed bill. Breeding adult has two long, nape plumes and light feathery plumage around breast and back. Juvenile similar in appearance to non-breeding adult, but has less striking colouration on feet and around eyes.

breeding

WESTERN REEF EGRET

Egretta gularis Ardeidae

Size 65 cm

Voice Rasping croaks

Range W, E coasts; often inland

Habitat River deltas; coasts; mangroves

Slim, medium-sized heron with skinny neck. Thick, pale and heavy bill. Polymorphic and varies from all white to light to dark grey. Throat usually white. Breeding adult has red lores and plumes on head, breast and back. Sexes alike. Usually solitary or seen foraging with other egrets. More active at twilight. Often both phases seen feeding together.

intermediate morph

white morph

RED-BILLED TROPICBIRD

Phaethon aethereus Phaethontidae

Adult has bright red bill; white tail-streamers, black barring on mantle and scapulars and much black on primaries. Juvenile has yellow bill with black tip, black band across nape and shows more black on primaries, with black primary coverts when compared with juvenile Red-tailed and White-tailed.

BROWN BOOBY

Sula leucogaster Sulidae

Dark coffee-brown booby with white underbody and underwing-coverts, distinctly demarcated between brown head, neck and upper breast. Juvenile has dusky brown underbody with pale-panel across underwing-coverts, though overall appearance similar to adult.

RED-FOOTED BOOBY

Sula sula Sulidae

Smallish, graceful booby with red legs and feet. White, brown and intermediate morphs occur; white morphs most likely to be encountered in the Indian Ocean. Adult white morph smaller in size than Masked, and has variable yellow wash on crown and hindneck, bluish bill and no mask on chin.

GREAT FRIGATEBIRD

Fregata minor Fregatidae

Adult male almost overall black above, except for pale brown wing-bar; greenish-purple gloss on head, neck and upper back; scissor-shaped tail; large, red, distensible gular pouch in breeding male. Female larger, and less glossy; non-distensible gular pouch; white upper breast; light grey; pale brown wing-bar. Juvenile has reddish-brown patch on head and white underparts.

WHITE-TAILED TROPICBIRD

Phaethon lepturus Phaethontidae

Small tropicbird with very long tail streamers, extending from wedge-shaped tail. Mostly white with strong black eye-stripe, black wing-bar and black tips to wings; robust decurved bill. Long, pointed wings. Juvenile soft, downy grey. Strong flier, but moves awkwardly on land, as its short legs are set far back.

MASKED BOOBY

Sula dactylatra Sulidae

Large and robust booby. Adult predominantly white with black mask and black flight feathers and tail; white head and neck, black tail and black tertials help distinguish it from the Red-footed.

LESSER FRIGATEBIRD

Fregata ariel Fregatidae

Smaller and more finely built than the other frigatebirds. Adult male mostly black except for white spur extending from breast sides on to inner underwings. Adult female has black head and throat, white neck sides, white spur extending from breast, also white, on to inner underwings, black belly and vent. Juvenile has rufous on white head.

GREAT WHITE PELICAN

Pelecanus onocrotalus Pelecanidae

Size 175 cm

Voice Grunts and croaks. Rarely heard

Range Resident, Rann of Kutch. Winters in parts of N, S and SE India

Habitat Large jheels; lakes; coastal lagoons

Enormous bird with dramatic azure blue bill with central red stripe. Bright yellow, expandable pouch extends from lower jaw to base of throat. Bare, fleshy pink face; white, bushy crest; creamy white plumage with pale pinkish wash; pink feet and yellowish tuft on breast; black primaries and underside of secondaries. Social. Feeds on large fish early in the morning; rarely settles on land; strong flier.

SPOT-BILLED PELICAN

Pelecanus philippensis Pelecanidae

Size 125-152 cm

Voice Mostly silent

Range Breeds in the well-watered parts of S, SE and E India, but population spreads in non-breeding season

Habitat Large jheels; lakes

Relatively small pelican, mostly white with greyish-brown tint; pinkish rump and lower back; browny-grey crest; black primaries and dark brown secondaries visible in flight; large spotted bill has orange-yellow tip; pinkish elastic throat pouch with large pale spots. In breeding adult, skin at base of bill dark, pink orbital patch. Sexes alike. Juvenile lacks spots on bill. Purely aquatic. Breeds in colonies in tall trees. Feeds in open water, mostly on fish.

LITTLE CORMORANT

Phalacrocorax niger Phalacrocoracidae

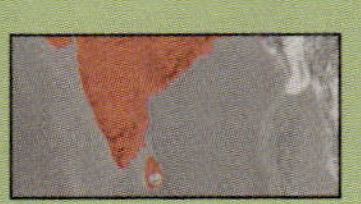

Size 50 cm

Voice Vocal, low roaring sounds near nest and roost

Range Subcontinent, south of the Himalayas

Habitat Village tanks; jheels; lakes; rivers and coastal areas

Small, glossy black cormorant with few white head plumes. Short, thick neck. Breeding adult has some white spots and filoplumes on face; short silky white crest on back of head; dark eyes, gular skin and face. Non-breeding adult and juvenile more brownish with white throat-patch and more crest. Sexes similar. Forages in small loose groups; swims underwater to capture fish. Roosts communally, often in the company of other waterbirds.

juvenile

INDIAN CORMORANT

Phalacrocorax fuscicollis Phalacrocoracidae

Size 63 cm

Voice Harsh croaks at nest

Range Throughout the region. Locally common breeding resident

Habitat Large freshwater wetlands; marshes; estuaries; brackish tidal creeks and mangrove swamps

Small to medium-sized slender cormorant mainly black in breeding season, with white neck plumes and whitish throat. Silvery wing-coverts; longish tail; white ear tufts, white-flecked feathers on neck, blackish gular pouch and no crest. Non-breeding adult more brown, with no ear tufts or white plumes and more yellow gular pouch. Sexes alikes. Juvenile more brown and lacks neck plumes. Gregarious, often found in larger bodies of water and rivers. Feeds in shallow water.

GREAT CORMORANT

Phalacrocorax carbo Phalacrocoracidae

Size 80 cm

Voice Usually silent

Range Resident in most areas; subcontinent

Habitat Jheels; lakes; mountain torrents; occasionally coastal lagoons

breeding

Sexes alike. Breeding adult has black plumage with metallic blue-green sheen; white facial skin and throat; bright yellow gular pouch and white thigh-patches; silky white plumes on head and neck. Non-breeding adult has no white thigh-patches gular pouch less bright. First year juvenile dull brown above, white below. Aquatic. Not gregarious outside breeding season; usually one or two birds feeding close by; dives underwater.

DARTER

Anhinga melanogaster Anhingidae

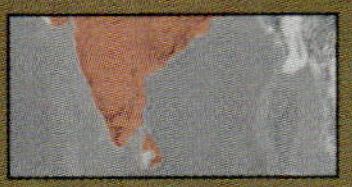

Size 90 cm

Voice Calls include loud croaks and squeaks

Range Subcontinent, south of the Himalayan foothills

Habitat Freshwater lakes; jheels

Long, snake-like neck, pointed bill and stiff, fan-shaped tail. Black upperparts, streaked and mottled with silvery-grey on back and wings; chocolate-brown head and neck; white stripe down sides of upper neck; white chin and upper throat; entirely black below. Juvenile brown with rufous and silvery streaks on mantle. Bird of deep freshwater; small numbers scattered along with Little. Highly specialised feeder, entire structure of bird modified for following and capturing fish underwater. Swims low in water with only head and neck uncovered; chases prey below water with wings half open, spearing fish with sudden rapier-like thrusts made possible by bend in neck at 8th and 9th vertebrae, which acts as spring as it straightens. Tosses fish into air and swallows it head-first. Basks on tree stumps and rocks, cormorant style.

immature

LESSER KESTREL

Falco naumanni Falconidae

Size 30 cm

Voice Call a diagnostic harsh *chay-chay-chay*

Range Migrant mostly to N and W India

Habitat Open country

Small bird of prey, similar to Larger Common but more delicate-looking, with shorter wings and shorter tail. Rufous-brown back; barred grey underparts; grey head; grey patches in wings; blue-grey greater coverts; wing-tips reach, or almost reach, the tip of the tail. In flight, underwings look whiter and darker trailing edges and wing-tips more clearly pronounced; tail looks more wedge-shaped; whitish-horn-coloured talons. Female and juvenile slightly paler. Feeds on insects, small birds, reptiles and rodents. Nests colonially on cliffs, or in tree holes; like other falcons, no nest structure is built.

♀

COMMON KESTREL

Falco tinnunculus Falconidae

Size 32–39 cm

Voice Infrequent clicking sound. Also *kee-kee-kee*

Range Resident; local migrant; several races

Habitat Open country; cliffsides

♀

Overall light chestnut brown falcon, with dark spotting on upperparts and buff underparts with narrow blackish streaking. Ash-grey crown, neck sides and nape; prominent black malar stripe; white tip to grey tail with black subterminal band. Bright yellow cere, feet and eye-ring; dark bill. Female has more black spots and streaking on pale rufous upperparts and pale buff underparts. Juvenile similar to female, but broader streaks on underparts and yellow parts paler. Solitary or in pairs; often hovers when hunting.

RED-NECKED FALCON

Falco chicquera Falconidae

Size 35 cm

Voice Calls include shrill, trilling screams

Range Resident; all over India, south of Himalayan foothills

Habitat Avoids dense forests; prefers open country; wide cultivated plains with groups of trees

Smallish stout falcon, with short, blunt-ended wings, long, rounded tail and distinctive chestnut head and neck. Overall blue-grey plumage with black primary feathers; white-tipped grey tail, whitish underparts mottled and streaked black and rufous; black banding on belly. Sexes similar, but female slightly larger. Juvenile darker brown, with paler rufous-brown underparts. Hunts from sheltered perch. Rapid, direct flight; rarely hovers.

AMUR FALCON

Falco amurensis Falconidae

Size 26–30 cm

Voice Call a high-pitched *kew… kew…kew* at roost

Range Scarce passage migrant (mainly in autumn) between NE Asia and SC Africa

Habitat Open country; often near water

Small, slender falcon with long, pointed wings. Male overall dark grey, with rusty-cinnamon lower abdomen and thighs; white underwing, prominent in flight; bright orange-red legs and facial skin; orange base to beak; white claws. Female similar in size to male, with cream or rusty underparts, streaked and barred; grey upperparts; slaty-grey head with cream forehead; barred tail with dark tip; white cheeks and throat; dark eye-patch and moustache. Juvenile similar to female, but paler, with rusty-brown or buff-edged feathers. Very sociable.

EURASIAN HOBBY

Falco subbuteo Falconidae

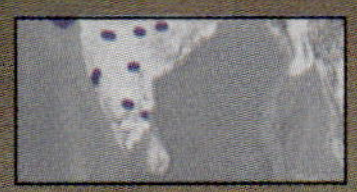

Size 33 cm

Voice Call a hurried *ki ki ki ki*

Range Breeds in the Himalayas; scarce passage migrant mainly in the NW India. Scattered records throughout lowlands

Habitat Open, wooded country often over or near water

juvenile

Small, slender falcon with long square-tipped tail. Upperparts and crown slaty-grey; creamy buff underparts heavily streaked black; chestnut thighs and vent; underwings and undertail barred; pale throat and cheeks; dark moustache; thin white line above eye. Sexes alike. Juvenile more brownish and mottled; creamish thighs and vent, and bluish-grey to greenish legs and facial skin. Aerial feeder, pursuing bats and small birds. The rarer Oriental Hobby, *F. severus*, is even darker with chestnut underparts.

ORIENTAL HOBBY

Falco severus Falconidae

Size 27–30 cm

Voice Call includes a shrill trill of 3- to 4-notes

Range Resident to the Himalayas, NE India

Habitat Forested, hilly country

Small, robust falcon with slaty-grey upperparts; deep black head and cheeks; rich chestnut underparts, paler on throat. Long, pointed wings; short, powerful bill with 'tooth' on sides; black teardrop-shaped patch on sides of head. Juvenile has rufous breast, streaked black and some mottling on back. Fast flying birds attaining high speed as they dive from high altitudes to knock out birds; eats on wing or on perch. Nests in holes in trees or in nest of another species; in trees, building ledges or cliffs.

LAGGAR FALCON

Falco jugger Falconidae

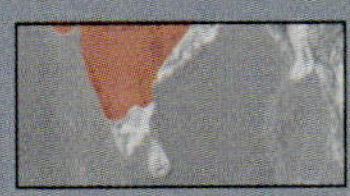

Size 45 cm

Voice Call a 2-or 3-noted scream, mostly when breeding

Range Resident, local migrant; all over India, to about 1,000 m in the Himalayas

Habitat Open country; scrubs

Overall dark greyish-brown falcon with white head; rufous crown; narrow, dark moustache. Whitish underparts streaked densely on flanks. In flight, pale breast contrasts with darker flanks and thighs; longish tail. Sexes alike, but female larger. In juvenile, underbody below throat dark brown. Juvenile similar to adult, but has more heavily streaked underparts. Usually in pairs, often seen in towns and cities; pair often hunts in concert, chasing prey; spectacular displays at onset of breeding season. Returns to favourite perch.

PEREGRINE FALCON

Falco peregrinus Falconidae

Size 42 cm

Voice Variety of calls including loud, harsh, persistent chatter, used against intruders

Range Resident; all over India, to about 3,000 m in the Himalayas; not found in semi-arid regions

Habitat Mostly rugged, mountainous areas; cliffs

calidus

One of the fastest fliers, the Peregrine is fairly large; stocky falcon with pointed wings and relatively short, square tail. Upperparts bluish-grey; underparts reddish-brown with variable dark spotting and barring; barred underwing and tail; pale throat and cheeks; broad, dark moustachial stripe. Yellowish-orange facial skin and legs; bluish beak, tinged yellow at base and black at tip. Sexes similar, but female substantially larger. Juvenile more brown with heavily streaked underparts, and blue-grey or greenish legs and facial skin.

peregrianator

OSPREY

Pandion haliaetus Accipitridae

Size 55-58 cm

Voice Short, nasal scream. Calls rarely

Range In parts of the Himalayas, between about 2,000-3,500 m. Winter visitor all over India

Habitat Lakes; rivers; coastal lagoons

Large bird whose long wings have characteristic bend at carpal joints. Underparts sharp white, with dark brown patches at carpal joints and mottled dark brown necklace. Dark eye-stripe; dark brown back; pale blue-grey feet; black beak. Female heavier and darker with more defined necklace. Solitary, or in scattered pairs; circles over water; hovers characteristically; dives with feet dangling; often splashes into water; carries fish on to perch.

ORIENTAL HONEY-BUZZARD

Pernis ptilorhynchus Accipitridae

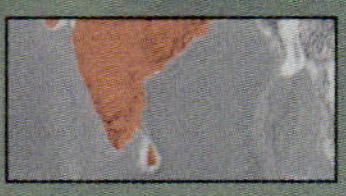

Size 65 cm

Voice Call a high-pitched, long-drawn *weeeeeu…*

Range Resident and local migrant; subcontinent to about 2,000 m in the Himalayas

Habitat Forests; open country; cultivation; vicinity of villages

Highly variable buzzard. Upperparts greyish-brown; grey head, underparts range from cream to blackish-brown and marked and streaked; slender head; longish neck distinctive; tail rarely fanned; crest rarely visible; pale underside of wings barred; broad dark subterminal tail-band; two or three more bands on tail; tarsus unfeathered. Scale-like feathers around eyes and forehead protect from stings of wasps, bees and hornets the bird preys upon. Specialises in feeding on larvae and honey of bees and wasps.

BLACK-WINGED KITE

Elanus caeruleus Accipitridae

Size 32 cm

Voice Generally silent. Call a weak *weeet…weeet…weeet* when agitated

Range All over India, to about 1,500 m in the outer Himalayas

Habitat Open scrub and grass country; light forests

Striking bird of prey with pure white head and breast and ruby-red eyes surrounded by black patches. Grey crown, back of neck and upperparts; black patch on upper edges of wings. Juvenile similar but with more brown upperparts and dusky streaks on crown; yellowish-brown breast and head. Solitary, or in pairs; sits on exposed perch or flies over open scrub and grass country; mostly hunts on wing.

BLACK KITE

Milvus migrans Accipitridae

Size 47-60 cm

Voice Call a loud, musical whistle

Range Resident; subcontinent upto about 2,200 m in the Himalayas, co-existing with Black-eared in some localities

Habitat Mostly neighbourhood of humans

Medium-sized raptor; overall very dark brown plumage with light brown and rufous markings, particularly on head, neck and underparts. Light brown bar on shoulder; tail forked and barred darker brown; edges of wings appear 'fingered', dark brown eye; black bill with yellow cere. Sexes similar. Juvenile lighter brown with less pronounced fork in tail.

BRAHMINY KITE

Haliastur indus Accipitridae

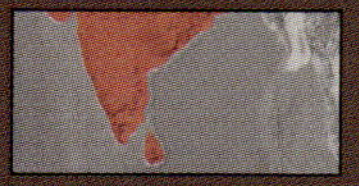

Size 50 cm

Voice Loud scream

Range Resident and local migrant; subcontinent

juvenile

Habitat Margins of lakes; marshes; rivers; sea coasts

White head, neck, throat, upper belly and flanks diagnostic. Chestnut wing-coverts, thighs and tail; black outer flight feathers; white-tipped tail. Sexes similar in appearance; female tends to be slightly larger. Juvenile various shades of brown, with darker upperparts and lighter head and underparts and rounder tail. Solitary, or in pairs, scavenging; also hunts for live food including crabs, crustaceans, amphibians, small reptiles, fish, insects, small mammals and birds.

juvenile

WHITE-BELLIED SEA EAGLE

Haliaeetus leucogaster Accipitridae

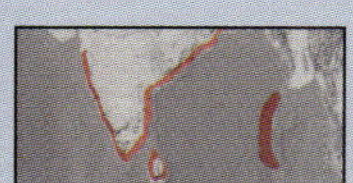

Size 70 cm

Voice Call a loud goose-like honking *hank…hank…hank* typically heard during breeding season

Range Resident; coast of Bombay and all along the E coast; flies many miles inland to freshwater lakes, rivers

Habitat Islands; rocky coasts; large inland waterbodies; wetlands

Ash-brown and white bird with pure white head, neck and short white tail. Black flight feathers; white underwing-coverts; pale blue-grey hooked bill with dark tip and grey cere; dark brown eyes; pale greyish yellow legs and feet. Sexes similar, but female larger. Juvenile has dark brown upperparts and wings, white-edged feathers on back and wing-coverts; white tail with brown subterminal band.

GREY-HEADED FISH EAGLE

Ichthyophaga ichthyaetus Accipitridae

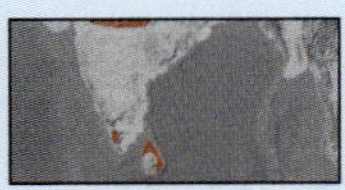

Size 61-75 cm

Voice Calls include *awh-awhr* and *chee-warr* repeated

Range Resident; from E Delhi to Assam; south through the peninsula

Habitat Lakes, rivers in forested country

Striking bird with relatively small head, longish neck and powerful, grey beak. Upperparts brownish-grey and white underparts. Rounded tail; sandy-yellow eyes; long, black talons; relatively short legs; and tail with broad, black terminal band. Female larger and heavier than male. Juvenile has white belly mottled with brown.

EGYPTIAN VULTURE

Neophron percnopterus Accipitridae

Size 60-70 cm

Voice Usually silent

Range All over India; plains to about 2,000 m in the Himalayas

Habitat Open areas or semi-open areas

Small vulture with mostly bare head that shows yellow to orange coloured skin. Ruff long whitish feathers on hindneck; brownish neck and back. Long pointed wings and long wedge-shaped tail; dark flight feathers; long, slender bill with curved tip; blood red iris; yellow or light grey legs. Immature uniformly brown. Nests solitarily, sometimes in loose colonies. Seen in small numbers on ground or gliding downhill slopes.

ginginianus

rubripersonatos

juvenile

INDIAN VULTURE

Gyps indicus Accipitridae

Size 90 cm

Voice Quieter than White-rumped

Range Formerly common breeding resident except in extreme south and Sri Lanka. Now globally threatened and very local. Most frequent in large wildlife sanctuaries

Habitat As White-rumped. Nests colonially exclusively on cliff ledges and buildings

Scruffy-looking bird with bald head, very broad wings, and short tail feathers. Pale yellow bill; pale eye-rings; white neck-ruff, black neck and head. Brown upperwings graduating to cream below. Dark flight feathers and tail form striking contrast to pale underparts. Cream feathered thighs. Juvenile has dark bill with pale culmen, pinkish head and neck with pale below; brown and cream-streaked undersides.

WHITE-RUMPED VULTURE

Gyps bengalensis Accipitridae

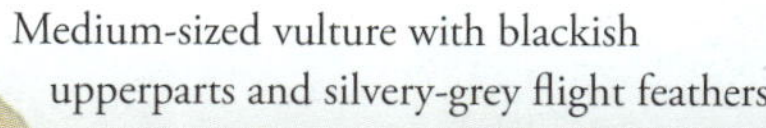

Size 85 cm

Voice Utters sounds mainly at carcass, when disputes and interactions occur

Range Formerly very common breeding resident throughout. Now globally threatened

Habitat Open country

Medium-sized vulture with blackish upperparts and silvery-grey flight feathers. Pure white rump, giving the bird its name. Brown-black underparts, finely streaked cream. White underwings, coverts visible in flight; black undertail-coverts; dark brown head and neck; downy, cream crown and nape with buff-white ruff. Brownish-black bill and cere; black legs and feet and brown eyes. Sexes alike. Eyes brown. Legs and feet black. Juvenile dark brown with streaked underparts. Often seen on thermal currents, circling with almost motionless wings.

juvenile

GRIFFON VULTURE

Gyps fulvus Accipitridae

Size 100 cm

Voice Quiet. Grunts and hisses when feeding

Range Common breeding resident to W Pakistan hills, N India and Nepal to E Sikkim. Winters widely in lowlands of Pakistan and NW India, south to Gujarat and Madhya Pradesh

Habitat Mountains and semi-desert, wandering into nearby dry plains in winter

Large, carnivorous scavenger, with impressive creamy-white ruff. Plain pale reddish-brown upperparts; white head and neck; yellow bill; dark flight feathers on rest of wings and tail; pale underwing-coverts with bands of white. Juvenile has very pale upperwing feathers and grey bill. Breeds colonially containing 15 to 20 pairs. Builds nest on cliff-face, preferably in protected ledge or cave. Usually in pairs or small groups, often with other vultures.

RED-HEADED VULTURE

Sarcogyps calvus Accipitridae

Size 85 cm

Voice Call a hoarse croak

Range Scarce resident; all over India, upto about 2,800 m in the Himalayas

Habitat Open country; village outskirts

Medium-sized, bulky vulture with wingspan of over two metres. Unmistakable with its black feathers and bald red head. Two lappets attached to neck; thin, white margin on underside of wings at base of remiges; white patches on thigh. Sexes similar, male has white or yellow eyes while female has dark. Juvenile overall paler with more mottled plumage and dark eyes. Usually found alone, or in breeding pair.

SHORT-TOED SNAKE EAGLE

Circaetus gallicus Acciptridae

Size 65 cm

Voice Call a loud *kee yo*

Range Scarce breeding resident in lowlands, more common and widespread winter visitor except in NE India, Bangladesh and Sri Lanka

Habitat Open country with preference for scrubby grasslands

Large, long-winged eagle with large head, relatively small beak and long, bare legs. Upperparts, head, throat and chest brown; white underparts, marked with dark bars and blotches. Dark flight feathers of tail marked with three to four dark bands; bright yellow eye and grey legs. Sexes similar, female heavier with slightly longer tail. Feeds on snakes, usually eaten whole.

EURASIAN MARSH HARRIER

Circus aeruginosus Accipitridae

Size 55 cm

Voice Usually silent

Range Winter visitor; common; subcontinent, south of the Himalayan foothills; most common in N India

Habitat Marshes; jheels; wet cultivation

Large broad-winged harrier, with sexes dissimilar. Male overall dark reddish-brown with buff-yellow streaks, more dense on breast; dull rufous head and breast; silvery-grey wings, tail; black wing-tips visible in flight; legs, feet, iris and cere yellow; black bill. Female and juvenile uniform chocolate brown; throat, crown and shoulders have yellowish wash; lack grey tail and wing-patch.

juvenile

juvenile

juvenile

CRESTED SERPENT EAGLE

Spilornis cheela Accipitridae

Size 65-75 cm

Voice Call a loud whistling scream *keee…kee…ke…*

Range Subcontinent, to about 3,000 m in the Himalayas

Habitat Forested country

juvenile

Medium-sized eagle with brown upperparts and light brown underparts. Wing-coverts and scapulars heavily streaked and mottled; black flight feathers with broad bands; black crown and nape; brown crest barred white; rusty orange thighs and belly barred and mottled white; short, broad wings; bright yellow eyes. Fans crest when alarmed. Solitary, or in pairs; flies high over forests and swoops down on prey.

HEN HARRIER

Circus cyaneus Accipitridae

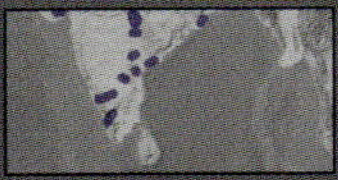

Size 40 cm

Voice Usually silent

Range Winter visitor to mainly Pakistan, the Himalayas and N India

Habitat Open country, grasslands and cultivation in plains and foothills

♀

Slender, medium-sized raptor with flat owl-like face and broad wings. Long, rounded tail; sharp, hooked bill. Upperparts grey; underparts whitish; black wing-tips, dark trailing edge to wing; black-banded tail; white patch on rump, conspicuous in flight. Female brown, with black bands on tail; whitish underparts streaked brown. Juvenile also brown, but more buffy and less streaked. Roosts gregariously on ground. All Northern Harriers have white rump patch obvious in flight, with wings held in V-shape.

PIED HARRIER

Circus melanoleucos Accipitridae

Size 45–49 cm

Voice Usually silent

Range Resident: Manas and adjoining areas in Assam. Winter visitor over parts of E India and erratically in parts of C and S India

Habitat Grassy areas; cultivation; reedy edges of jheels

♀

Slim and long-winged raptor, overall white and grey. Black head, back, throat and breast; grey tail, wings; black primaries; black band across median coverts. Female dark brown above; pale white nape-patch, rump; pale buffy-rufous below; marked underside of flight feathers. Juvenile has pale marking on head, rufous brown underparts, dark upperwings; pale patch on primaries, white uppertail-covert patch. Solitary, or in pairs.

MONTAGU'S HARRIER

Circus pygargus Accipitridae

Size 48 cm

Voice Usually silent; alarm a high-pitched chatter

Range Rather scarce winter visitor throughout peninsula. Passage migrant through NW India. Rare in the east

Habitat Open country including cultivation; often in scattered groups

♀

♀

Slender, medium-sized, slim bird with long narrow wings and long tail. Extensive black marking on wing-tip; distinct black band on both lateral and dorsal sides of wing. Head, breast, back and inner wing dark grey; rest of wing and tail lighter grey; narrow white rump; chestnut streaking on belly and underwing. Female and immature streaked brown with flat owl-like faces and white rumps. Juvenile similar to female but has reddish-brown underparts. Roosts communally in long grass. Hunts birds, rodents and large insects.

CRESTED GOSHAWK

Accipiter trivirgatus Accipitridae

Size 42 cm

Voice Call a high-pitched scream *ke...ke...ke...ke*

Range Fairly common breeding resident

Habitat Forests

Large dark brown hawk with diagnostic black mesial-stripe from chin to breast. Long, brown tail has four wide black bands; brownish-black head with slight crest; black neck and white throat. White undertail; breast vertically streaked rufous; belly marked with horizontal dark brown bands. Iris, legs and feet yellow. Watches prey from perch, capturing it in rapid attack.

SHIKRA

Accipiter badius Accipitridae

Size 35 cm

Voice Call a loud, drongo-like *titew...titew*

Range Subcontinent, upto 1,600 m in the Himalayas

Habitat Light forests; open country; neighbourhood of villages. Also in cities

Adult male has uniform grey upperparts, with faint rufous half-collar. Dark grey primaries tipped black. Underparts white, with narrow black streak from chin to throat centre; greyish red face and neck sides; breast and belly finely barred chestnut; grey tail has five dark bands and dark tip. Underwings rufous to buff; orange to red eye; yellowish-orange legs. Female larger, more slaty-brown and boldly barred.

♀

juvenile

BESRA

Accipiter virgatus Accipitridae

Size 32 cm

Voice Quite noisy. Call a high-pitched *chew…chew…chew*, when perched and in flight

Range Scarce breeding resident: The Himalayan foothills, Nepal, NE India, Western Ghats, Sri Lanka. Winters in N plains

Habitat Forests; open woodlands

Medium-sized raptor with short broad wings and long tail. Similar to Shikra, but darker and distinct dark vertical throat-stripe. Upperparts dark bluish-grey and whitish underparts barred rufous. Female larger and more brown. Juvenile has dark brown upperparts and white underparts barred brown with barred tail.

EURASIAN SPARROWHAWK

Accipiter nisus Accipitridae

Size 35 cm

Voice Rather quiet. Call a rapid *kew… kew…kew…kew* when nesting

Range Fairly common breeding resident

Habitat Open wooded country, including cultivation. Probably overlooked

Smallish sparrowhawk with long legs and short, rounded wings. Upperparts dark grey with pale underparts finely barred reddish-brown. Hooked beak; pale line above eye; white chin-patch. Female significantly larger, with darker, more brown upperparts and white underparts barred. Juvenile similar to female, but more brown upperparts, with rusty feather margins, broader barring on underparts; yellow iris. The Himalayan resident, *A.n. melaschistos*, is blackish-grey above.

WHITE-EYED BUZZARD

Butastur teesa Accipitridae

Size 45 cm

Voice Musical, plaintive *te…twee.* Calls frequently when breeding

Range Subcontinent, upto about 1,200 m in the Himalayas

Habitat Open and dry forests; cultivated country. Moves considerably

Ash-brown hawk with white throat, two dark cheek-stripes. Underparts brown-and-white; orange-yellow cere; whitish eyes with white and nuchal-patch buff shoulders. Solitary, or scattered pairs; seen on exposed perches, trees, poles or telegraph wires; seems to prefer certain sites; soars high and does aerial displays when breeding. Feeds on locusts, grasshoppers, crickets and other large insects as well as mice, lizards and frogs. Nests in loose, unlined cup of twigs in fork of thickly foliaged trees.

Juvenile

COMMON BUZZARD

Buteo buteo Accipitridae

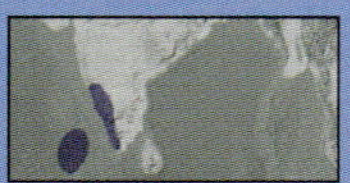

Size 51 cm

Voice Mostly silent in winter

Range Widespread winter visitor but status uncertain

Habitat Open wooded or cultivated areas

Large buzzard with broad, rounded wings, and short neck and tail. Plumage highly variable, ranging from darkish-brown to russet to pale buff. Upperparts darker; wing-tip and trailing edge of wing also darker than rest of wing feathers. Barred tail and flight feathers; streaked throat and breast. Wings held in shallow V-shape and tail fanned when gliding and soaring.

Steppe Buzzard

LONG-LEGGED BUZZARD

Buteo rufinus Accipitridae

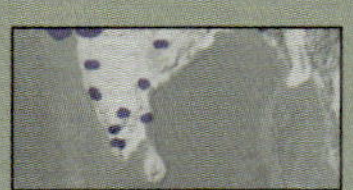

Size 43–58 cm

Voice Rather quiet

Range Breeds in a few parts of N India. Winters commonly in NW India, particularly Pakistan. Rare elsewhere

Habitat Open, uncultivated areas with high bushes, trees, cliffs or hillocks favoured nesting areas

Largest of buteo species with many colour morphs from pale white to dark brown but with clear orangish tint to plumage. Tail reddish and head pale. Underwings whitish; rump mostly dark brown. Hunts mostly small and medium-sized mammals. Often seen sitting on electricity posts, pylons and other vantage points.

rufous morph

GREATER SPOTTED EAGLE

Aquila clanga Accipitridae

Size 62-74 cm

Voice Call a loud, shrill *kaek… kaek…* often from perch

Range Globally threatened. Breeds in parts of NW India; spreads south in winter

Habitat Tree-covered areas in vicinity of water

Large eagle with massive wingspan. Adult almost entirely blackish except for some white in wings and base of tail. Immature has broad white bars on wings and white rump. Huge wings hold out straight from body when soaring. Seen mostly in open country, near freshwater. Often perches on low trees. Regularly seen on carcass; impressive master of the air.

fulvescens

BLACK EAGLE

Ictinaetus malayensis Accipitridae

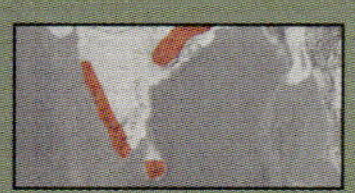

Size 69-81 cm

Voice Rather quiet. Call a loud *kee… kee…kee* when courting

Range Local breeding resident to N hills from E Punjab to Myanmar border, Bangladesh, and hills of Eastern and Western Ghats, Sri Lanka

Habitat Hills; mangrove forests

Almost entirely black eagle with yellow cere and yellow feet. Brown eyes; yellow-grey beak tipped black; white patches at base of primary feathers; extended primary feathers; long wings reach tail-tip at rest. Wings held in shallow V-shape with long upturned fingers when gliding. Juvenile has dark brown crown, nape, back, and wings, speckled buff-yellow; tail barred with grey; heavily streaked underparts. Normally seen soaring alone, or in pairs over canopy.

INDIAN SPOTTED EAGLE

Aquila hastata Accipitridae

Size 59-67 cm

Voice Very high-pitched cackling call

Range N subcontinent; largely unrecorded in Pakistan

Habitat Wooded areas interspersed with cultivation in lowlands. Globally threatened

Medium-sized eagle with short, broad wings and short tail. Adult overall brown. Broad head with wide mouth. Fleshy gape extending to middle of eye. Upperparts medium-brown; uppertail-coverts light brown barred white; large creamy spots on median coverts. Wings angled down at shoulder. In flight, shows rounder wings, lighter and slimmer than Greater Spotted. Seizes prey from ground whilst quartering over areas within, or near forests.

TAWNY EAGLE

Aquila rapax Accipitridae

Size 70 cm

Voice Loud crackling notes; high-pitched call

Range Sporadically over parts of the country; *nipalensis* is a winter visitor

Habitat Open country; vicinities of villages; towns and cultivation

Large, handsome bird with variable plumage ranging from very dark brown to light brown. Blackish flight feathers and tail, light bars on wings; short, rounded tail; pale lower back; brown eyes; yellow beak with dark tip; heavily feathered legs. Holds tail straight and parallel to body in flight. Female larger than male. Immature paler and more streaked, almost white.

juvenile

STEPPE EAGLE

Aquila nipalensis Accipitridae

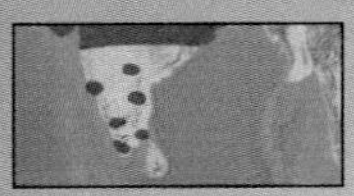

Size 80 cm

Voice Usually silent

Range Fairly common winter visitor

Habitat Lightly wooded and open country. Also villages and towns

juvenile

Adult overall dark brown, with well-defined bars on flight and tail feathers; pale-tipped secondaries; reddish-brown patch on nape of neck; long, wide gape; small head; pale throat; dark iris; yellow legs. Juvenile resembles adult, but paler brown, with characteristic broad white band running along underside of wing.

BONELLI'S EAGLE

Aquila fasciata Accipitridae

Size 70 cm

Voice Call a shrill scream of 3- to 6 notes

Range All over India, sporadically from about 2,400 m in the Himalayas

Habitat Forests

Large brown-and-white eagle with short, rounded wings and long tail. Dark brown back and wings; white belly and underparts mottled brown; white trailing edge to wing; black terminal band; grey patch at carpal joint; long, feathered legs; yellow-orange eyes; yellow feet and cere. Juvenile has pale chestnut underside and hazel eyes.

♀

juvenile

BOOTED EAGLE

Hieraaetus pennatus Accipitridae

Size 52 cm

Voice Call a loud scream of several notes

Range Breeds in the Himalayas

Habitat Open forests; scrubs

Has two distinct colour phases. In lighter phase, head paler as uppertail and upperwing-coverts. Buffy white wing linings, underbody and tail with blackish flight feathers distinctive. In darker phase, chocolate-brown below. Pale-banded tail makes it easily identifiable in flight. Often seen alone, or sometimes in pairs hunting in concert. Often roosts together at night.

pale morph

RUFOUS-BELLIED EAGLE

Lophotriorchis kienerii Accipitridae

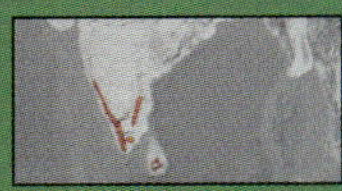

Size 60 cm

Voice Normally silent, but has plaintive scream when breeding

Range Rare breeding resident: Western Ghats, Sri Lanka, Nepal, Bangladesh, NE India and the Himalayan foothills

Habitat Humid forests

Medium-sized raptor with black hood and short crest. Black upperparts; white to rufous throat and chest; rufous belly and legs streaked black; brown, square tail; undertail barred black-and-white; barred wings; white base to primary feathers; red-brown eyes; yellow cere and feet; feathered legs. Juvenile has dark brown upperparts, brown crown and nape, and two black eye-patches white underparts and grey tail with dark, narrow barring and white tip. Normally seen soaring over canopy.

CHANGEABLE HAWK EAGLE

Nisaetus c limnaeetus Accipitridae

Size 70 cm

Voice Similar to Crested, but slower

Range The Himalayan foothills; NE India, Andaman Islands and Bangladesh

Habitat Well-wooded country

Recently split from Crested Hawk to which it is very similar. Mostly distinguished by its prominent crest. Also, lacks dark morph. Tail more heavily barred. Usually solitary, or in pairs; soars infrequently.

MOUNTAIN HAWK EAGLE

Nisaetus nipalensis Accipitridae

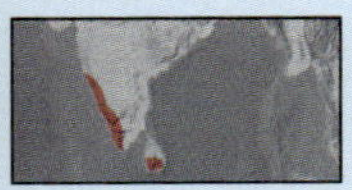

Size 72 cm

Voice Call a high whistling *peeo… peeo* during breeding season

Range Locally common breeding resident: N mountains, Western Ghats and Sri Lanka

Habitat Upland forests

Large brown-and-white raptor with brown upperparts, rufous head and black, pale-tipped crest. Belly and underwing-coverts barred dark brown; tail has three bands and grey-brown from above and white below. Juvenile dark brown with buff to tawny underparts, barred tail and white legs. Broad wings with curved trailing edge, held in shallow V-shape in flight.

juvenile

GREAT INDIAN BUSTARD

Ardeotis nigriceps Otididae

Size Male 120 cm; Female 92 cm

Voice Call a loud *whonk*... often audible for over a mile

Range Resident and local migrant; distant areas of Rajasthan, Gujarat, Maharashtra, Karnataka; numbers and erstwhile range much reduced today

Habitat Open grasslands and scrubs; semi-desert

Large, long-necked, long-legged bird. Male has black crown, short crest; sandy-buff upperbody, finely marked back; white neck and underparts; black band on lower breast; well-developed gular pouch. Female smaller; breast gorget broken and only rarely full. Scattered pairs, or small parties; shy, difficult to approach; enters immediate vicinity of Bishnoi villages and other rural habitation; fast runner; hides in shade of bushes; flies low over ground.

LESSER FLORICAN

Sypheotides indicus Otididae

Size 45 cm

Voice Call a rattling click in display; whistles when flushed

Range Globally threatened endemic breeding visitor to few sites in NC India. Reportedly moves to SE India after breeding, but rarely recorded there

Habitat Dry, scrubby grasslands; tall crops

Small, slender bustard, with long, curved neck and long, thin legs. Adult male has distinct, black head plumes with spatulate tips. Black head, neck and belly; brown back and wing feathers brown edged black; whitish collar and white coverts. Female larger and more sandy brown with black streaks on head, neck and underparts. Juvenile similar to female. Jumps suddenly out of grass, into air in courtship display. Solitary, or in pairs. Lays eggs on ground in small patch of grass. Omnivorous, eats both invertebrates as well as plant shoots.

SLATY-LEGGED CRAKE

Rallina eurizonoides Rallidae

Size 25 cm

Voice Noisy mix of double-notes

Range All over India

Habitat Well-watered areas

Rich brown bird with short, rounded wings. Rufous head and breast, reddish-brown iris, bold, strong black-and-white barring on flanks, underparts and undertail; small white throat-patch, yellowish or greyish bill, greenish-grey legs. Sexes similar. Walks through leaf litter, foraging on berries, insects, worms and molluscs.

SPOTTED CRAKE

Porzana porzana Rallidae

Size 22 cm

Voice Silent in winter

Range Winter visitor over most of the country

Habitat Reed-covered jheels, vegetation in and around marshes

Adult brown above, with rufescent wash, streaked black; grey supercilium, sides of head and neck; whitish chin, throat; greyish breast spotted white; white barring on grey-brown flanks. Sexes alike. Solitary, or in pairs; crepuscular.

SLATY-BREASTED RAIL

Gallirallus striatus Rallidae

Size 27 cm

Voice Call a harsh, repeated *gelek*

Range Scarce but overlooked resident throughout peninsula, NE India, Bangladesh and Sri Lanka. Also occurs in China and SE Asia

Habitat Well-vegetated freshwater marshes and adjacent scrubs

Medium-sized bird with longish, straight bill. Chestnut forehead, hindneck and neck sides; rest of upperparts olive-brown, spotted and barred white; blackish underparts, barred white; white chin and throat; grey breast; red iris. Female has duller head and neck; paler upperparts and whitish belly. Extremely shy and somewhat crepuscular. Feeds on insects and seeds. Nests well-hidden on ground.

WATER RAIL

Rallus aquaticus Rallidae

Size 25-28

Voice Shrill squeal

Range Breeds in Kashmir

Habitat Marshes; reed beds; paddy cultivation; ponds

Similar to Brown-cheeked Rail, from which it has recently been split.

BROWN CRAKE

Amaurornis akool Rallidae

Size 28 cm

Voice Mostly silent, but a plaintive note and long-drawn, vibrating whistle

Range Local migrant; south from Kashmir lowlands down through the peninsula, at least to Karnataka and Odisha

Habitat Reed-covered marshes; irrigation channels; dense growth on jheels

Overall olive-brown crake with white chin and throat that fades into ash-grey underparts; more brown on breast, flanks and abdomen. Sexes alike, but female slightly smaller. Solitary, or in pairs; mostly crepuscular; extremely elusive and secretive; feeds in early mornings and late evenings on edges of jheels, flicking stub tail and generally moving very suspiciously.

RUDDY-BREASTED CRAKE

Porzana fusca Rallidae

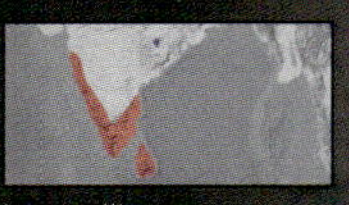

Size 22 cm

Voice Rather quiet, but makes soft crake calls, sometimes accelerated into trill

Range Scarce breeding resident, local migrant. Most often recorded from N Pakistan, Nepal, Bangladesh, Sri Lanka and Western Ghats

Habitat Secretive; crepuscular and thus easily overlooked. Well-vegetated marshes; jheels and riverbanks

Medium to small, uniformly reddish-brown crake. Upperparts brown; deep chestnut forehead, forecrown and sides of head; pale throat, deep red underparts and white-barred black undertail-coverts; bright pink legs and feet. Sexes similar, but female paler. Juvenile more brown with faint white barring on underparts.

BAILLON'S CRAKE

Porzana pusilla Rallidae

Size 19 cm

Voice Call a frog-like or grasshopper-like dry rattling *trrr…trrr.* Unlikely to be heard unless breeding

Range Common breeding visitor to Kashmir. Scarce passage migrant and winter visitor throughout the region

Habitat Marshes; reedy jheel edges; small ponds; wet paddy. Much overlooked

Very small crake with streaked black-and-white upperparts. Pale grey underparts that stretch from breast to around eyes. Pale green bill and legs. Sexes similar in appearance, but female often has reddish-brown streak over ear and paler grey upperparts; stout, well-muscled legs with three forward-facing toes and one hind toe. Juvenile has mottled-white breast and more barred. Walks with bobbing head and flicking tail.

WHITE-BREASTED WATERHEN

Amaurornis phoenicurus Rallidae

Size 32 cm

Voice Very noisy when breeding during rains, series of loud croaks and chuckles, the commonest being a harsh *krr… khwakk…* . Often calls through the night; silent during dry season

Range South from the Himalayan foothills

Habitat Reed-covered marshes; ponds; tanks; monsoon cultivation; streams

midnicobarica

juvenile

Large, distinctive-looking bird with white forehead and sides of head and dark slaty-grey upperparts. Underparts silky white; slaty-grey sides of breast and flanks; rufous on vent and undertail-coverts; stump-like tail. Sexes alike. Solitary, or in small groups; often around village ponds and tanks. Walks with long strides; climbs trees easily, especially when breeding.

WATERCOCK

Gallicrex cinerea Rallidae

Size 36 cm

Voice Booming call when breeding

Range Scarce local migrant throughout lowlands, breeding mainly in NE India, Bangladesh and Sri Lanka. Also occurs in E and SE Asia

Habitat Extensive reed beds, marshes and wet paddy. Also tidal estuaries when migrating.

Mainly blue-black bird; conical red bill an extended 'frontal shield'; green legs. Female smaller with dark brown upperparts and paler below with streaked and barred plumage; yellow bill and green legs. Probes mud for insects, small fish and seeds, but also picks food by sight. Secretive, but seen in the open. Crepuscular; secretive, stacking flight.

♀

COMMON COOT

Fulica atra Rallidae

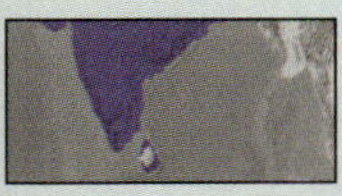

Size 40 cm

Voice Quite noisy. Calls include abrupt *towk*, sharper *pseek*; various conversational chucklings

Range Common winter visitor throughout lowlands but rather sporadic breeder

Habitat Large swimming flocks on open water of jheels and rivers, often mixing with duck. Walks on floating vegetation

Roundish bird with greyish body, black head, neck and white bill. Has distinct white 'frontal shield'; almost no tail; white-tipped secondary flight feathers; pale grey underwing; pale pinkish-white bill; deep red eyes. Greenish-yellow legs with grey, lobed feet. Breeding male shows broader white shield than female. Juvenile has whitish head sides, breast and foreneck; brownish-grey body; no white frontal shield. Gregarious in non-breeding season when it forms large flocks. Weak and reluctant flier.

COMMON MOORHEN

Gallinula chloropus Rallidae

Size 32 cm

Voice Extremely vocal; capable of bizarre, distinctive sounds, including a variety of clucks and chattering calls

Range All over India, upto about 2,400 m in the Himalayas; breeds commonly in Kashmir

Habitat Vegetation and reed-covered ponds; tanks; jheels

Medium-sized, striking looking waterbird Distinctive red shield; short, yellow bill; dark olive-brown upperparts; grey underparts; white centre of abdomen; bright yellowish-green legs; white trim on undertail. Sexes alike but female slightly larger. Juvenile has brown-grey crown, neck and back, paler and whitish throat and belly. In small feeding groups in marsh vegetation. Jerks head and tail while swimming.

juvenile

DEMOISELLE CRANE

Grus virgo Gruidae

Size 95 cm

Voice Call a high-pitched, sonorous *kraak...kraak...*

Range Winter visitor; most common in NW India and over E Rajasthan, Gujarat and Madhya Pradesh, though sporadically over much of area

Habitat Winter crop fields; sandy riverbanks; ponds

Overall grey bird with black head and neck, prominent white ear tufts. Long black feathers of lower neck fall over breast; brownish-grey secondaries sickle-shaped and drooping over tail. Juvenile has grey head and much shorter drooping secondaries over tail than adult. Sexes alike. Huge flocks in winter, often many thousands. Feeds early mornings and early evenings in cultivation; rests during hot hours on marsh edges and sandbanks; flies en masse when disturbed.

juvenile

SARUS CRANE

Grus antigone Gruidae

Size 165 cm

Voice Call includes a very loud, far-reaching trumpeting, often a duet between pair; elaborate dancing rituals

Range Most common in N and C India (E Rajasthan, Gujarat, N and C Madhya Pradesh, Gangetic plains)

Habitat Marshes; jheels; well-watered cultivation; village ponds

juvenile

Grey crane with naked red head and upper neck. Small pale grey ear-patch on head sides; sparse black feathers on chin and upper neck; pale brown to orange eyes. Long, pointed, grey bill; pinkish-red legs. Sexes alike, but female slightly smaller than male. Juvenile brownish-grey, with rusty-brown on head. In pairs, family parties or flocks; also feeds along with other waterbirds; known to pair for life and usually well-protected in Northern and West-Central India, but habitat loss continues to be a grave threat; flies under 12 m off ground.

COMMON CRANE

Grus grus Gruidae

Size 140 cm

Voice Call a loud, strident trumpeting *krr...oohk...*; calls on ground and from high in sky; also other harsh, screeching notes

Range Winter visitor; commonest in NW India, progressively less towards the east, rarely straying south of S Maharashtra and N Andhra Pradesh

Habitat Cultivation of wheat, gram, groundnut; also riverbeds

Large, impressive crane with pale slaty-grey plumage; slight red on crown; black face, throat and white stripe on sides of head, neck; black flight-feathers and dark, drooping tail plumes diagnostic; bright red or reddish-brown eye. Sexes alike. Juvenile has yellowish-brown tips to feathers; lacks drooping wing feathers, neck pattern; fully-feathered crown. Gregarious in winter; feeds in mornings and evenings in cultivation; rests during day; rather shy and suspicious, ever alert; slow, but strong flight.

YELLOW-LEGGED BUTTONQUAIL

Turnix tanki Turnicidae

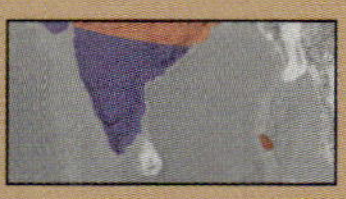

Size 15–16 cm

Voice Loud, drumming call

Range All over India, from about 1,200 m in the Himalayas

Habitat Damp grasslands; scrubs; cultivation

Grey-brown bird. Blackish crown has rufous and buff; pale stripe through centre of crown; white chin, throat; buffy underparts with dark spots on sides of breast; yellow legs and beak; beak reddish-brown above and chrome-yellow below. Female slightly larger than male.

BARRED BUTTONQUAIL

Turnix suscitator Turnicidae

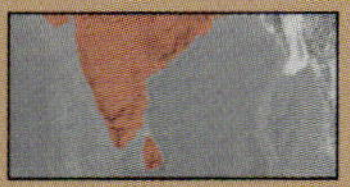

Size 15 cm

Voice Loud, drumming call of female during breeding

Range All over India, south of the Himalayas

Habitat Grass; scrubs

Distinctive white eye; dark brown crown; black specks on white sides of head; back speckled with white, black and brown. Pale buff on wing shoulders seen in flight diagnostic. Sexes alike. Female slightly larger and more brightly coloured.

♀

♀

SMALL BUTTONQUAIL

Turnix sylvaticus Turnicidae

Size 13 cm

Voice Female has a far-carrying, low-pitched, intermittent hoot at dusk and dawn

Range Probably fairly common resident throughout lowlands, but much overlooked

Habitat Scrubby, dry grasslands

Small bird with round body, small head and short, pointed wings, small grey bill, yellowish legs and white iris. Mostly brown with broad buff feather edgings above; paler, speckled head with crown-stripe. Orangish-buff below with black spotting on flanks. Female slightly larger.

INDIAN THICK-KNEE

Burhinus o indicus Burhinidae

Size 41 cm

Voice Plaintive, curlew-like call at dusk; also sharp *pick…pick…* notes

Range Drier parts of the subcontinent, upto about 1,200 m in the outer Himalayas

Habitat Light, dry forests, scrubs, dry riverbanks; Stony country; orchards; open *acacia* clad areas

Sandy-brown bird streaked darker; whitish underparts; thick head, long, bare, yellow legs and large goggle-eyes diagnostic; white wing-patch in flight; black-tipped bill with yellow base. Sexes alike. Solitary, or in pairs; strictly a ground bird; crepuscular and nocturnal.

GREAT THICK-KNEE

Esacus recurvirostris Burhinidae

Size 50 cm

Voice Harsh call-note, somewhat whistle-like; wild, piping calls at night

Range Almost all over India, south of the Terai; uncommon in NE regions

Habitat Dry, open country; barren lands; riverbanks; rocky areas; islands; jheels

Sandy-grey bird with large head and large upturned, black and yellow beak; large goggle-eyes surrounded by white, two black bands on face; white below, washed grey on neck, breast; white in-flight feathers, visible at night. Sexes alike. Solitary, or in pairs on open barren land, riverbanks or rocks in mid-river; mostly crepuscular and partly nocturnal; spends day under strong sun resting; usually very difficult to spot; extremely wary.

EURASIAN OYSTERCATCHER

Haematopus ostralegus Charadriidae

Size 42 cm

Voice Call a piping *kleeeep*… in flight; also a shrill whistle, often double-noted, uttered on ground as well as in flight

Range Winter visitor, especially to the coastal regions; most common on western seaboard

Habitat Rocky and sandy coastal areas

Large oystercatcher with distinct pied plumage. Black head, upperparts and breast; white underparts; long orange beak and pinkish legs distinctive. White on throat in winter. White rump and broad wing-bar conspicuous in flight. Juvenile more brown than adult. Sexes alike. Most common on sea coasts; frequently associates with other shorebirds; runs and probes mud; beak highly specialised for feeding on molluscs.

CRAB PLOVER

Dromas ardeola Glareolidae

Size 41 cm

Voice Call a goose-like honking *qurk...qurk...qurk*

Range Very local winter visitor to most coasts

Habitat Sandy coasts; reefs

Distinctly-patterned, large, ungainly wader. Overall black-and-white with long, bluish legs; heavy, straight black bill; large, white head with black-edged eye; short, grey tail. Juvenile more uniform grey-brown. Feeds in plover-like manner, scattered over flats or among exposed reefs, mainly on crabs but also mudskippers. Nests in deep burrows in sandbanks. Feeds at low tide. Often confiding.

juvenile

BLACK-WINGED STILT

Himantopus himantopus Charadriidae

Size 35 cm

Voice Calls include shrill notes in flight, very tern-like. Noisy when breeding

Range Resident and local migrant all over India, south from about 1,800 m in W Himalayas

Habitat Marshes; salt pans; tidal creeks; village ponds; also riversides

Characterised by long, red legs and black-and-white plumage. Jet-black mantle has greenish iridescence; rest of plumage glossy white. Underparts white, sometimes with pale pinkish wash on breast. Pointed wings. Female dark brown with black spots on head; duller overall in winter. Gregarious; seen in large numbers, often along with other waders in wetlands; long legs enable to enter relatively deep water; clumsy walk; submerges head when feeding.

♀

juvenile

PIED AVOCET

Recurvirostra avosetta Charadriidae

Size 45 cm

Voice Call a loud, somewhat fluty *klooeet* or *kloeep*, mostly on wing; also some harsh, screaming notes

Range Breeds in Kutch, N Balochistan; winter visitor, sporadically over most parts of the country; most common in NW regions

Habitat Freshwater marshes; coastal tidal areas; creeks

Long-legged, black-and-white wader with slender upcurved beak, long bluish-black, long legs extend much beyond tail in flight. Black head, upper neck and inner scapulars; dark brown greater coverts; rest of plumage pure white. Sexes alike. Usually gregarious, frequently enters shallow water; characteristic sideways movement of head when feeding with head bent low as upcurved beak sweeps along bottom mud; also swims and upends. Nests in colonies on sandbanks.

YELLOW-WATTLED LAPWING

Vanellus malabaricus Charadriidae

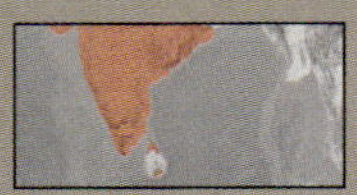

Size 27 cm

Voice Quiet. Calls include short, plaintive notes; quick-repeated notes when nest site intruded upon

Range From NW India, south through the area; does not occur in extreme NE India

Habitat Dry, open country

Medium to large wader with jet-black crown, bordered with white. Upperparts sandy-brown; black trailing edge to secondaries. In flight, white bar in black wings; black chin and throat; sandy-brown breast; white belly; black band on lower breast; white below; lemon-yellow wattles above and in front of eyes and yellow legs diagnostic. Sexes alike.

juvenile

SOCIABLE LAPWING

Vanellus gregarius Charadriidae

Size 27-30 cm

Voice Rather quiet

Range Winter visitor, now mainly to Pakistan, N and NW India

Habitat Dry fallow fields, stubbles and scrub desert. Globally threatened

Distinctly marked plover with olive-brown upperparts, throat and breast. Olive-brown head with conspicuous white supercilium from forehead to neck; black crown and lores; fine black eye-line extending to rear of eye; white chin; black and chestnut belly; white vent and undertail-coverts; white rump and uppertail feathers; subterminal white crescent-shaped patch visible in flight. Black bill; dark brown eyes; blackish feet. Female duller than male. Juvenile similar to adult, but has heavily streaked face, crown and breast. Feeding behaviour similar to that of Red-wattled.

RED-WATTLED LAPWING

Vanellus indicus Charadriidae

Size 35 cm

Voice Quiet. Calls include short, plaintive notes; quick-repeated notes when nest site intruded upon

Range From NW India, south through country; does not occur in extreme NE India

Habitat Dry, open country

Jet-black head, neck, breast; bronze-brown upperbody; white below, continuing to broad bands up the neck-sides towards eyes; fleshy crimson facial wattles diagnostic. Solitary or pairs when breeding; often large flocks in winter; moves on open ground, feeds during mornings and evenings; vigilant species, its loud cries heraldng any new activity in an area; feeds late into evening.

atronuchalis

indicus

juvenile

WHITE-TAILED LAPWING

Vanellus leucurus Charadriidae

Size 28 cm

Voice Mostly silent in winter except for an occasional soft, double-noted whistle

Range Winter visitor, NW India; smaller in number east to Uttar Pradesh, parts of Bihar, C India

Habitat Open marshy areas; edges of lakes and jheels

Elegant looking bird with unusually long, bright yellow legs. Upperparts greyish-brown tinged with pink and streaked black; pinkish-brown head and back; long, dark bill; grey-white forehead, supercilium; ash-grey chin, throat, turning dark-grey on breast; rusty-red ring around eye. Sexes alike. Juvenile has mottled, grey-brown neck and breast, dark-centred feathers on upperparts. In small to medium-sized flocks, often with other waders.

RIVER LAPWING

Vanellus duvaucelii Charadriidae

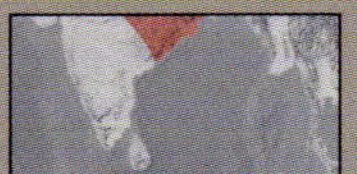

Size 30 cm

Voice Rather like that of Red-wattled, only bit softer and less shrill; also sharp *deed...did...did...*

Range Breeds in parts of E and C India, including Odisha, Andhra Pradesh and E Madhya Pradesh; may disperse in winter

Habitat Stony riverbeds, sandbanks; sometimes collects around jheels in winter

Striking bird in flight with black primaries, white underwings and upperwing secondaries, and brown upperwing-coverts. Black crest, crown, face and central throat and greyish-white nape and neck sides. Underparts white; grey-brown breast-band; black belly-patch brown back; white rump, black tail. Sexes alike, but male slightly larger. Juvenile has brown tips to black head feathers, sandier brown back, pale fringes to upperpart and wing-covert feathers. Usually pairs in close vicinity; may collect into small parties during winter, sometimes with other waders.

PACIFIC GOLDEN PLOVER

Pluvialis fulva Charadriidae

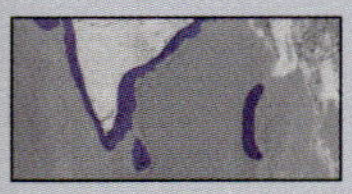

Size 25 cm

Voice Distinct *tu…leep* like a soft Spotted Redshank

Range Locally common winter visitor to all coasts and inland in Bangladesh and NE India. Most common in SE India and Bangladesh. Scarce but regular passage migrant to inland and elsewhere

Habitat Coastal mudflats; salt pans and grasslands. Inland on marshes, jheels

breeding

non-breeding

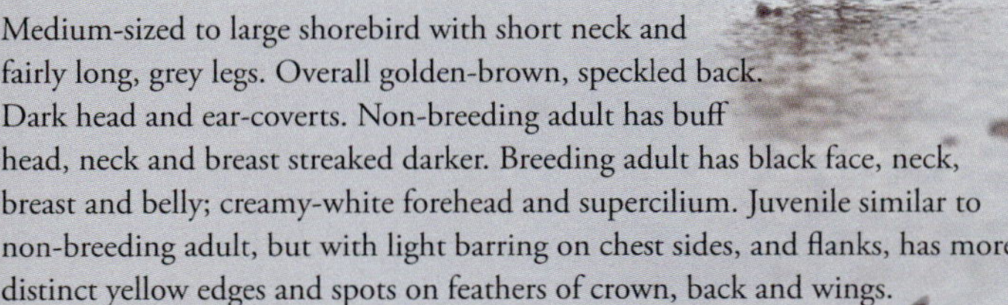

Medium-sized to large shorebird with short neck and fairly long, grey legs. Overall golden-brown, speckled back. Dark head and ear-coverts. Non-breeding adult has buff head, neck and breast streaked darker. Breeding adult has black face, neck, breast and belly; creamy-white forehead and supercilium. Juvenile similar to non-breeding adult, but with light barring on chest sides, and flanks, has more distinct yellow edges and spots on feathers of crown, back and wings.

GREY PLOVER

Pluvialis squatarola Charadriidae

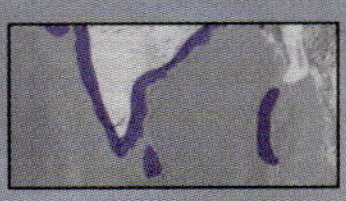

Size 30 cm

Voice Call a loud, penetrating *pee-ou ee*

Range Uncommon winter visitor to most coasts. Rare inland on passage

Habitat Coastal, open mudflats. Inland on open jheels, floods and rivers

Medium-sized, long-legged plover distinguished by large head and sturdy, black beak. Upperparts dark greyish-brown with white edges; distinctive black axillaries visible beneath wings in flight. Upperparts pale grey above with fine mottling; whitish forehead and eyebrow; strongly barred white tail. Whitish underparts. Breeding adult boldly marked black-and-white.

breeding

non-breeding

COMMON RINGED PLOVER

Charadrius hiaticula Charadriidae

Size 19 cm

Voice Call a rising disyllabic *poo…eep*

Range Rare winter visitor to Pakistan, Sri Lanka and Indian E coast

Habitat Muddy and sandy margins of lakes, rivers and the coast. Mixes with other waders

Small, plump bird with sandy-brown upperparts, white underparts and short orange or orange-yellow legs and short orange bill with black tip. Broad black neck-band; black eye mask; black stripe across forehead. Juvenile duller; often incomplete grey-brown breast-band, dark bill and dull yellowish-grey legs. Known for 'broken wing display' where it feigns a broken wing to draw predators away from nesting chicks.

juvenile

LITTLE RINGED PLOVER

Charadrius dubius Charadriidae

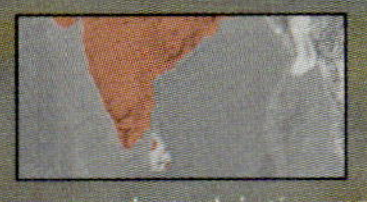

Size 16 cm

Voice Call a *few…few…* whistle, high-pitched but somewhat plaintive, uttered mostly on wing. Warning or attention-seeking call a loud *piuu*

Range Resident and local migrant; all over India

Habitat Shingle-covered riverbanks; tidal mudflats; estuaries; edges of lakes

breeding

Similar to Ringed, but has yellow eye-ring and almost non-existent wing-bars. Upperparts sandy-brown; white forehead; brown cap; black eye masks and breast, white neck-ring diagnostic; white chin and throat; white belly; short, dark bill; flesh-coloured legs. Sexes alike. Walks with fast steps, stopping suddenly, then runs a small stretch again. Tramples around on sand or mud to flush prey out of hiding places. Flies rapidly, low over ground; zigzag flight.

KENTISH PLOVER

Charadrius alexandrinus Charadriidae

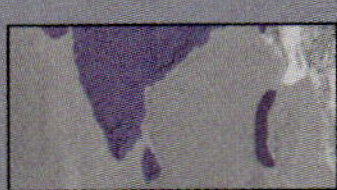

Size 17 cm

Voice Call a soft *dri…ip…*; alarm a *whi…it* on ground. In flight, an abrupt *tit…tit*

Range Fairly common winter visitor, local breeding resident to most coasts and throughout lowlands

Habitat Coastal sandflats, salt pans but inland on river sandbars, open lakeshores and drying floods

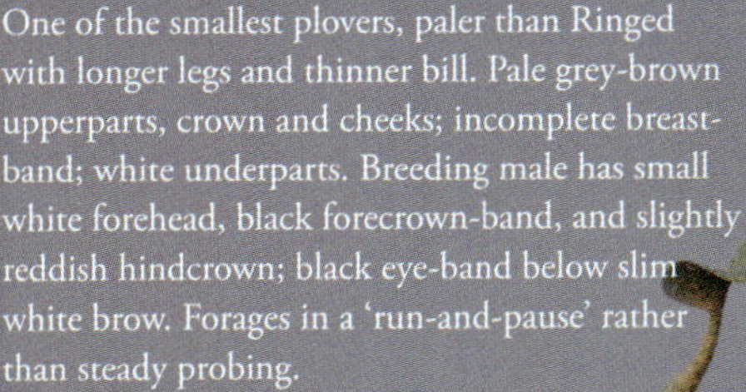

One of the smallest plovers, paler than Ringed with longer legs and thinner bill. Pale grey-brown upperparts, crown and cheeks; incomplete breast-band; white underparts. Breeding male has small white forehead, black forecrown-band, and slightly reddish hindcrown; black eye-band below slim white brow. Forages in a 'run-and-pause' rather than steady probing.

LESSER SAND PLOVER

Charadrius mongolus Charadriidae

Size 19 cm

Voice Call a hard, repeated *tri… ip*. Also a trilling *trrp*. Flight call a hard trill

Range Common winter visitor to most coasts. Scarce on passage inland

Habitat Coastal sand and mudflats. River and jheel margins and flooded inland fields

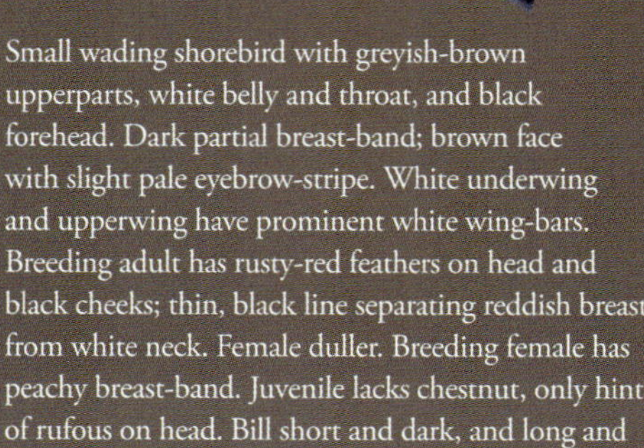

Small wading shorebird with greyish-brown upperparts, white belly and throat, and black forehead. Dark partial breast-band; brown face with slight pale eyebrow-stripe. White underwing and upperwing have prominent white wing-bars. Breeding adult has rusty-red feathers on head and black cheeks; thin, black line separating reddish breast from white neck. Female duller. Breeding female has peachy breast-band. Juvenile lacks chestnut, only hint of rufous on head. Bill short and dark, and long and greenish-brown legs.

non-breeding

breeding

GREATER SAND PLOVER

Charadrius leschenaultii Charadriidae

Size 22 cm

Voice Call a trilling *trrr…t*

Range Rather scarce winter visitor to most coasts. Commonest in NW India. Rare on inland

Habitat Behaviour as Lesser Sand, with which it often mixes

breeding

Relatively dull looking in non-breeding plumage. Dark lores, bill and upperwing; dusky ear-coverts; prominent white plumage on forehead, chin, throat and underparts, including underwing.
In breeding, crown and breast turn dull brick-red, and area around ear changes to black. Chin and throat remain white throughout the year, while nape and forehead greyish-brown colour all year round. Greenish legs distinguish it from Lesser.

GREATER PAINTED-SNIPE

Rostratula benghalensis Rostratulidaet

Size 25 cm

Voice Common call a long-drawn, mellow note that can be likened to the noise made by blowing into a bottle mouth

Range All over India, upto about 2,000 m in the Himalayas

Habitat Wet mud; marshes; areas where there is a mix of open water and heavy low cover

Medium-sized waterbird polyandrous. Breeding female metallic-olive above, marked buff and black; buff stripe down crown centre; white patches around eyes; chestnut throat, breast and sides of neck; white below breast. Breeding male duller overall; lacks chestnut. Sexes difficult to distinguish when not in breeding plumage. Crepuscular and nocturnal. Solitary, or a few scattered birds; feeds in squelchy mud but also moves on drier ground; runs on landing.

♀

♀

PHEASANT-TAILED JACANA

Hydrophasianus chirurgus Jacanidae

Size 30 cm

Voice Loud, mewing call when breeding, two birds often calling in duet

Range All over India, upto about 1,500 m in Kashmir; occasionally seen much higher

Habitat Ponds and jheels covered with floating vegetation

non-breeding

juvenile

Male in breeding plumage chocolate-brown and white; golden-yellow hindneck; dull brown-and-white when not breeding, also has blackish necklace and lacks long tail; very long toes diagnostic. Sexes alike. Solitary, or in pairs when breeding; small flocks in winter; purely aquatic, moves on vegetation-covered pond surfaces; unusually long toes enable walk on lightest of floating leaves; quite confiding on village ponds.

BRONZE-WINGED JACANA

Metopidius indicus Jacanidae

Size 30 cm

Voice Loud harsh notes; also a shrill piping call

Range Most of India, except some NW regions

Habitat Vegetation-covered jheels, ponds

Glossy black head, neck, breast; glistening bronze-green back, wings; broad white stripe over eyes; chestnut rump, tail; long legs with massive toes distinctive. Immature has rufous-brown crown; black terminal band to tail and whitish underbody, tinged rufous-buff around breast. Sexes alike. Female slightly larger. Small gatherings during winter and summer, keeps to leafy, floating growth on jheel beds, village tanks; wary, moves slowly and silently; flies low with long legs trailing.

juvenile

EURASIAN WOODCOCK

Scolopax rusticola Scolopacidae

Size 33–38 cm

Voice Usually silent in winter

Range Breeds in the Himalayas

Habitat Dense forests

Medium to small wader with intricately patterned reddish-brown upperparts and buff underparts; long straight bill; head barred black; eyes set far back on head to give 360° vision; rounded wings; base of bill flesh-coloured with dark tip; legs vary from grey to pinkish. Probes ground for food with long bill. Crepuscular; rarely active during the day unless flushed.

JACK SNIPE

Lymnocryptes minimus Scolopacidae

Size 21 cm

Voice Invariably silent when flushed

Range Winter visitor: Plains of N Afghanistan, Indus Valley

Habitat Marshes; paddy fields

Extremely small, secretive bird and exceptionally well-camouflaged within habitat. Lacks central crown-stripe; two pale lateral crown-stripes separated from supercilium by dark patch; dark eye-stripe. Mottled brown upperparts and pale underparts; streaked breast; narrow, pointed wings; conspicuous long straight golden scapular and mantle-stripes; short, wedge-shaped tail; yellow back-stripes visible in flight. Forages in soft mud for insects, earthworms and plant material. Feeds in characteristic bouncing motion. Crouches in undergrowth. Low and rapid zigzag flight when flushed. Male performs an aerial display during courtship.

WOOD SNIPE

Gallinago nemoricola Scolopacidae

Size 28-32 cm

Voice Invariably silent when flushed

Range Breeds in the Himalayas and winters in the foothills and in S India and Sri Lanka

Habitat Marshes; paddy fields

Large, relatively short-billed snipe with broad wings. Dark-tipped pale yellow bill; distinct chestnut and black head-stripes; dark upper back with chestnut stripes running down towards tail; chestnut neck and breast; buff underparts streaked brown; creamish belly; dense barring on underwing; pale green-yellow legs. Heavy, direct flight.

PINTAIL SNIPE

Gallinago stenura Scolopacidae

Size 28 cm

Voice Call said to be *squik* or *chef*

Range Winter visitor to peninsula from about Mumbai south and to EC India and S Nepal to Arunachal Pradesh, Assam Valley

Habitat Marshes; paddy fields

Small, stocky wader with short greenish-grey legs and long, straight dark bill. Upperparts mottled brown with linear cream markings down back. Underparts pale with streaked buff breast and white belly; dark stripe through eye with lighter stripes above and below. Sexes similar. Wings less pointed than Common, lacks white trailing edge. Distinguished by shorter tail and flatter flight path when flushed.

SWINHOE'S SNIPE

Gallinago megala Scolopacidae

Size 28 cm

Voice In flight, a sudden *chrek* with abrupt ending. Pintail has more subdued *tesch;* coarse shriek

Range Probably fairly common but overlooked winter visitor mainly to E and S of the region

Habitat Marshes; wet paddy

Cryptically-patterned black, brown buff and white snipe, with extremely long bill. Very similar to *Pintail G. stenura* but distinguished by proportionately longer bill. Pale, dull upperparts. Greyish legs extend just beyond tail. Greyish flight feathers contrast with heavily barred white wing-coverts. Sexes alike. Lumbering flight. Feeds by deep, vertical probing.

COMMON SNIPE

Gallinago gallinago Scolopacidae

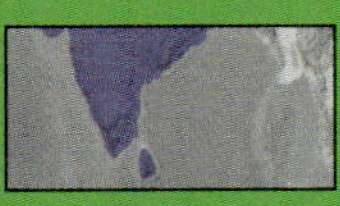

Size 28 cm

Voice Call a loud *scaaap* when flushed

Range Breeds in parts of W Himalayas; mostly winter visitor over the subcontinent, most common in N and C India

Habitat Marshlands; paddy cultivation; edges of jheels

Well-camouflaged bird, usually seen when flushed. Mottled-brown upperparts, with pale stripes on back and dark streaks on chest; paler underparts. Short legs; long wings; short tail and very elongated beak. Sexes alike, female may have slightly longer bill. Juvenile's wing feathers fringed with cream. Fast, zigzag flight. Probes with long beak in mud, often in shallow water; feeds mostly during mornings and evenings, often continuing through the night.

ASIAN DOWITCHER

Limnodromus semipalmatus Scolopacidae

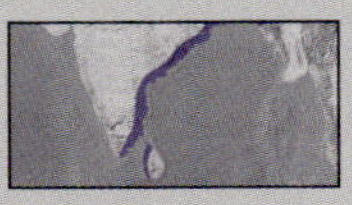

Size 34 cm

Voice Usually silent. Sometimes a soft *maou*

Range Rare passage migrant: E, S coasts. Rarer inland

Habitat Mudflats and if inland, jheels and flooded fields. Mixes with other waders

Medium to large-sized wader similar to Bar-tailed Godwit but distinguished by straight, completely black bill. Upperparts brown; breeding adult reddish from crown to belly; barred black-and-white tail; dark legs and long straight dark bill. Non-breeding adult overall grey; obvious white supercilium and barred flanks. Feeds on insects, molluscs, crustaceans and marine worms, and some plant material by probing in shallow water or on wet mud.

WHIMBREL

Numenius phaeopus Scolopacidae

Size 43 cm

Voice Noisy. Call a trilling, usually 7-note whistle *tee…tee…tee…tee…tee…tee…tee*

Range Fairly common winter visitor to most coasts. Rare inland

Habitat Coastal muddy and rocky shores, particularly favouring mangroves on which it perches at high tide

Large shorebird with long downcurved bill, long neck and long legs. Streaked brown upperparts, neck, and breast; white belly and rump; dark brown crown; greyish line above eye, and dark brown line on eye mask. Immature similar to adult, but with light spotting on back and has less distinct crown-stripe. Uses bill to probe deep in sand for invertebrates; also feeds on berries and insects. Aggressive nest protectors.

EURASIAN CURLEW

Numenius arquata Scolopacidae

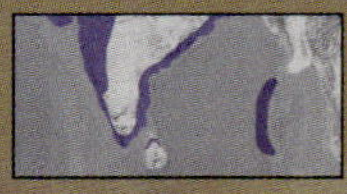

Size 58 cm

Voice Famed scream; wild, rather musical *cour…leeor…cooodee…*, first note longer

Range Winter visitor: Sea coast, W to E; large inland marshes; rivers

Habitat Estuaries; creeks; large remote marshes

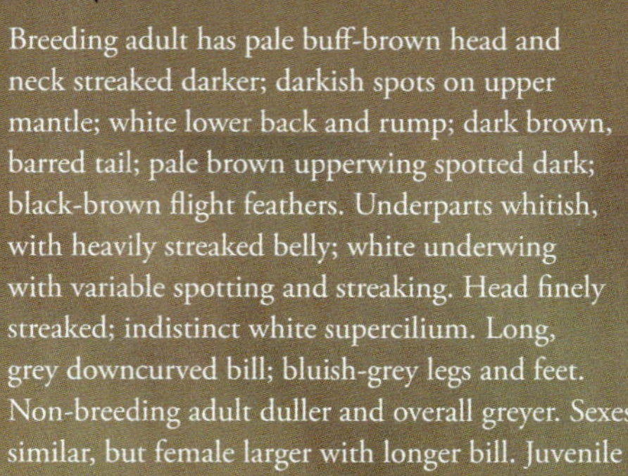

Breeding adult has pale buff-brown head and neck streaked darker; darkish spots on upper mantle; white lower back and rump; dark brown, barred tail; pale brown upperwing spotted dark; black-brown flight feathers. Underparts whitish, with heavily streaked belly; white underwing with variable spotting and streaking. Head finely streaked; indistinct white supercilium. Long, grey downcurved bill; bluish-grey legs and feet. Non-breeding adult duller and overall greyer. Sexes similar, but female larger with longer bill. Juvenile has more buff on breast, flanks less streaked.

non-breeding

BAR-TAILED GODWIT

Limosa lapponica Scolopacidae

Size 35 cm

Voice Rather quiet. Call a soft *kik…kik…kik* in flight

Range Rather scarce winter visitor. Commoner on NW coasts. Rare inland

Habitat Coastal. Favours open mudflats

Large wader with long neck, bill and legs. Has wedge-shaped white rump-patch and no wing-bars. Stockier than Black-tailed with shorter, slightly upturned bill and shorter legs. Size varies; female and eastern race larger. Non-breeding adult finely streaked brown above and on head and neck; latter turns rich orange, as do all underparts, when breeding. Back turns darker and wing-coverts silvery-grey.

non-breeding

breeding

BLACK-TAILED GODWIT

Limosa limosa Scolopacidae

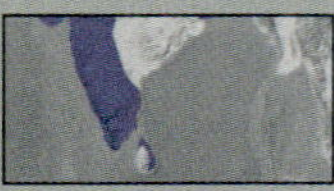

Size 35 cm

Voice Occasional, fairly loud *kwika…kwik*

Range Winter visitor, fairly common over N India; lesser numbers towards E and S India

Habitat Marshes; estuaries; creeks

non-breeding

Large, graceful bird with rather small head, long neck, very long, straight or slightly curved bill and very long legs. Distinguished from Bar-tailed by straighter and blunter bill, longer neck, shallower forehead, slimmer body and longer legs. In flight, broad white wing-bars, white rump and black tail-tip distinctive. Female slightly larger with longer bill, but overall duller. Solitary, or in groups, often with other waders. Feeds in sea-edge flocks. Fast, low flight.

breeding

SPOTTED REDSHANK

Tringa erythropus Scolopacidae

Size 33 cm

Voice Noisy. Call an explosive *chew it*

Range Fairly common winter visitor throughout lowlands. Scarce on the coast, NE India

Habitat Marshes; jheels; rivers

Slightly larger, slimmer and longer-legged than Common. No wing-bars; long cigar-shaped white patch on back between wings, extending to rump; long red legs. Non-breeding adult has light grey, speckled upperparts and whitish underparts; paler head and neck with short, white supercilium. Red lower mandible, downcurved. Breeding adult has black underparts, head and neck; dark grey upperparts, spotted white. Juvenile resembles pale Redshank.

COMMON REDSHANK

Tringa totanus Scolopacidae

Size 28 cm

Voice Quite musical, fairly loud and shrill *tleu…ewh…ewh*

Range Breeds in Kashmir, Ladakh; winter visitor all over India. Fairly common

Habitat Marshes; creeks; estuaries

breeding

Elegant-looking bird with greyish-brown upperparts, spotted dark brown and black. Whitish underparts streaked and spotted dark brown on breast, flanks and belly. White secondary flight feathers, rump, lower back and barred tail visible in flight. Breeding adult more brown above, marked black and fulvous, and more heavily streaked below. Brown head streaked and spotted darker. Orange-red legs and base of beak; long, straight bill with red base and black tip; dark brown eyes with white eyelids. Legs and feet bright red.

COMMON GREENSHANK

Tringa nebularia Scolopacidae

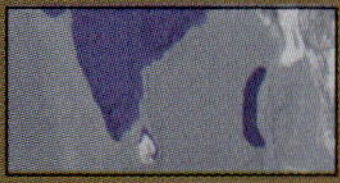

Size 32 cm

Voice Call a wild, ringing *tew…tew…tew…*

Range Winter visitor, fairly common over most of the region

Habitat Marshes; estuaries

Medium-sized slim wader with dark grey back and white underparts. Diagnostic long, greyish-green legs, slightly upturned, blackish-grey bill. Long neck; white rump extending into distinctive white wedge up the back, visible in flight; grey streaking on head and neck; whitish tail. Breeding adult heavily streaked, spotted darker on upperparts, head, neck and upper breast. Juvenile similar to non-breeding adult, but upperparts more brown and feathers edged buff; neck and breast more heavily streaked.

MARSH SANDPIPER

Tringa stagnatilis Scolopacidae

Size 23 cm

Voice Rather quiet. Call a briefly repeated *klew*, rather like first note of Common Redshank

Range Fairly common winter visitor throughout lowlands. Less common on coasts

Habitat Shallow freshwater jheels; village ponds; wet paddy; river shoals

Distinctive wader with long needle-like bill and very long greenish legs, often mistaken for Common Greenshank. Non-breeding adult has greyish-brown upperparts and white underparts; grey crown and hindneck; white eyebrow. Breeding adult has heavily streaked head and neck; flanks and lower breast show bars or chevrons. Juvenile has more heavily patterned upperparts than non-breeding adult; dark outer wing and slightly lighter inner wing, white wedge on lower back and rump visible in flight. Feeds upright with slow graceful movements breaking into quick dashes.

breeding

non-breeding

GREEN SANDPIPER

Tringa ochropus Scolopacidae

Size 23 cm

Voice Call a ringing *tlu…eet…weet*

Range Widespread but rather scarce winter visitor

Habitat Well-vegetated pools; streams; mangroves; village ponds

Medium-sized sandpiper, similar to Wood, but larger and stockier; shorter legs; darker and less spotted back; more uniform white flanks. Overall brown and spotted white; blackish underwings and tail with broad black lateral-stripes; white rump square. Wings dark above and below, tail white; indistinct eye-stripe; black beak with reddish base; dark brown eyes with white eye-ring.

WOOD SANDPIPER

Tringa glareola Scolopacidae

Upperparts greyish-brown, spotted white; breast and neck white and striped brown. White supercilium, extending from behind eye to back of ear-coverts; short, straight beak with deep olive-green base; long yellow to greenish-yellow legs; brownish tail contrasts with white rump-patch. Breeding adult more olive-brown, spotted white and bill has pale base. Juvenile similar to non-breeding adult, but upperparts much darker, warmer brown; more spotting and streaking on breast.

Size 21 cm

Voice Quite noisy; sharp, trilling notes on ground. Call a shrill, somewhat metallic *chiff…chiff* when flushed; sometimes loud, sharp *tluie…*

Range Winter visitor throughout the region

Habitat Wet cultivation; marshes; tidal creeks; mudflats

breeding

COMMON SANDPIPER

Actitis hypoleucos Scolopacidae

Size 20 cm

Voice Vocal in flight. Call includes a 3-note sound with distinctive 3-note, piping-like cry; often represented as *twee-wee-wee*

Range Breeds in the Himalayas, Kashmir to Uttarakhand to about 3,000 m; winter visitor all across the region

Habitat Freshwater marshes; lakes; tidal areas; creeks

breeding

Small to medium-sized bird, with relatively long legs. Upperparts olive-brown, streaked on head and neck sides; white underparts; lightly streaked, brown breast; narrow white wing-bar, brown rump; white 'hook' at shoulder conspicuous in flight. Breeding adult has darker and more speckled upperparts. Active; feeds on ground on crustaceans, insects, worms, and other coastal creatures; makes short dashes, bobbing and wagging short tail; stiff-winged flight.

TEREK SANDPIPER

Xenus cinereus Scolopacidae

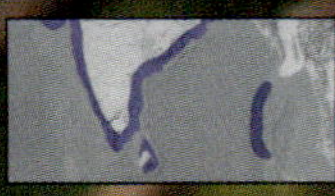

Size 24 cm

Voice Call a ringing *twoot…wee…wee*

Range Rather scarce winter visitor to most coasts. Most numerous on Arabian Sea coast. Rare inland

Habitat Muddy coasts and mangroves. When inland, mostly on sandy rivers or muddy jheels

non-breeding

Resembles Common, but has long bill with dull yellow to orange base, visibly upcurved. Brownish-grey upperparts; grey face; neck and breast speckled pale grey, but other underparts white. Breeding adult has stronger and increased streaking across head and prominent irregular dark stripes on upper scapulars. White trailing edge to wings; black lengthwise stripe over each wing. Orange legs; blackish-brown eyes. Sexes alike. Juvenile similar to breeding adult but upperpart feathers have buff fringes and dark subterminal marks; yellow legs.

breeding

RUDDY TURNSTONE

Arenaria interpres Scolopacidae

Size 22 cm

Voice Call a rapid *tuka…tuk…tuk* in flight

Range Scarce winter visitor to most coasts. Commonest in the NW. Rare inland

Habitat Mainly rocky coasts. Also sandy flats and by large rivers

Medium-sized, attractively-patterned stocky shorebird. Short, thick and dark bill has slight upturn; black-and-white or black and grey clown-like patterning on face; bold wing pattern visible in flight; white lower back; short, orange legs. Adult turns rich chestnut in breeding. Juvenile resembles winter adult, but overall more brownish and paler head.

GREAT KNOT

Calidris tenuirostris Scolopacidae

Size 28 cm

Voice Rather quiet. Call a low *chukka…chukka*

Range Rare winter visitor, could occur on any coast and even inland

Habitat Coastal mudflats; salt pans

Easily confused with Red, but distinguished by longer bill and whitish rump that is conspicuous in flight. Non-breeding adult has bolder chevron-shaped markings on sides, darker streaks on breast and forehead, less obvious supercilium, heavier streaking on forehead, and feathers of upperparts more brown with darker centres than Red. Breeding adult easily identified by gorget of black spots across breast, large red spots and patches on scapulars. Sexes alike.

RED KNOT

Calidris canutus Scolopacidae

Size 24 cm

Voice Rather quiet. Sometimes a soft *chuk…chuk*

Range Rare winter visitor to E coast and particularly Sri Lanka

Habitat Coastal mudflats

Medium-sized shorebird that has conspicuous plumage during breeding season, when face, chest and undersides turn bright rust and wings dark brown; tail develops dark stripe. Non-breeding adult has grey head, chest and upperparts; white belly; blackish primaries and white stripe across wing; white patch above throat and eye. Long greenish legs; pointed black bill. Sexes alike. Juvenile variable grey; feathers edged darker; dark grey primaries and white wing-stripe.

breeding

RED-NECKED STINT

Calidris ruficollis Scolopacidae

Size 15 cm

Voice Call a hoarse *chrit…it…it*

Range Scarce but overlooked winter visitor, most regular in Bangladesh, Tamil Nadu and Sri Lanka

Habitat Coastal mudflats; salt pans. Also inland in Bangladesh

Rather small shorebird with small head, round forehead, short legs and attenuated rear end. Longish body; short, very slightly decurved bill; white wing-bars, white sides to black-centered rump visible in flight. In breeding plumage, head turns russet, crown acquires brown streaks and breast gorget. Sexes alike. Juvenile plainer and duller. Forages by walking, on shore edge rapidly picking food from surface. Sometimes probes mud. Highly sociable; often found in mixed flocks.

breeding

TEMMINCK'S STINT

Calidris temminckii Scolopaidae

Size 14 cm

Voice Call a dry, high-pitched trilling in flight

Range Common winter visitor throughout lowlands. Scarce on the coast

Habitat Vegetated freshwater habitats favouring flooded short grass and paddy fields

Small, uniform brown bird, similar in size to Little, but darker and greyer. Greyish-brown head and chest; blackish-brown bill and brown iris; thin, downcurved bill; well-defined line between breast and white belly; greenish-brown legs. Uniform chest-patch and greyish upperparts similar to Common Sandpiper. V-shaped white mark on back; extensive white edge to black-centered tail conspicuous in flight.

breeding

non-breeding

LONG-TOED STINT

Calidris subminuta Scolopacidae

Size 14 cm

Voice Call a trilling, slightly throaty *krrrt*

Range Mainly E, NE India and Bangladesh

Habitat Marshes; riverbanks; mudflats

Tiny, delicate wader with distinctive shape, small head, and long slim neck. Variegated rufous, black and buff upperparts; brown scapulars and tertials with broad rufous fringes; roundish belly, short rear-end, long legs and long toes, short, pointed bill; yellow-green legs and feet, pale-brown or yellow base to lower mandible. Brown crown and white supercilium; brown spots on cheek and brown forehead. Similar to Red-necked, but has darker and brighter upperparts.

LITTLE STINT

Calidris minuta Scolopacidae

Size 14 cm

Voice Call a piercing, repeated *stit...it*

Range Abundant winter visitor throughout lowlands; all coasts

Habitat Coastal mudflats; salt pans; shallow open freshwater; muddy lakes; river margins

breeding

Tiny wader. In breeding plumage, edges of back feathers, flanks and cheeks turn rusty-red with darker mottling, and white underparts. Dark and split cap; white supercilium. Short, straight and narrow-tipped beak. Thin wing-bars and distinct white V on back, prominent in flight. White lengthwise stripes on back and grey on tail feathers diagnostic. Black legs, beak and iris. Sexes similar. Juvenile similar to Temminck but with pale forehead and pale eyebrow-stripe split into two. Swift flight with extremely rapid wingbeats.

CURLEW SANDPIPER

breeding

Calidris ferruginea Scolopacidae

Size 21 cm

Voice Call a trilling *chirrup* in flight

Range Common winter visitor to most coasts, particularly in S and E. Scarce passage migrant inland

Habitat Coastal mud, sandflats, salt pans. Inland on floods, muddy jheels, sandy rivers

Very similar to Dunlin, but larger, slender with longer bill, neck and legs and divided eyebrow-stripe. Obvious downcurved bill. Breeding adult has deep chestnut head, neck and belly (paler in female) black, white and reddish patterning on upperparts; bright white rump and white wing-stripe and white chin. Non-breeding adult greyer with distinct white supercilium. Toes extend beyond tail-tip in flight. Juvenile has greyer underparts and pale red breast. In mixed flocks with other waders. Feeds mainly on insects and small invertebrates and worms, occasionally feeds on seeds and other plant material.

breeding

SANDERLING

Calidris alba Scolopacidae

Size 20 cm

Voice Call a metallic *plit*

Range Local winter visitor to most coasts. Very rare inland

Habitat Almost entirely restricted to sandy coasts

Small, active shorebird with short, stout, black beak and black legs that lack hind toe. Breeding adult has cinnamon-red upperparts, head and breast mottled black-and-white. Non-breeding adult largely white; pale grey upperparts; pure white underparts; distinct, dark shoulder-patch; broad, white wing-bar bordered black; Sexes similar, but female larger and paler, less reddish-brown. Juvenile similar to non-breeding adult, but more streaked black; buff breast and head; back more darkly marked with black-and-white.

breeding

SPOON-BILLED SANDPIPER

Eurynorhynchus pygmeus Scolopacidae

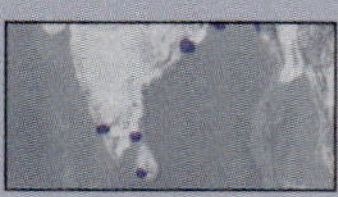

Size 15 cm

Voice Call includes a series of short *zhree…zhree…zhree…*

Range Rare winter visitor to coastal Bangladesh, West Bengal

Habitat Usually found in small numbers among stint flocks, at water's edge or in wettest parts of mudflats

Sparrow-sized wader with unique spoon-shaped bill. Non-breeding adult has pale brown-grey upperparts, with edge to feathers; white underparts. Breeding adult has russet-red head, neck and breast streaked brown, and dark upperparts with pale brown-and-red trim to feathers. Strongly territorial; returns year after year to breed at the same nest site.

DUNLIN

Calidris alpina Scolopacidae

Size 19 cm

Voice Call a trilling *creep* in flight

Range Locally common winter visitor to most coasts. Most common in NW. Rare inland

Habitat Coastal mudflats. Inland; occurs on sandy rivers, muddy jheels

breeding

non-breeding

Medium-sized sandpiper with bright reddish upperparts, black belly, and long, drooping bill. Relatively short neck and long, blackish legs. Breeding adult has black belly, rufous back and crown. Non-breeding adult overall dull brownish-grey with whitish belly; black bill and legs. Juvenile has more red on back and brownish-black markings on belly. Slightly hunched appearance.

BROAD-BILLED SANDPIPER

Limicola falcinellus Scolopacidae

Size 18 cm

Voice Call a buzzing, metallic *brr…eet* in flight

Range Scarce winter visitor to most coasts, most regular in Tamil Nadu. Rare inland

Habitat Mudflats; sandbanks; salt pans

Small wader, slightly smaller than Dunlin, but with longer, straighter bill and shorter legs. Breeding adult has patterned dark grey upperparts and white underparts with blackish markings on breast; pale crown-stripe and supercilium. Non-breeding adult has pale grey upperparts and white underparts; neck, breast, and belly intensely speckled darker. Dark grey legs and dark brown iris. Juvenile similar to adult but duller with rusty-brown edges to back feathers and faint streaking on underparts.

RUFF

Philomachus pugnax Scolopacidae

Size Male 30 cm; Female 23 cm

Voice Silent. No call recorded

Range Abundant winter visitor mainly to W and S parts of the region

Habitat Marshes; jheels; stubble; cultivation; mudflats; salt pans

Medium-sized wader with long neck, small head, rather short, slightly droopy bill and medium-long orange or reddish legs. Non-breeding adult has scalloped brown-grey upperparts. Breeding male has striking ruff ranging from black or brown to orange or white with pronounced black stripes and ear tufts. Female (known as Reeve) and male in non-breeding plumage similar, with orange bills and white feathers at bill base, but male much larger; upper flanks marked with dark spots. Shows white U on tail, separating dark rump and dark tail-tip in flight.

♀

breeding

breeding

breeding

RED-NECKED PHALAROPE

Phalaropus lobatus Scolopacidae

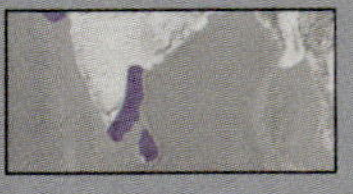

Size 20 cm

Voice Call a husky *chet*

Range Scarce winter visitor to Arabian Sea and Sri Lankan coast. Rare inland

Habitat Marine. Inland, prefers salt lakes

Female more brightly-coloured than male, especially on neck. In breeding, both sexes have distinct white cheek-patch, dark grey head and back. Male has whitish underparts; female has grey breast. Non-breeding adult more drab with greyish upperparts and white below; strong, black eye-stripe; thin, black, needle-like bill; narrow wing-bar visible in flight. Juvenile darker brown. Feeds by swimming rapidly.

non-breeding

breeding

INDIAN COURSER

Cursorius coromandelicus Glareolidae

Size 23 cm

Voice Soft, hen-like clucking call in flight, when flushed

Range Most of the area south of the Himalayas, but distribution rather patchy; absent in NE India

Habitat Open scrub; fallow lands; dry cultivation

Similar to Cream-coloured, but brighter and with broader eye-stripe. Bright chestnut crown; white and black stripes above and through eyes to nape; sandy-brown above; chestnut throat and breast and black belly; long, whitish legs; in flight, dark underwings. Sexes alike. Juvenile has dull buff, irregularly barred with blackish-brown upperparts and has pale supercilium; breast dull rufous, more or less barred with blackish; chin and abdomen white. In small parties in open country; strictly ground bird, runs in short spurts and feeds on ground; flies strongly for a short distance and lands; can fly very high.

JERDON'S COURSER

Rhinoptilus bitorquatus Glareolidae

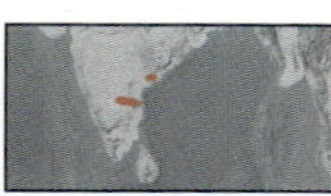

Size 27 cm

Voice Call a clear *tuick...ttuuu... tuick...tuuu...tuickt...*

Range Resident; foothills of S Andhra Pradesh

Habitat Scrubs

Small bird, with cryptic sandy-brown plumage. White underparts with banded lower breast; distinct rufous neck-patch; dark brown hindneck and crown; broad, cream eye-stripes joined to form V; straight, yellow bill with black tip; black tail with white base. Walks with upright stance. Thought to be extinct, it was rediscovered in 1986, after a lapse of 86 years since the previous sighting.

ORIENTAL PRATINCOLE

Glareola maldivarum Glareolidae

Size 25 cm

Voice Call a tern-like *krek…krek* in flight

Range Resident, local migrant; common breeding resident. Most frequent in N and extreme S, including Sri Lanka

Habitat As Collared; more tolerant of dry fallow away from water. Favours river sandbanks

Very similar to Collared, but distinguished by brown breast extending down to belly and merging into white; long, narrow wings and short, forked tail; much less contrast above and no white trailing edges seen in flight. Short bill; brown back and head; wings brown with black flight feathers. Sexes alike.

juvenile

SMALL PRATINCOLE

Glareola lactea Glareolidae

Size 17 cm

Voice Call a sharp *tirrit tirrit tirrit*

Range Resident and local migrant; subcontinent south of outer Himalayas, from about 1,800 m

Habitat Large and quiet riversides, sandbars, marshy expanses, coastal swamps, tidal creeks

Similar, but much smaller and paler than Oriental. Brown forehead; pale sandy-grey mantle and grey crown. Breeding adult has black stripe from eye to beak; white, squarish tail, tipped black; smoky-brown underbody has rufous wash; whiter on lower breast and abdomen; long, narrow wings; pale grey wing-coverts, white base to secondaries, black flight feathers and short legs. Sexes alike. Gregarious; large, loose flocks over open expanse, close to water; very swallow-like in demeanour; strong and graceful flight over water surface, catching insects on wing; flies high during late evening.

SOOTY GULL

Ichthyaetus hemprichii Laridae

Size 39 cm

Voice Call musical but nasal, fairly high-pitched

Range Resident; Balochistan to Sind coast

Habitat Follows offshore fishing boats

Exceptionally long, thick beak. Heavy looking with broad pointed wings and dull yellowish legs; prominent crescent above eye and sometimes faint crescent below; dark hood forming bib on chest, bordered above by white partial collar. Breeding adult has distinct red-tipped mustard bill and black subterminal ring; inconspicuous white spot above eye and tiny indistinct one below; white trailing edge of wings inconspicuous owing to lack of dark band on secondaries.

CASPIAN GULL

Larus cachinnans Laridae

Size 41 cm

Voice Nasal, ringing call

Range Rare vagrant

Habitat Coasts; inland waters

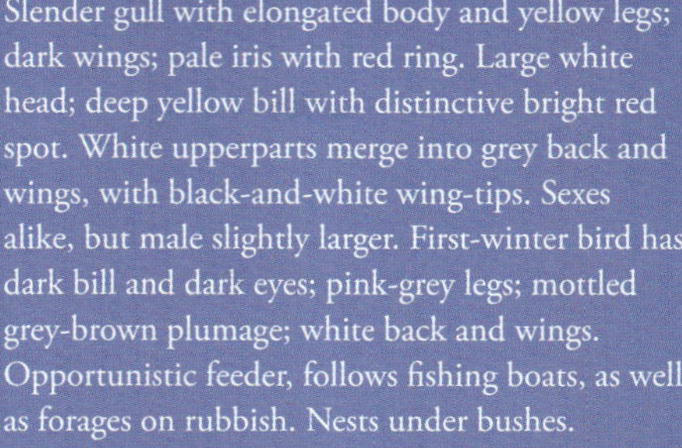

Slender gull with elongated body and yellow legs; dark wings; pale iris with red ring. Large white head; deep yellow bill with distinctive bright red spot. White upperparts merge into grey back and wings, with black-and-white wing-tips. Sexes alike, but male slightly larger. First-winter bird has dark bill and dark eyes; pink-grey legs; mottled grey-brown plumage; white back and wings. Opportunistic feeder, follows fishing boats, as well as forages on rubbish. Nests under bushes.

HEUGLIN'S GULL

Larus heuglini Laridae

Size 65 cm

Voice As Yellow-legged

Range Scarce winter visitor to W and S coasts from Pakistan to Andhra Pradesh. Also Sri Lanka

Habitat As Yellow-legged but probably even more coastal

Elongated gull with small rounded head, relatively fine bill, slender legs and short tail. Male has flatter crown and bulbous tip to bill. Very similar to Black-headed and almost indistinguishable in field, but for slimmer bill, smaller head and more slender legs. Breeding adult has white head. Non-breeding adult streaked slightly dark, particularly on hindneck; duller bare parts. Juvenile has paler bill and less darkly marked head and body.

BROWN-HEADED GULL

Chroicocephalus brunnicephalus Laridae

Size 42 cm

Voice Call a deep *kraaa*

Range Breeds in Ladakh. Common winter visitor to most coasts, sometimes inland

Habitat Coasts, rivers and lakes. Very gregarious, often with Black-headed

breeding

breeding

Slightly larger than Black-headed; summer adult has pale brown head, pearl-grey body, chocolate-brown partial hood, red bill and legs. In non-breeding adult, mask reduced to brown ear-patch. Black-tipped primary wing, feathers have large, conspicuous white spots; grey underwing; black flight feathers. Juvenile has brownish tinge to wings, black tail-bars, pale iris and white eye-rings. Sexes alike. Light, easy flight. Swims buoyantly, often among ducks and coots. Breeds colonially in high-altitude bogs.

breeding

BLACK-HEADED GULL

Chroicocephalus ridibundus Laridae

Size 38 cm

Voice Noisy. Call includes querulous *kree…ah…* screams

Range Common winter visitor; most common on W seaboard; also strays inland, both on passage and for short halts

Habitat Sea coasts; harbours; sewage outflows; refuse dumps. Disciplined skeins

breeding

non-breeding

Greyish-white plumage; dark ear-patches; white outer flight feathers, with black tips. Breeding adult has coffee-brown head and upper neck. Sexes alike. Highly gregarious; large flocks on sea coasts, scavenges in harbours; wheels over busy seaside roads or beaches; large numbers rest on rocky ground and sand; follow boats in harbours.

breeding

SLENDER-BILLED GULL

Chroicocephalus genei Laridae

Size 43 cm

Voice Slightly deeper than that of Black-headed

Range Resident: Pakistan; winter visitor: Nepal, India, Bhutan and Sri Lanka

Habitat Coastal waters; lagoons; estuaries; large tidal creeks; salt pans

Distinguished by remarkably long and slender blood-red bill, very flat forehead, pale iris and long neck. Breeding adult usually has strong pink wash on underparts. Very similar to Black-headed, but lacks black hood in summer. Pale grey body, white head and breast; black tips to primary wing feathers. Dark red legs; yellow iris. First-year immature has black terminal tail-band, and dark areas on wings. Flies above water surface diving on prey; probes mud for invertebrates.

breeding

PALLAS'S GULL

Ichthyaetus ichthyaetus Laridae

juvenile

juvenile

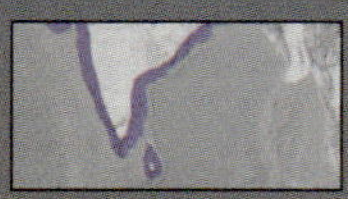

Size 69 cm

Voice Rather quiet. Call a nasal *argh*

Range Rare winter visitor to most coasts, inland

Habitat Coasts; large rivers; lakes

Large, striking-looking, long-winged gull with long-sloping forehead and strong black and orange-tipped yellow bill. Breeding adult has velvety-black hood and white eye-rings. Non-breeding adult has duskier head. Upperparts pale grey; whiter outer wing with black speckles near tips. Orangish-yellow bill; greenish-yellow legs with orange web. Immature pale grey-brown; grey mantle and wing panel. Solitary; mixes with smaller gulls and turns where fish is in abundance. Displays heavy buoyant heron-like flight.

breeding

GULL-BILLED TERN

Gelochelidon nilotica Laridae

Size 38 cm

Voice Normally rather quiet but occasionally, call a guttural *ger…erk*

Range Common winter visitor; coasts; inland. Local breeder

Habitat Rivers; jheels; coasts

Medium-sized tern with broader wings and thicker bill than most other terns and long, black legs. Tail short and notched; sleek, black cap when breeding. Non-breeding adult has white head and dark smudge behind eyes. Pale grey, black-tipped wings; white body; black legs; dark trailing edge to primaries visible in flight. Sexes alike. Hawks for flying insects, often over dry land but also picks fish from water surface. Nests on ground.

CASPIAN TERN

Hydroprogne caspia Laridae

juvenile

juvenile

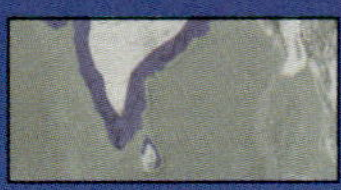

Size 53 cm

Voice Call a deep heron-like *kaarrh*

in flight

Range Scarce winter visitor to some coasts and inland. Most frequent in W and S. Breeds in Gujarat and Pakistan

Habitat Coasts; large rivers; lakes

Large, gull-like tern, with white body and black cap. Large, thick brilliant red bill with black band near yellow tip. Breeding adult has black crown becoming speckled white in non-breeding season. Pale grey upperparts; blackish outer primaries visible in flight. Juvenile has blackish crown, black edging to back feathers. Sexes alike.

LESSER CRESTED TERN

Thalasseus bengalensis Laridae

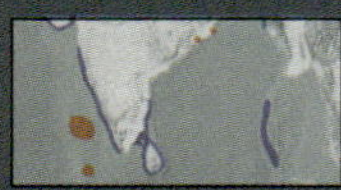

Size 35-37 cm

Voice Call a high-pitched *krrreeep...*

Range Over the entire Indian sea coast in winter; possibly breeds in parts of W Pakistan coast, and some islets off the W coast of India

Habitat Open sea; coastal regions

Typical-looking tern with greyish upperparts washed lilac; jet-black forehead, crown and nuchal crest in summer; whitish forehead and white-streaked crown diagnostic in winter. Blackish primaries, bright orange-yellow beak and black feet diagnostic. Sexes alike. Small parties out at sea, sometimes coming into coastal waters; flies leisurely between 2 and 8 metres over water, hovering occasionally; dives headlong for fish.

SANDWICH TERN

Thalasseus sandvicensis Laridae

Size 36–41 cm

Voice Call an upward-inflected, hoarse *kree…it*

Range Visitor to mainly W coasts

Habitat Frequents coasts, tidal creeks and open sea

breeding

Medium-sized marine tern with long, thin, black bill with pale yellow tip and short black legs. Overall almost uniformly plain grey; small shaggy crest behind head; white rump and tail; white forehead and crown. Breeding adult has black cap which turns pale in winter plumage. In flight, grey wedges on wing-tips and short-forked tail noticeable. Similar to Gull-billed but wings narrower and more pointed and sharply angled. Juvenile similar to non-breeding adult, except for dusky crown and dark markings on back, bill may lack yellow tip.

GREATER CRESTED TERN

Thalasseus bergii Laridae

Size 47 cm

Voice Call a coarse *kerrick*

Range Local resident. Most regular off Pakistan coast; Sri Lanka, W and S Indian coasts

Habitat Seen mainly offshore or around archipelagos, where it nests on islets

Large, grey-backed marine tern with distinctive black cap and long crest. Upperparts dark grey; blackish wing-tips; white forehead in all plumages; large greenish-yellow bill; black legs. Non-breeding plumage, black cap reduced. Dark legs. Sexes alike. Juvenile has more heavily mottled or barred brown upperparts. Smaller and slimmer; Lesser Crested Tern *S. bengalensis* paler grey above and has thinner orange bill.

RIVER TERN

Sterna aurantia Laridae

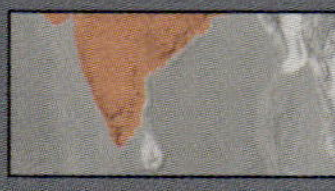

Size 42 cm

Voice Occasional harsh, screeching note

Range All over India; most common in N and C India

Habitat Inland waterbodies, rivers, tanks; almost completely absent on the sea coast

Graceful bird with pearly-grey upperparts; jet-black cap and nape, when breeding; white below; narrow, pointed wings; deeply-forked tail; bright yellow, pointed beak and red legs diagnostic. In winter, black on crown and nape reduced to flecks. Sexes alike. Solitary or small flocks, flying about erratically; keeps to riversides, calm waters, large tanks; scans over water, plunges if possible prey in sight; rests on riverbanks, noisy and aggressive, especially at nesting colonies (March to mid-June).

breeding

juvenile

ROSEATE TERN

Sterna dougallii Laridae

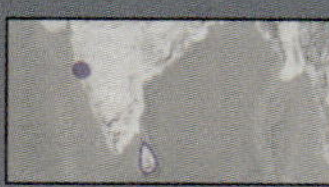

Size 41 cm

Voice Typical call a *chivy* or *cherr…rrick*

Range Summer visitor to Vengurla Rocks on W coast. Sri Lanka

Habitat Flocks with similar tern species; often follows fishing boats

Called so for its pinkish tint on underparts. Very similar to Common, but distinguished by long streamer tails and less black on wing-tips. Paler grey upperparts, long fine bill with extensive black tip, longish legs. Breeding adult has extensive black forehead, crown and nape. Non-breeding adult has white forehead. Feeds by plunge-diving.

BLACK-NAPED TERN

Sterna sumatrana Laridae

Size 33 cm

Voice Call a sharp *kik*

Range Local breeding resident; restricted to Maldives; Andaman and Nicobar Islands. Very rare off coasts of Bangladesh, S India and Sri Lanka

Habitat Strictly maritime

Crisply-marked, slim white tern with narrow black lines from eyes to black nape and deep-forked tail. Upperparts washed very pale grey with dark shafts to outer primary only. May show pink flush below when breeding. Black legs and bill. Sexes alike. Juvenile black-flecked above. Looks whiter than Roseate, which is similar in non-breeding plumage.

COMMON TERN

Sterna hirundo Laridae

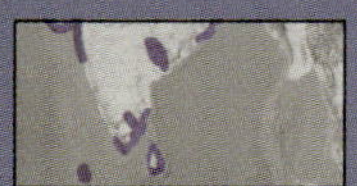

Size 35 cm

Voice Call a loud, harsh *kirrah…kirrah*

Range Breeds in Ladakh. Local winter visitor; most coasts and sometimes inland. Most common: Pakistan, S India and Sri Lanka

Habitat Coasts; rarely, inland lakes and rivers

Similar to Roseate, but distinguished by shorter tail, red bill with black tip and more black on wing-tips. Greyish wash to underparts; mantle and wings pale grey contrasting with white rump and white deeply-forked tail. In flight, shows darker tips to primaries. Non-breeding and juvenile have mottled head. Sexes alike. Feeds by plunge-diving.

WHITE-CHEEKED TERN

Sterna repressa Laridae

Size 32-34 cm

Voice Similar to Common's; also has diagnostic hoarse *kee…err* or *kee…ceek*

Range Breeds off Maharashtra coast; offshore waters of Pakistan, W India

Habitat Offshore waters

Very similar to Common but distinguished by darker grey upperparts and uniform grey rump and tail with back; underwing has darker trailing edge and pale central panel. Breeding adult has dirty-grey back, wings, rump, tail and underparts; black crown; white cheeks. Non-breeding adult has almost completely white head with brownish patch around eye and nape. Brownish-red legs and feet; bill graduates from dark red base and black towards pale tip. Juvenile similar to non-breeding adult, but has more brown upperparts.

SAUNDERS'S TERN

Sternula saundersi Laridae

Size 23 cm

Voice Call a penetrating, wiry, nasal worried *ker…wick*

Range W coasts

Habitat Coastal waters

Often confused with Little. Pale grey upperparts; white underparts, rump and tail; black streaks on outer primaries, conspicuous in flight. Legs and feet vary from olive-brown to reddish-brown or pinkish-brown. Breeding adult has black cap, white patch on forehead; yellow bill with black tip. Non-breeding adult has white head, with black plumage extending from hindneck through eye; black bill. Juvenile has sandy-buff plumage, with each feather having darker centre.

LITTLE TERN

Sternula albifrons Laridae

Size 23 cm

Voice Call a high, hurried *kink…kink*

Range Local breeder in N, S coasts and Sri Lanka. Disperses widely, mainly to coasts in non-breeding season

Habitat Sandy coasts; large rivers; lakes

Tiny tern with short tail and fast flight. Distinctive yellow bill with black tip and yellow legs; white forehead; pale grey back and wings with dark outer primaries. Forehead-patch extends like a point above eye. Non-breeding has black bill and smaller black cap. Sexes alike. Hovers over surface of water with fast wingbeats; plunges to catch fish. Male's aerial display involves calling and carrying fish to attract female, which soars high before descending by gliding with wings in a V. Juvenile has black on grey upperparts and wings.

non-breeding

BLACK-BELLIED TERN

Sterna acuticauda Laridae

Size 33 cm

Voice Calls include a shrill *krek… krek* and fast *kek…kek…kek*

Range Globally threatened, local resident; now very local breeding resident throughout most of the region

Habitat Inland rivers; lakes

Small, slender tern with very long tail and black underparts. Similar to River, but distinguished by deep orange bill with variable black tip. Black cap; darkish-grey upperparts, white face, neck. Breeding adult has black from lower breast to vent. Non-breeding adult white, streaked on crown. Sexes alike.

BRIDLED TERN

Onychoprion anaethetus Laridae

Similar to Sooty, but smaller and less pied, with paler upperparts and black nape and crown; narrower white forehead-patch. In flight, has prominent white leading edge to wings and whiter outer rectrices. Variation, as many as three races once recognised in the region.

juvenile

Size 33 cm

Voice Call low-pitched, includes a robust yapping *wup…wup*

Range Breeding visitor; (or resident), Vengurla Rocks

Habitat Flocks regularly; gathers where fish shoals near surface, or near fishing boats

adult

SOOTY TERN

Onychoprion fuscata Laridae

Size 33-36 cm

Voice Call a loud, piercing *wide…a…wake*

Range Breeds off Maharashtra coast, Lakshadweep and Maldives, seas adjacent to breeding islands in non-breeding season

Habitat Pelagic

Largish black tern with white underparts, forehead and tail-streamers and thin white leading edge to inner wing; extensive blackish underside to primaries, black tail with white outer-tail feathers; white forehead-patch with narrower black loral-stripe. Non-breeding adult may show white spotting on crown and white fringed-upperparts; upperparts may appear brownish and white feather bases may be visible. Juvenile similar but greyer with white scallops above and grey breast.

WHISKERED TERN

Chlidonias hybrida Laridae

Size 25 cm

Voice Sharp, wild notes

Range Breeds in Kashmir and Gangetic plains; common in winter over the area

Habitat Inland marshes; wet cultivation; coastal areas; tidal creeks

breeding

Slender tern with black markings on crown; silvery-grey-white plumage; long, narrow wings and slightly forked, almost squarish tail; short red legs and red beak distinctive. Breeding adult has jet-black cap and snow-white cheeks; black belly. At rest, closed wings extend beyond tail. Sexes alike. Large numbers fly about marshes or tidal creeks, leisurely but methodically, beak pointed down; dives from about 5 m height, taking turn when just about to touch ground, picking up insects in the process; also hunts flying insects over standing crops.

non-breeding

WHITE-WINGED TERN

Chlidonias leucopterus Laridae

breeding

non-breeding

Size 23 cm

Voice Quiet. Call a rasping *chree*

Range Scarce passage migrant, winter visitor

Habitat Rivers, lakes and estuaries. Feeds by surface-dipping. Does not dive

Breeding adult has velvety-black head, neck, breast and belly; almost white tail and rump; pale grey upperwings with broad, white leading edge; red bill and short, red legs. Non-breeding adult has largely grey upperparts and tail; white rump; white head and neck, and black-and-white streaked cap. Juvenile similar in appearance to non-breeding adult, but has an entirely black cap.

WHITE TERN

Gygis alba Laridae

Size 29 cm

Voice Call a harsh *grich…grich*

Range Common resident; only in Maldives. In non-breeding season, wanders Indian Ocean and could be storm-blown to mainland coasts

Pristine white, elegant seabird with slender body and long tapering wings. Short, deeply forked-tail; black bill, curves slightly upwards and tapers to sharp point; blackish legs with yellow webs between toes, small eyes surrounded by black rings. Sexes alike. Juvenile has brownish-grey back; grey neck; black mark behind eye. Feeds offshore on small fish shoals, usually catching them in air as they jump to escape predators. Flies with deliberate, slow wingbeats in undulating pattern for long periods. Extremely confiding at nest.

BROWN NODDY

Anous stolidus Laridae

Size 42 cm

Voice Call a dry growling *hrrrrarrhh*

Range Resident: Lakshadweep, Maldives

Habitat Pelagic. Breeds in huge colonies

Tropical seabird and largest of the noddies, distinguished from the closely-related Black by larger size and dark brown plumage and greyish-white cap. Broadish wings and longish wedge-shaped tail; white forehead, narrow white half-ring below eye; black lores. Juvenile has narrower, often brown-mottled white forehead and pale edges on upperparts; pale grey underwings and dark brown tail visible in flight. Known to perch on heads of brown pelicans to capture fish that escape from the bill of pelican.

LESSER NODDY

Anous tenuirostris Laridae

Size 33 cm

Voice Call includes varied short rattling notes; generally squeakier and more cackling than in the other two noddies

Range Non-breeding visitor; Sri Lanka

Habitat Similar to Brown's

Similar to Black, but distinguished by smaller size and paler, greyer body and shorter bill. Distinguished from Brown by longer, thinner bill and darker brownish-black colour; shorter and broader wings and shorter tail. Non-breeding adult has whiter forehead and crown. Pale grey cap grading evenly into grey face sides; white half-ring below eye; pale grey lores; dark brown underwings and belly visible in flight. Flight somewhat faster and more fluttery than Brown's. Juvenile whiter on head than adult and shows pale fringes to upperparts. Distinguished from juvenile Brown by slimmer shape, dark underwing and overall darker colour.

INDIAN SKIMMER

Rynchops albicollis Laridae

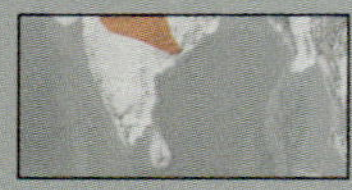

Size 40 cm

Voice Call a shrill scream; twittering cries at nest colony

Range Most common in N and C India, east to Assam. Less common in S Maharashtra, N Andhra Pradesh

Habitat Large rivers; fond of placid waters

Diagnostic yellowish-orange beak, much longer lower mandible; slender, pointed wings and tern-like pied plumage, blackish-brown above, contrasting with white underbody; white forehead, neck-collar and wing-bar; red legs. Sexes alike, but female slightly smaller. Juvenile has dusky orange bill with blackish tip, dull orange legs, paler, brownish-grey upperparts and white-buff fringes to mantle and wing-coverts. Solitary, or loose flocks fly over water; characteristic hunting style to skim over calm waters, beak wide open, longer projecting lower mandible partly submerged at an angle to snap up fish on striking; many rest together on sandbars.

ARCTIC SKUA

Stercorarius parasiticus Stercorariidae

Size 45 cm

Voice Usually quiet at sea

Range Probably regular off Pakistan coast in non-breeding season

Habitat Pelagic

Region's smallest skua (although vagrant Long-tailed is smaller). Bill relatively fine and head small; except when in moult shows at least slight projection of pointed central rectrices even in juvenile. In flight, inner wing narrower than in Pomarine; wings look long, with less white in primary bases. Adult has all-dark bill.

POMARINE SKUA

Stercorarius pomarinus Stercorariidae

Size 56 cm

Range Occurs as vagrant in the region's seas

Habitat Pelagic

Small skua with short and thick bill, with prominent dark tip. Breeding adult paler grey than other skuas, and bears unusual spoon-shaped central tail feathers. Non-breeding adult lacks streamers. Dark morph generally dark brown all over and has dark cap, while pale morph has dark wings, dark cap and pale breast. Powerful, steady flight.

CHESTNUT-BELLIED SANDGROUSE

Pterocles exustus Pteroclidae

Size 28 cm

Voice Call note a deep, clucking *kut…ro…*, uttered mostly on wing

Range All over India except NE and extreme S; most common in NW, C India

Habitat Open areas; semi-desert; fallow lands

More plain-looking sandgrouse. Male has sandy-buff upperparts speckled brown and dull yellow; black gorget and chocolate-black belly. Female buffy above, streaked and barred darker; black-spotted breast; rufous and black-barred belly and flanks. Pointed central tail feathers and black underside of wings distinctive in flight. Large flocks at waterholes in dry season; regularly arrives at water; prefers to stay on ground.

♀

PAINTED SANDGROUSE

Pterocles indicus Pteroclidae

Size 28 cm

Voice Call a thick, clucking *wuko… wuko* in flight

Range Scarce breeding, endemic resident mainly in dry parts of N and C India

Habitat Dry, open woodlands and thorn scrub usually on hillsides

Small, blunt-tailed sandgrouse. Male has broad black-and-buff and chestnut breast-bands and black-and-white crown pattern; plain sandy head and neck; intensely barred black-and-white; plain, sandy wing-coverts; plain underwings. Both sexes have barred upperparts and foreneck. Female has plainer face and finer barring on body and plain greyish throat. Feeds mainly on seeds. Gregarious; flocks congregate at waterholes.

♀

NILGIRI WOOD PIGEON

Columba elphinstonii Columbidae

Size 42 cm

Voice Call a loud *who*, followed by 3-to-5 deep and eerie sounding *who...who...who...* notes

Range Western Ghats south from Mumbai

Habitat Evergreen forests; shoals; cardamom plantations

Strikingly beautiful bird with reddish-brown upperparts and metallic purple-green sheen on upper back. Grey head and underbody; whitish throat; black-and-white chessboard on hindneck diagnostic. Sexes alike. Solitary, or in small gatherings; arboreal but often descends to forest floor to pick fallen fruit; strong flier, wheeling and turning amidst branches at fast speed; occasionally along with other frugivorous birds.

PALE-CAPPED PIGEON

Columba punicea Columbidae

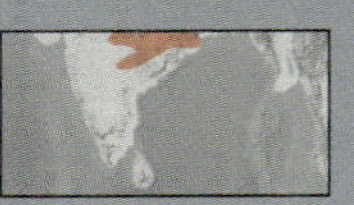

Size 36 cm

Voice Unknown

Range Rare breeding resident Odisha and Assam

Habitat Tall trees

Rich chestnut-maroon upperparts, pale vinous-chestnut underparts. Pale bluish-grey cap; maroon-brown mantle and wing-coverts with green-and-purple sheen. Sexes similar, but female darker with dark grey crown. Juvenile lacks cap; upperparts more brown, with chestnut fringes, and underparts mixed grey and rufous-buff.

ROCK PIGEON

Columba livia Columbidae

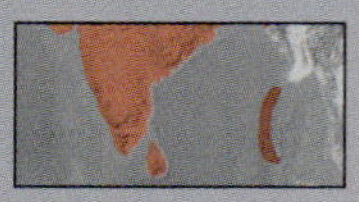

Size 33 cm

Voice Call a deep *tru…troo…tru*

Range Abundant feral and wild breeding resident throughout

Habitat Urban areas; cultivation

intermedia

Common bird in urban areas around the world; medium-sized, blue-grey pigeon with darker head and neck and black wing-bars, interbreeds with domestic pigeons, so several colour varieties possible. Blue-grey with green-purple sheen across neck. Wings darker. Some races have white lower back. Always has two long black bars across wing-coverts. Gregarious, mixing with other doves. Feeds in flocks on split grain and sprouting cereals. Also in remote rocky places with cliffs and ruins. Nests colonially in cavities and on ledges in buildings and cliffs.

neglecta

ORIENTAL TURTLE DOVE

Streptopelia orientalis Columbidae

Size 32 cm

Voice Call a deep and grating *ghur…ghroo…goo…*

Range Several races, resident and migratory, distributed over much of the Indian region

Habitat Mixed forests; vicinity of cultivation; orchards

meena

Large, stocky dove with grey-and-black spotted patch on neck sides. Rufous-brown back and scapulars, with black markings diagnostic; slaty-grey lower back, rump; whitish border to roundish tail, best seen when tail fanned during landing. Sexes alike. In pairs or loose parties, occasionally solitary birds; feeds mostly on ground; rests during hot hours in leafy branches; perches on overhead wires.

erythrocephala

EURASIAN COLLARED DOVE

Streptopelia decaocto Columbidae

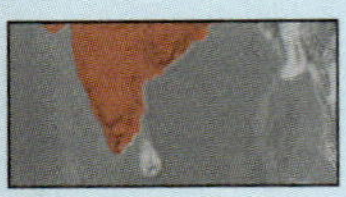

Size 32 cm

Voice Call a characteristic *kukkoo…kook…*

Range Most of the region, except extreme NE Himalayas; resident and local migrant; most common in NW, W and C India

Habitat Cultivation; open scrub; dry forests

Similar to Red Collared female but larger with different tail pattern. Greyish-brown plumage; lilac wash around head and neck; black half-collar on hindneck distinctive; broad whitish tips to brown tail feathers, seen as terminal band when fanned during landing; dull lilac breast and ash-grey underbody. Sexes alike. Small parties, when not breeding; often associates with other doves; large gatherings glean in cultivated country; strong flier, chases intruders in territory.

RED COLLARED DOVE

Streptopelia tranquebarica Columbidae

Size 23 cm

Voice Call a quick repeated *gru... gurgoo...*, with more stress on first syllable

Range Throughout the region, south of the Himalayan foothills

Habitat Cultivation; scrubs; deciduous country

Male has deep ash-grey head; black hindneck-collar; rich wine-red back; slaty grey-brown lower back, rump and uppertail; whitish tips to all but central tail feathers. Female much like Eurasian Collared, but smaller size and more brownish colouration distinctive. Solitary, in pairs or small parties; associates with other doves but less common; feeds on ground, gleaning on harvested croplands; perches and suns on leafless branches and overhead wires.

SPOTTED DOVE

Stigmatopelia chinensis Columbidae

Size 30 cm

Voice Familiar bird sound of India, a soft, somewhat doleful *crook...cru...croo or croo...croo...*

Range Subcontinent, upto about 3,500 m in the Himalayas

Habitat Open forests; scrubs; habitation; cultivation

Slender dove with long wedged tail. Grey and pink-brown above, spotted white; white-spotted black hindneck-collar (chessboard) diagnostic; dark tail with broad white tips to outer feathers seen in flight; vinous-brown breast, merging into white on belly. Sexes alike. Juvenile barred above and lack chessboard. In pairs or small parties on ground; frequently settles on paths and roads, flying further on intrusion; quite tame and confiding in many areas; drinks often; at harvest, seen along with other doves in immense gatherings.

LAUGHING DOVE

Stigmapelia senegalensis Columbidae

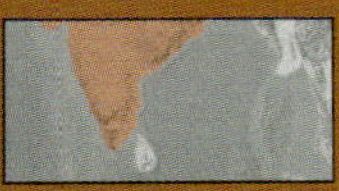

Size 27 cm

Voice Call a somewhat harsh but pleasant *cru…do…do…do…do*

Range Almost across India upto about 1,200 m in the outer Himalayas; uncommon in NE states

Habitat Open scrub; cultivation; neighbourhood of habitation

Pinkish grey-brown plumage with black-and-buff chessboard on sides of foreneck; white tips to outer-tail feathers and broad grey wing-patches best seen in flight; small size distinctive. Sexes alike. In pairs, or small flocks; associates freely with other doves in huge gatherings at harvest time; feeds mostly on ground, walking about silently.

EMERALD DOVE

Chalcophaps indica Columbidae

Size 26 cm

Voice Call a deep, plaintive *hoo…oon…hoo…oon…*, many times at a stretch

Range Almost throughout the subcontinent upto about 2,000 m. Absent in Pakistan

Habitat Forests, bamboo clearings; foothills

Bronze emerald-green upperbody; white forehead and eyebrows; grey crown and neck; white on wing shoulder and across lower back; whitish rump diagnostic in flight; rich pinkish-brown below; coral-red beak and pink-red legs. Sexes similar with female duller. Solitary, or in pairs; moves on forest paths and clearings or darts almost blindly through trees, usually under 5 m off ground; difficult to spot on ground.

♀

ORANGE-BREASTED GREEN PIGEON

Treron bicinctus Columbidae

Size 33 cm

Voice Call a typical whistle; quiet gurgle

Range Throughout the region

Habitat Subtropical moist deciduous broadleaved evergreen forests; secondary growth; well-wooded country

Smallish green pigeon with blue eyes. Male has distinctive bright orange breast with lilac border above; face and forehead yellowish green; nape and hindneck bluish-grey; unmarked plain green mantle. Female has yellower wash on underparts. Both have dark uppertail-coverts; central tail feathers grey; light grey banding on tail; yellow bordered wing-coverts. Gregarious; in small flocks; often in large groups or mixed feeding parties with other frugivores; arboreal; in fruiting trees; quiet; hard to detect; acrobatic.

YELLOW-FOOTED GREEN PIGEON

Treron phoenicopterus Columbidae

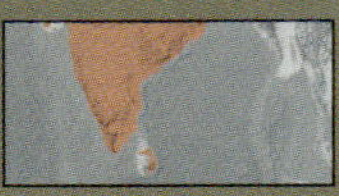

Size 33 cm

Voice Call includes rich, mellow whistling notes

Range South roughly of line from S Rajasthan to N Odisha to Sri Lanka; rarer in Pakistan

Habitat Forests; orchards; city parks; cultivated village vicinities

Male ash olive-green above; olive-yellow collar, dark, slaty tail has band; lilac-red shoulder-patch (mostly absent in female); yellow legs and underbody. Female slightly duller than male. The nominate (northern) race has grey lower breast and belly. Small flocks; mostly arboreal, rarely coming to salt-licks or cropland; remains well hidden in foliage but moves briskly; has favourite feeding trees.

GREEN IMPERIAL PIGEON

Ducula aenea Columbidae

Size 43 cm

Voice Deep chuckling notes, quite pleasant-sounding and somewhat ventriloquistic

Range Forested parts of N India, from Garhwal Terai eastwards; forested regions of C and E India, Western Ghats south of Mumbai; resident in many areas but also moves considerably

Habitat Evergreen forests

Large forest pigeon, often confused with similar Mountain Imperial, but much smaller. Greyish head, neck and underbody with distinct pinkish wash; metallic bronze-green upperbody, unbanded tail; chocolate-maroon undertail; reddish legs. Sexes alike. Juvenile overall duller. Known for aerial display, repeatedly rises to dive with half-closed wings. In pairs, or small parties on fruiting trees, not infrequently with other species; chiefly arboreal but comes to ground, at salt-licks and water; strong flight; has favourite feeding spots. Several regional variations.

MOUNTAIN IMPERIAL PIGEON

Ducula badia Columbidae

Size 45 cm

Voice Call a booming *oomp…oomp*

Range Fairly common breeding resident: Western Ghats, NE India, parts of Nepal

Habitat Closed forests

Very large pigeon with grey head and neck tinged with pink. Wings and mantle brownish-maroon, throat and chin white. Pinkish-grey underparts; dark-based tail with broad, pale terminal band. Red-based bill and red eye-rings with pale iris. Pinkish feet. Sexes alike.

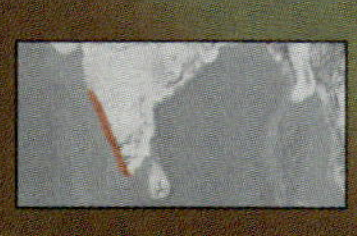

VERNAL HANGING PARROT

Loriculus vernalis Psittacidae

Size 15 cm

Voice Quiet but distinctive and rapid *zzit…zzit* in flight

Range Scarce breeding resident of lower hills of SW, E India and Bangladesh, subject to local movements

Habitat Forests

Small short-tailed and primarily emerald green-plumaged bird with blue patch on throat; red rump and uppertail-coverts; red bill; white eye. Female similar to male but with little or no blue on throat. Juvenile similar to adult but has dull greyish-green on forehead and cheeks; no blue on throat; dull red rump washed green; pale orange bill; brown eye. Unique for its ability to sleep upside down. Very arboreal.

ALEXANDRINE PARAKEET

Psittacula eupatria Psittacidae

Size 53 cm

Voice Call a high-pitched *kreeak…* scream, on wing as well as on perch; popular cage bird, learns to imitate some notes and few human words

Range Almost throughout the region, south of the Himalayan foothills

Habitat Forests; orchards; cultivated areas; towns

Rich, vibrant-coloured bird. Male has rich grass-green plumage; hooked, heavy red beak; deep red shoulder-patch; rose-pink collar and black stripe from lower mandible to collar distinctive. Female smaller and lacks collar and black stripe. Yellow undertail in both sexes. Seen in small flocks and large gatherings; feeds on fruiting trees in orchards and on standing crops; strong flier; roosts along with other birds at favoured sites.

ROSE-RINGED PARAKEET

Psittacula krameri Psittacidae

Size 42 cm

Voice Call a shrill *keeak…*; screams

Range Subcontinent, south of the Himalayan foothills

Habitat Light forests; orchards; towns; villages

Male has grass-green plumage; short, hooked, red beak; rosy-pink and black collar distinctive (attained only during third year). Female lacks pink-and-black collar; instead, pale emerald-green around neck. Gregarious; large flocks of this species familiar sight in India; causes extensive damage to standing crops, orchards and garden fruit trees; also raids grain depots and markets; large roosting colonies, often along with mynas and crows.

PLUM-HEADED PARAKEET

Psittacula cyanocephala Psittacidae

Size 36 cm

Voice Call includes loud, interrogative *tooi...tooi...* notes in fast flight; also other chattering notes

Range Subcontinent, south of the Himalayan foothills

Habitat Forests; orchards; cultivation in forest

Male has yellowish-green plumage; plum-red head washed purplish-blue on hindcrown; black chin strap; black and bluish-green collar; maroon-red wing shoulder-patch; dark red spot on inner median wing-coverts; white tips to central tail feathers distinctive. Female dull, greyer head; yellow collar; almost non-existent maroon shoulder-patch. In pairs, or small parties; arboreal, but descends into cultivation in forest clearings and outskirts; sometimes huge gatherings in cultivation; strong, darting flight over forest.

MALABAR PARAKEET

Psittacula columboides Psittacidae

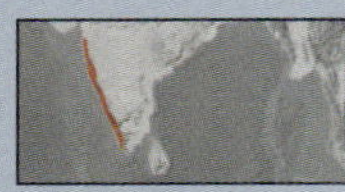

Size 38 cm

Voice Call a hard squeaky *screet…screet*, harsher than Plum-headed

Range Fairly common endemic breeding resident restricted to Western Ghats

Habitat Mainly evergreen hill forest, feeding high in canopy on fruits and flowers

Long-tailed, mainly blue and grey parakeet with bluish-grey head, breast and mantle, blue flight feathers and yellow-edged blue tail. Green patch around eyes. Both sexes have black collar but male's edged with blue-green band; pale iris. Bluish-green collar band absent in female and has less green on face and forecrown. Juvenile has greenish head, bluish-green band under black stripe absent. Very sociable. Nests in tree holes.

♀

JACOBIN CUCKOO

Clamator jacobinus Cuculidae

Size 33 cm

Voice Noisy; loud, metallic *plew…piu…* call notes

Range Chiefly SW monsoon breeding visitor

Habitat Open forests; cultivation; orchards

Earlier known as Pied Crested Cuckoo, this summer visitor has black upperparts; noticeable crest; white in wings and white tip to long tail feathers diagnostic in flight; white underbody. Juvenile, seen in autumn, dull sooty-brown with indistinct crest; white areas dull fulvous. Sexes alike. Solitary, or in small parties of four to six; arboreal; occasionally descends to ground to feed on insects. Brood-parasite, laying eggs in other birds' nests (usually bulbuls), arrives just before SW monsoon by end of May. Noisy and active, chasing one another; mobbed by crows on arrival.

juvenile

CHESTNUT-WINGED CUCKOO

Clamator coromandus Cuculidae

Size 45 cm

Voice Call a whistling *peep… peep* in breeding season. Also, hoarse screech

Range Scarce, local breeding summer visitor to N foothills

Habitat Forests; thick scrub

Slender, long-tailed cuckoo with chestnut wings, white collar and long, black, erect crest. Top of head and upperparts to tail of adult glossy metallic black, pale orange-brown throat to upper breast, and upper belly; white belly; blackish undertail-coverts; tail tipped white. Juvenile has dark brown head and upperparts, feathers edged paler, smaller crest; white underparts; rufous-edged wing-coverts and buff edge and tip of tail. Swift direct flight with rapid wingbeats.

LARGE HAWK CUCKOO

Hierococcyx sparverioides Cuculidae

Size 38 cm

Voice Call a measured *kee… keeah…kee…keeah* usually without crescendo. Heard at night as well as day

Range Fairly common breeding summer visitor: Himalayas and hills of NE India. Winters sparsely in lowlands

Habitat Broadleaved evergreen forests

Large greyish-brown bird with rufescent subterminal bar to white-tipped tail; rufous-washed belly, barred brown-and-white; black chin; orange iris; pale yellow feet; bill black above and greenish-yellow below. Immature has chestnut-brown upperparts, barred with rufous; buff underparts with black streaks.

COMMON HAWK CUCKOO

Hierococcyx varius Cuculidae

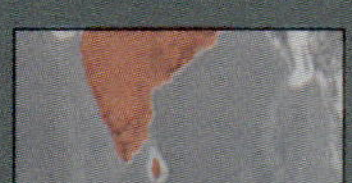

Size 34 cm

Voice Famous call notes; interpreted as brain-fever, uttered untiringly in crescendo; also described as *pipeeha… pipeeha…*; very noisy in overcast weather

Range Subcontinent, south of the Himalayan foothills; uncommon, even during rains, in arid zones

Habitat Forests; open country; near habitation

juvenile

Popularly known as the Brainfever bird; medium-sized cuckoo with ash-grey upperparts; dark bars on rufescent-tipped tail; dull white below, with pale ash-rufous on breast; barred below. Juvenile broadly-streaked dark below; pale rufous barrings on brown upperbody. Sexes alike. Solitary, rarely in pairs; strictly arboreal; noisy during May–September; silent after rains. Brood-parasite, laying eggs in nests of babblers.

INDIAN CUCKOO

Cuculus micropterus Cuculidae

Size 33 cm

Voice Very distinct call; 4-noted mellow whistle, variously interpreted, *bo…ko…ta…ko or crossword…puzzle* best known

Range Subcontinent, south from the Himalayas to about 2,500 m, except drier and arid parts of NW India; absent in Pakistan

Habitat Forests; orchards

Medium-sized, solitary and shy bird. Slaty-brown above; greyer on head, throat and breast; whitish below, with broadly spaced black cross-bars; broad subterminal tail-band (characteristic of the non-hawk cuckoos of genus *Cuculus*); female often has rufous-brown wash on throat and breast; call notes most important identification clue. Sexes alike. Arboreal, not easy to see; overall appearance very hawk-like, but distinctly weaker-looking flight.

EURASIAN CUCKOO

Cuculus canorus Cuculidae

Size 33 cm

Voice Well-known, repetitive *cuc…koo*. Also, rapid bubbling, mainly by female

Range Common breeding summer visitor to N mountains. Scarce winter visitor elsewhere in lowlands

Habitat Woodlands and scrubs, where brood-parasites. Winters in wooded country and cultivation. Typically flies with wings held low and rather humped back

♀

hepatic

Medium-sized grey bird. Adult male has bluish-grey upperparts and finely barred white belly with dark barring; bluish-grey head, throat and upper breast. Darker flight feathers and black tail bordered white; yellow iris and eye-rings. Female occurs in two morphs, one similar to male but with buff-brown breast, barred darker, buff coloured with dark barring; other more reddish-brown, intensely barred darker. Juvenile slaty-grey with hints of reddish-brown.

LESSER CUCKOO

Cuculus poliocephalus Cuculidae

Size 25 cm

Voice Strong, cheerful song, rendered as pretty *peel…lay…ka*

Range Breeds in the Himalayas from N Pakistan east to Arunachal Pradesh

Habitat Forests; well-wooded country

hepatic

Adult male has slaty-grey upperparts, pale slaty-blue head, neck, throat and upper breast; white lower breast and rest of underparts, boldly-barred black. Grey morph female similar to male, but has rufous wash on upper breast; hepatic morph has rufous upperparts with blackish barring except on rump, white underparts barred black, tail barred rufous and black with white tip. Juvenile has dark grey-brown upperparts with variable, narrow whitish to rufous barring and broadly barred underparts.

BANDED BAY CUCKOO

Cacomantis sonneratii Cuculidae

Size 24 cm

Voice Call a shrill whistle

Range From N Uttar Pradesh east to Assam and Bangladesh

Habitat Dense broadleaved forests in Nepal; lightly wooded country in India; edges of forests, patches of shifting cultivation and open forests in Sri Lanka

Small cuckoo with longish, curved bill. Upperparts rufous-brown, strongly barred, uniformly and regularly, dark brown. Adult male has broad white supercilium (cross-barred with black), which encircles brown ear-coverts; dark eye-stripe; whitish cheeks; white-tipped tail. Whitish underparts, washed pale buff from belly to flanks, finely and uniformly barred; central tail feathers barred and darker on each side of shaft. Juvenile similar to adult, but whiter on head and upper mantle; less barring on underparts.

GREY-BELLIED CUCKOO

Cacomantis passerinus Cuculidae

Size 23 cm

Voice Noisy, with good range of calls. Call a mournful (plaintive) single-noted *piteeer*…; sometimes 3-noted, second note shortest, third long-drawn

Range India, south from the Himalayas to about 2,500 m, except arid NW regions

Habitat Open forests, orchards and gardens in vicinity of habitation

hepatic

Grey head; grey-brown glossy upperparts; white tail-tip and patch under the wing seen in flight; grey throat, upper breast; paler, almost white below. Female also has hepatic (reddish) phase. Bright chestnut upperparts and throat, with reddish-brown wash; cross-barred black on back; white below throat, narrowly cross-barred black. Sexes alike. Mostly solitary; keeps to foliage.

DRONGO CUCKOO

Surniculus lugubris Cuculidae

Size 23 cm

Voice Diagnostic; noisy during monsoon. Call a short whistled *pee...pee...pee...pee*

Range Hills of C and SW India. Summer visitor to the Himalayas, hills of NE India

Habitat Open forests; orchards; shade trees

Smallish, mainly glossy black cuckoo, similar to Black Drongo but with smaller, slimmer, downcurved bill, long, black, square-cut tail, with only slight fork or notch; tail and vent white-barred, unlike those of true drongos; white thighs; sometimes, white nape spot; no white rictal spot of Black Drongo. Juvenile duller, white-spotted; quieter, shyer, more inconspicuous than the bolder and more active drongos; cuckoo-like flight; mostly arboreal; sometimes in lower growth or ground; sings from bare branches. The square-tailed and forked-tailed forms are sometimes considered to be separate species.

square-tailed

forked-tailed

ASIAN KOEL

Eudynamys scolopaceus Cuculidae

Size 43 cm

Voice Familiar call of Indian countryside. Very noisy between March and June, coinciding with breeding of crows; loud *kuoo...kuooo...* whistling calls in crescendo by male koel, first syllable longish; water-bubbling call of female

Range Subcontinent, upto about 1,800 m in the outer Himalayas; uncommon in drier areas

Habitat Light forests; orchards; city parks; cultivation; open areas

Large cuckoo with metallic, bluish-green black plumage; greenish beak and crimson eyes. Female dark brown, thickly-spotted and barred white; whitish below, dark-spotted on throat, barred below. Solitary, or in pairs; arboreal; mostly silent between July and February; fast flight.

♀

GREEN-BILLED MALKOHA

Rhopodytes tristis Cuculidae

Size 51 cm

Voice Rather silent, sometimes croaks quietly

Range Scarce breeding resident: N foothills, NE India, Eastern Ghats

Habitat Forests; scrub undergrowth

Large, long-tailed bird with pale green, robust bill. Overall greenish-grey with paler head and underparts; grey underparts, darker on breast; glossy green, graduated tail, black with white feather-tips; red facial skin; black bristles around gape. Juvenile duller than adult with shorter rectrices and narrower white tail-tip. Narrow white border surrounding red orbital skin. Holds tail straight when running through tangled vegetation.

BLUE-FACED MALKOHA

Rhopodytes viridirostris Cuculidae

Size 39 cm

Voice Rather silent; sometimes croaks quietly

Range Scarce, but overlooked endemic breeding resident in S India, Sri Lanka

Habitat Thick thorn scrub and open forest undergrowth

Large, dark greenish-grey cuckoo with diagnostic blue, bare and warty orbital skin. Head and upperparts dark grey; iridescent greenish-grey wings and tail; dark grey underparts, washed rufous on abdomen; bluish streaked throat; very long black-and-white tail. Deep brown to red iris with white eye-ring. Sexes alike. Juvenile duller and less glossy. Soliary, or in pairs. Scrambles in tangled vegetation, foraging. Seldom seen in open.

SIRKEER MALKOHA

Taccocua leschenaultii Cuculidae

Size 43 cm

Voice Fairly loud and sharp clicking notes; mostly vocal when breeding

Range Most of the subcontinent, upto about 1,800 m in the Himalayas; absent in NW India and Kashmir

Habitat Open jungles, scrubs, ravines, dense growth around habitation. Endemic resident of thorn scrub and semi-desert regions

Sandy-brown head, hindneck and upperparts; shiny black shaft streaks on head and nape. Long, graduated tail, with broad white tips to blackish outer feathers distinctive in flight; cherry-red beak, with yellow tip. Sexes alike. Solitary, or in pairs; sometimes four or five birds in neighbourhood; moves mostly on ground, in dense growth; may clamber out on some bush-tops or low trees. Laboured and flapping flight. Shy. Runs low and rat-like when disturbed.

LESSER COUCAL

Centropus bengalensis Centropodidae

Size 33 cm

Voice Call a deep, rapid *oop…oop…oop* varying in tone. Also *kutook…kutook* and variants

Range Local breeding resident and summer visitor: N foothills from Uttarakhand east to Myanmar border, throughout NE India, south to Odisha and including Bangladesh. Also SW India

Habitat Grasslands; open country

Small coucal with short decurved beak. Breeding adult glossy bluish-black. Bright buff shaft streaks on scapulars and lesser wing-coverts; wings mottled dark brown and rufous. Non-breeding adult has dark brown head and mantle, dark brown rump barred rufous; pale buff throat and breast streaked darker. Juvenile similar to non-breeding adult, but has dark and light buff streaking on head and upperparts. Usually solitary, or in pairs. Feeds mainly on grasshoppers.

juvenile

GREATER COUCAL

Centropus sinensis Centropodidae

Size 50 cm

Voice Loud and resonant *coop…coop…coop…* call familiar; occasionally a squeaky call

Range Subcontinent, from outer Himalayas to about 2,000 m

Habitat Forests; scrubs; cultivation; gardens; derelict patches; vicinity of habitation

Beautiful terrestrial bird with glossy bluish-black plumage; chestnut wings; blackish, glossy dark green, long, graduated tail; strong, heavy, darkish bill; deep red eyes; dark grey feet. Female somewhat larger than male. Sexes alike. Solitary, or in pairs; moves amidst dense growth, fanning and flicking tail often; clambers up into trees, but poor flier, lazily flying short distances.

BARN OWL

Tyto alba Tytonidae

Size 35 cm

Voice Call a long-drawn, wild shriek; variety of snoring, hissing notes

Range Almost all over India, south of the Himalayan foothills

Habitat Grasslands; cultivation; human habitation; town-centres

Dull golden-buff above, finely speckled black-and-white; white below, often with fine, dark spots; heart-shaped, white facial disc with brown edge; brownish wash between lower edge of eyes and base of pale pink bill. Sexes alike. Solitary, or in pairs; nocturnal, but sometimes hunts during day; normally rests during day, mostly in tree-cavity, dense creepers or some dark loft; perches upright; flies silently, mostly under 4 m from ground; pounces on prey.

EASTERN GRASS OWL

Tyto longimembris Tytonidae

Size 36 cm

Voice Hissing scream, similar to that of Barn, though tends to be more silent than Barn

Range Resident; NE and SW India, and S Nepal

Habitat Tall grasslands

Similar to Barn in size but distinguished by darker eyes and whitish face and underparts. Adult male has white facial disc, while female has more beige facial disc. Dark brown upperparts mottled with fine white and ochre spots; creamy-white underparts blotched darker; long wings; three dark bars on primaries; shortish tail has three or four bars. Feathered legs with blackish-brown claws and yellowish-grey toes. Female similar, but slightly larger. Mainly nocturnal, but occasionally seen during day; ground bird; hides in grass. Breeds colonially; several birds hunt in same area.

ORIENTAL BAY OWL

Phodilus badius Tytonidae

Size 29 cm

Voice Calls include a series of eerie, upward-inflected whistles

Range Resident; NE India

Habitat Dense evergreen broadleaved forests

Sri Lanka Bay Owl

Medium-sized owl with whitish-vinaceous, elongated facial disc, short, rounded wings and short tail. Pale V-shaped, brownish-grey forehead and dark brown vertical eye-patches. Long legs feathered to feet. Large dark eyes; white necklace; rich chestnut and buff upperparts spotted and barred with black. Pale yellow-brown underparts, speckled with blackish-brown and buff. Chestnut tail has few narrow bars. Nocturnal bird, roosts in holes and hollows in tree trunks. The similar Sri Lanka Bay Owl *P. b. assimilis* is found in SW India and Sri Lanka.

COLLARED SCOPS OWL

Otus b lettia Strigidae

Size 23 cm

Voice Call fluty and questioning. Calls throughout the night

Range Resident of the Himalayas, NE India

Habitat Forests; cultivation; orchards; trees in vicinity of habitation

Small owl with buff and brown 'imitation face' on nape. Small ear tufts and upright posture. Greyish-brown above; buffy nuchal-collar diagnostic; buffy-white underbody, streaked and mottled dark. Sexes alike. Solitary, or in pairs; remains motionless during day in thick, leafy branches or at junctions of stems and branches; very difficult to spot; flies around dusk.

PALLID SCOPS OWL

Otus brucei Strigidae

Size 21 cm

Voice Resonant, extended *hoop...hoop...hoop*. Soft dove-like call

Range Little-known resident of N Pakistan mountains east to Ladakh. Some winter in NW India

Habitat Dry mountain ranges. Highly nocturnal

Small, cryptically plumaged owl. Overall sandy-grey plumage very sparsely streaked; small, often depressed ear tufts; narrow, well-defined black border to pale facial disc. Underparts finely streaked with black. Large eyes with yellow iris. Tail extends marginally beyond wing-tips, with tail-bands diffusing towards tip; legs feathered till base of toes. Similar to Oriental, but paler, less distinct scapular spots and darker and narrower streaking on underparts. Sexes alike. Juvenile has completely barred underparts. Nests in tree holes.

ORIENTAL SCOPS OWL

Otus sunia Strigidae

Size 19 cm

Voice Distinctive call of slowly repeated *wug-chug-chug*

Range Locally common breeding resident in plains and lower hills mainly in north from N Pakistan, east to Myanmar border, Bangladesh, Sri Lanka, Western Ghats and S peninsular India

Habitat Forests; groves; orchards

Small mottled brown owl with short ear tufts. Breast heavily streaked with black; orange-yellow iris; greyish bill and feet. Cryptic, mottled plumage in three morphs: rufous (shown), brown and grey. Latter two not readily separable from rarer Eurasian *O. Scops* and call only reliable identification factor. Well-streaked crown and underparts distinguish it from Mountain and Pallid. Prominent white scapular lines. Large vertical ear tufts often suppressed. Strictly nocturnal, roosts in day close to trunks in thickly-foliaged trees. Hunts in smaller trees on forest edge, clearings and secondary growth. Nests in holes.

rufous morph

EURASIAN EAGLE OWL

Bubo bubo Strigidae

Size 60 cm

Voice Call a deep, booming *bu… boo…*; snapping calls at nest

Range Northern hills of Pakistan and Himalayas, from about 1,500 m

Habitat Ravines; cliffsides; riversides; scrubs; open country

Large owl with conspicuous ear tufts and heavily feathered, powerful talons; tawny-buff facial disc, mottled blackish-brown; blackish bill; greyish-olive cere; bright orange-red to golden-yellow eyes; white chin and throat, continuing down to centre upper breast. Brownish-black and tawny-buff upperparts; tawny-buff underparts except for chin, throat finely-barred.

SPOT-BELLIED EAGLE OWL

Bubo nipalensis Strigidae

Size 63 cm

Voice Low, blood-curdling moan and scream

Range Uttarakhand eastwards, throughout NE Indian region; also in Western Ghats and Sri Lanka

Habitat Dense broadleaved evergreen forests

juvenile

Large, dramatic-looking bird of prey. Pallid, overall stark, greyish-brown with prominent horizontally-held ear tufts; characteristic dark heart or chevron-shaped markings on white underparts diagnostic; dark brown primaries striped lighter; heavily-barred secondaries; plain white facial discs; white supercilium; large, pale yellow bill, dark brown eyes. Juvenile overall whiter with distinctive crown and mantle. Nocturnal; roosts by day in thickly-forested areas; hunts deep in forests, but sometimes ventures to edges at dusk; formidable strength allows to take on large prey.

DUSKY EAGLE OWL

Bubo coromandus Strigidae

Size 58 cm

Voice Call a deep, hollow, somewhat eerie hoot of 5- to 8-notes fading towards end; interpreted as *woo...wo...wo...wo...o...o...o*

Range Throughout the region, south of outer Himalayas; status in extreme south of country unclear. Also spotted in Myanmar and Malaysia

Habitat Groves; light forests; roadside leafy trees; vicinity of habitation

Pale grey-brown plumage, profusely spotted, streaked and marked with white; pale buffish-grey underparts with dark shaft stripes and brown cross-bars; prominent ear tufts, erect when alert and dull yellow eyes diagnostic. Feathered tarsus and bristled toes. Sexes alike. Mostly in pairs, sometimes three to four scattered; has favoured roost sites in large, leafy trees; may call and fly during daytime.

juvenile

MOTTLED WOOD OWL

Strix ocellata Strigidae

Size 48 cm

Voice Call a loud, hooting note

Range All over India, south from the Himalayan foothills; absent in arid NW parts and much of NE India

Habitat Forests; orchards; vicinity of habitation; cultivation

Medium-sized owl with no ear tufts. Yellowish-red upperparts, profusely mottled and vermiculated red-brown, black, white and buff; whitish facial disc with narrow chocolate-black barrings forming concentric circles; white spots on crown, nape; chestnut and black throat, stippled white; rest of underparts whitish, barred golden-buff to orange-buff. Yellowish-brown toes, blackish talons. Sexes alike. Solitary, or in pairs; nocturnal, spends day in dense foliage of large trees; roosts after sunset.

BROWN WOOD OWL

Strix leptogrammica Strigidae

Size 47-53 cm

Voice Calls include *hoo... hoohoohoo...(hoo)* and loud eerie scream

Range The Himalayas, NE India, Eastern and Western Ghats, Bangladesh and Sri Lanka

Habitat Dense broadleaved subtropical or temperate forests

Medium-sized owl with warm-brown plumage; no ear tufts; fulvous or rufous-brown facial disc with narrow but distinct black rim. The Himalayan *S.l. newarensis* has dark brown face, with prominent white eyebrows, and striking white band across foreneck. Underparts greyish-white, heavily barred with brown.

juvenile

JUNGLE OWLET

Glaucidium radiatum Strigidae

Size 20 cm

Voice Noisy; musical *kuo…kak…kuo…kak…* call-notes, rising in crescendo for few seconds only to end abruptly, other pleasant bubbling notes

Range All over India, from about 2,000 m in the Himalayas; probably absent in extreme NE states

Habitat Forests; partial to teak and bamboo mixed forests

radiatum
malabaricum

Darkish-brown above, barred rufous and white; flight-feathers barred rufous and black; white moustachial stripe, centre of breast and abdomen; remainder of underbody barred-dark rufous-brown-and-white. Sexes alike. Solitary, or in pairs and sometimes in small groups; crepuscular, but sometimes also active and noisy by day; otherwise spends day in leafy branch; flies short distance when disturbed.

FOREST OWLET

Heteroglaux blewitti Strigidae

Size 23 cm

Voice Not well-known but *oh…hu* and *kweek…kweek* calls reported

Range Rare endemic breeder rediscovered in extreme NW Maharashtra in 1997 after no sightings for over a century. Also, now known from sites in Madhya Pradesh

Habitat Open, dry deciduous forests on low hills

Thought to be extinct for over a hundred years till rediscovered in 1997. Small, overall dark, greyish-brown bird with fairly small, round head. Tail and wings, heavily-banded; almost completely white underparts; white face; unspotted, brown crown; broad brown breast-band; barred flanks. Similar to Spotted but darker brown with whitish spotting and broader, but paler barring on tail and wings. Underparts white with large claws. Diurnal, shy and wary.

SPOTTED OWLET

Athene brama Strigidae

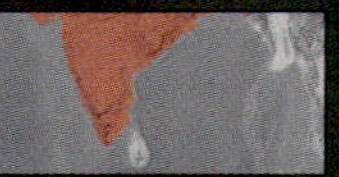

Size 21 cm

Voice Assortment of scolding and cackling notes, screeches and chuckles

Range Throughout the region, upto about 1,800 m in outer Himalayas

Habitat Open forests; orchards; cultivation; vicinity of habitation

Small, stocky owlet with greyish-brown upperparts, spotted white; no ear tufts; yellowish eyes; broken whitish-buff nuchal-collar. Juvenile more thickly-marked white; darkish streaks below breast. Sexes alike. In pairs, or small parties; roosts during day in leafy branches, tree cavities or cavities in walls; active in some localities during daytime; when disturbed flies to nearby tree or branch and bobs and stares at intruder.

BROWN HAWK OWL

Ninox scutulata Strigidae

Size 32 cm

Voice Call includes an extended, liquid *oowup… oowup…oowup*

Range Locally common breeding resident mainly in lower hills from Uttarakhand east to Myanmar border, Bangladesh, peninsular India and Sri Lanka

Habitat Well-wooded country, usually near water

Slender, dark owl. Dark brown facial disc has white radial streaks; chocolate-brown crown and nape with ochre streaks; mantle and wing-coverts plain chocolate-brown; some white on back and wings; underparts have intense, drop-shaped streaks, becoming chevron-shaped towards flanks; long, grey-banded tail with whitish tip; no ear tufts; yellow eyes; feathered legs. Andaman and Nicobar race all dark. Sexes alike, male larger than female. Hunts singly, or in pairs, insects, birds and other animals from favoured perch. Hawk-like flight with flaps and long glides. Crepuscular or nocturnal. Roosts during day in thick canopy.

SHORT-EARED OWL

Asio flammeus Strigidae

Size 38 cm

Voice Usually silent

Range Scarce but widespread winter visitor throughout lowlands

Habitat Dry, open country with scattered bushes

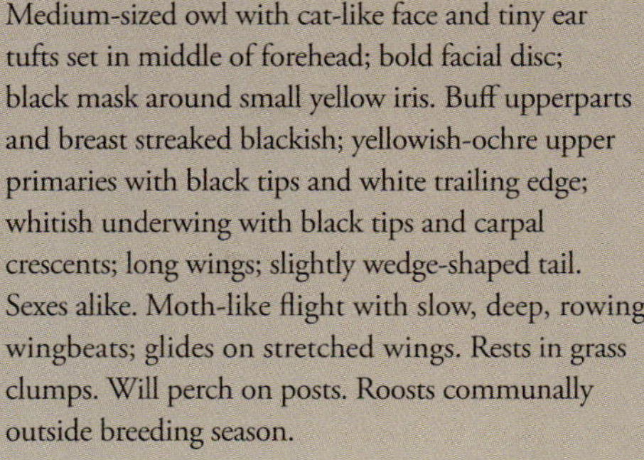

Medium-sized owl with cat-like face and tiny ear tufts set in middle of forehead; bold facial disc; black mask around small yellow iris. Buff upperparts and breast streaked blackish; yellowish-ochre upper primaries with black tips and white trailing edge; whitish underwing with black tips and carpal crescents; long wings; slightly wedge-shaped tail. Sexes alike. Moth-like flight with slow, deep, rowing wingbeats; glides on stretched wings. Rests in grass clumps. Will perch on posts. Roosts communally outside breeding season.

SRI LANKA FROGMOUTH

Batrachostomus moniliger Batrachostomidae

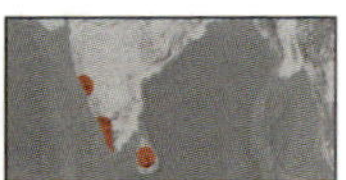

Size 23 cm

Voice Calls include harsh *chaak*; decelerating whistle *klok-klok*…

Range Scarce endemic breeding resident of Western Ghats and Sri Lanka, where it is the only frogmouth

Habitat Thick, wet evergreen forests

Large-headed nightjar with huge frog-like gape and flat, hooked, and feathered bill. Male grey-brown, heavily-mottled white with white neck bar. Female plainer orange-rufous, lightly spotted white. Hunts insects at night; roosts in thick undergrowth; perches vertically, camouflaged by its cryptic plumage. Points bill upwards when disturbed. Nests on branch. Secretive. Lays single white egg which is incubated by both parents, male during the day and female at night.

GREAT-EARED NIGHTJAR

Eurostopodus macrotis Caprimulgidae

Size 40-41 cm

Voice Call a clear, wailing *pee…wheeeu*

Range Mainly NE India, Bangladesh and Western Ghats

Habitat Tropical and subtropical broadleaved moist forests; secondary growth

Very large and vividly coloured nightjar. At rest, shows prominent ear tufts, and generally more richly-marked with golden buff and rufous than other nightjars.

GREY NIGHTJAR

Caprimulgus i jotaka Caprimulgidae

Size 32 cm

Voice Song a *kowrr…kowrr…kowrr*; guttural *tuk…tuk*

Range Himalayas and NE India

Habitat Forest clearings

Medium-sized nightjar with long pointed tail; short legs; short bill with rectal bristles larger than Sykes's, with longer wings and tail. Small dark arrowhead-shaped markings on crown, and irregular buff spotting on nape forms indistinct collar. Roosts on the tree along length of branch.

JERDON'S NIGHTJAR

Caprimulgus atripennis Caprimulgidae

Size 28 cm

Voice Call a series of liquid, tremulous *ch…wo…wo*

Range C and S peninsula; Sri Lanka

Habitat Edges of forests

Larger than Indian, distinguished by barred tail, rufous rear neck, and wing-bars. Male has white wing-patch; plumage mainly variegated buff and brown; buff edges to scapulars; unbarred brown breast, rufous neck-band; unbroken white gorget similar to Long-tailed's, but has a shorter tail. Roosts in bushes.

LARGE-TAILED NIGHTJAR

Caprimulgus macrurus Caprimulgidae

Size 30 cm

Voice Call a resounding, rather slow *chunk…chunk…chunk*

Range Fairly common resident along Gangetic plains and throughout NE India, south to Andhra Pradesh

Habitat Lowland forests; woodlands

Large, long and broad-tailed nightjar. Grey-brown upperparts streaked darker; more broadly on crown; indistinct buff collar; bright buff-edged black scapular lines; white moustache and breast-patch; small bill. Male has broad white (female buff) apical tips to tail and primary patches. Roosts on ground well-camouflaged by dead leaves. Hunts flying insects at night. Erratic, stiff-winged flight.

INDIAN NIGHTJAR

Caprimulgus asiaticus Caprimulgidae

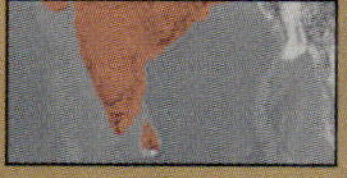

Size 24 cm

Voice Call a far-carrying *chuk…chuk…chuk…cli…uk…tukoroo*

Range Widespread resident; unrecorded in NW and most of NE India

Habitat Open-wooded country in plains and foothills

Medium-sized sandy-grey to brownish-grey nightjar with shortish wings and tail; boldly streaked crown; rufous-buff markings on nape forming distinct collar; bold black centres and broad buff edges to scapulars; bold rufous-buff or buff spotting on wing-coverts, and pale, relatively unmarked central tail feathers. Similar to Large-tailed, but with shorter tail.

SAVANNA NIGHTJAR

Caprimulgus affinis Caprimulgidae

Size 23 cm

Voice Calls on wing as well as on perch, fairly loud, penetrating *sweeesh*… or *schweee*

Range Throughout the region, south of outer Himalayas to about 2,000 m; moves considerably locally

Habitat Rocky hillsides, scrub and grass country, light forests, dry streams and riverbeds, fallow land, cultivation

Male has grey-brown plumage, mottled dark; buffy V on back, from shoulders to about centre of back; two pairs of white outer-tail feathers, with pale dusky tips; white wing-patches. Female similar to male, but lacks white outer-tail feathers, which are barred; conspicuous rufous-buff wing-patches; call most important identification clue. Solitary, or sometimes several scattered over open expanse; overall behaviour like that of other nightjars; remains motionless during day on open rocky, grass or scrub-covered ground; sometimes roosts on trees, along length of branches; flies around dusk, often flying high; drinks often.

INDIAN SWIFTLET

Collocalia unicolor Apodidae

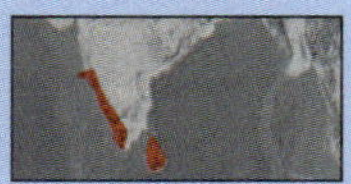

Size 12 cm

Voice Roosting birds keep up incessant, faint chatter

Range Western Ghats, south of Ratnagiri; associated hill ranges

Habitat Caves; cliffs on rocky; offshore islands

Diminutive blackish-brown swiftlet with slightly forked-tail visible in flight. Gregarious and colonial; huge numbers on cliffsides and caves; swarms leave before dawn in a rush of wings; spends day high over mountains and countryside, hawking insects, often along with other swifts and martins; arrives back to caves and cliff roosts around dusk, when bats are leaving.

WHITE-RUMPED SPINETAIL

Zoonavena sylvatica Apodidae

Size 11 cm

Voice Call a twittering *chick… chick*, uttered on wing

Range The Himalayas from N Uttar Pradesh, east to Sikkim

Habitat Broadleaved evergreen and moist deciduous forests

Small, stocky, broad-winged spinetail. Has bulging secondaries, with wings pinched in at base and pointed at tip. Typically, flight action fast with rapid wingbeats, and banking from side-to-side, interspersed with short glides on slightly bowed wings. Upperparts mainly blue-black with contrasting white rump; throat and breast grey-brown, merging into whitish lower belly and undertail-coverts. From below, long white undertail-coverts contrast with black of sides and tip of undertail. 'Spines' at tip of tail visible at close range.

BROWN-BACKED NEEDLETAIL

Hirundapus giganteus Apodidae

Size 23 cm

Voice Rather quiet. Calls include various soft squeaks and trills

Range Scarce breeding resident of Western Ghats, Sri Lanka and NE India

Habitat Forested areas

Large, dark, extremely fast-flying swift with white vent crescent and pointed tail. All sooty-brown with paler back, distinct white vent extending as crescent up the flanks. Needles in tail feathers visible and long enough to form pointed tail. Flapping of wings often audible in low flight. Roosts and breeds in large hollow trees. Flight exceptionally powerful and flexible; quite difficult to follow with binoculars. Hunts aerial insects low over forest in loose parties.

ASIAN PALM SWIFT

Cypsiurus balasiensis Apodidae

Size 13 cm

Voice Call a 3-note shrill scream, uttered very fast and always on wing

Range All over peninsular India, south of the Himalayan foothills (except NW); also in NE hill states

Habitat Open country, cultivation; this bird's life revolves around palms

Sooty-brown plumage; typical swift wings, long and sickle-like; deeply forked-tail distinctive, specially in flight. Sociable; small parties in open, palm-dotted country; strong in flight, and uttering lively screaming notes on wing; hawks insects all day, occasionally rising very high; roosts on underside of palm frond (leaf).

ALPINE SWIFT

Tachymarptis melba Apodidae

Size 23 cm

Voice Calls include shrill *chrrrr... chee...chee...* screams in fast flight; twittering notes at roost sites

Range All over India, from about 2,500 m in the Himalayas; uncommon over N Indian plains

Habitat Hill country; cliffsides

Very long, sickle-shaped, pointed wings; dark sooty-brown above; white underbody; broad, brown band across breast diagnostic in flight; dark undertail-coverts. Loose 'parties' dashing erratically at high speed in skies; extremely strong flier; seen high in skies around dusk, many birds wheeling and tumbling, their shrill screams rending the air; drinks at ponds and puddles by skimming over water surface. Sexes alike.

COMMON SWIFT

Apus apus Apodidae

Size 17 cm

Voice Call a high-pitched scream *screee…screee…screee*

Range Summer visitor to Balochistan, Pakistan, and the Himalayas from N Pakistan east to Nepal; Maldives

Habitat Chiefly in mountains, but can occur fleetingly over any habitat

Large, uniformly dark brown swift with long scythe-shaped wings and deeply forked-tail. Most likely to be confused with Fork-tailed, but has uniform brown upperparts, minus white rump, and lacks (or is much less distinct) pale scaling on underparts. Distinguished from the very similar Pallid and Dark-rumped. Juvenile has whiter forehead and more extensive white throat, and extensive pale scaling on underparts (although not so prominent as on Fork-tailed).

FORK-TAILED SWIFT

Apus pacificus Apodidae

Size 15 cm

Voice Call a hard *shkree* in flight

Range Locally common breeding summer visitor to N mountains. Wintering areas unknown

Habitat Open skies

Medium-sized, blackish, long-winged and fork-tailed swift with narrow white rump-band, its most striking feature. Blackish-brown with small white throat-patch. Deep and obvious tail-fork; sickle-shaped wings. Best chance of seeing the bird when flying low before weather front or passing thunderstorm. Very fast, lucid flight without fluttering, distinguishes it from House Martin. High aerial feeder (often out of sight) in loose flocks or singly with other aerial feeders.

LITTLE SWIFT

Apus affinis Apodidae

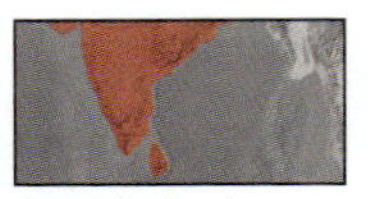

Size 15 cm

Voice Musical squeals on wing; very vocal at sunset, but also through the day

Range Throughout the region, upto about 2,400 m in the Himalayas

Habitat Human habitation; cliffs; ruins

Overall dark swift with white rump and throat distinctive; short, square tail. Highly gregarious; on wing during day, hawking insects, flying over human habitation, cliffs and ruins; strong flier, exhibiting great mastery and control in fast-wheeling flight; frequently utters squealing notes on wing; retires to safety of nest colonies in overcast weather.

CRESTED TREESWIFT

Hemiprocne coronata Hemiprocnidae

Size 23 cm

Voice Call a parrot-like *kea… kea…*; double-noted faint scream

Range Subcontinent, south of the Himalayan foothills; absent in arid parts of NW India

Habitat Open, deciduous forests

Male bluish-grey above, with faint greenish wash; chestnut sides of face and throat; ash-grey breast, whiter below. Female similar to male, but lacks chestnut on head. Backward-curving crest and long, deeply forked-tail diagnostic. In pairs or small, scattered parties; flies during day, hawking insects; has favourite foraging areas; flight graceful, not as fast as other swifts, but displays typical swift mastery; calls from perch and in flight; unlike other swifts, perches on bare, higher branches; drinks in flight from surfaces of forest pools.

MALABAR TROGON

Harpactes fasciatus Trogonidae

Size 30 cm

Voice Diagnostic, often a giveaway to bird's presence in forest; 3- to 8-noted, somewhat whistling *cue…cue…* calls

Range Forested areas of peninsular India; Satpura Range, Western Ghats, east to Odisha and parts of Eastern Ghats. Also Sri Lanka

Habitat Forests

♀

Male has sooty-black head, neck and breast; yellow-brown back; black wings narrowly-barred white; rich crimson underbody; white breast gorget. Female duller overall; lacks black on head and breast; orange-brown underbody. Long, squarish tail distinctive. Solitary, or in pairs; strictly arboreal; difficult to see because duller back mostly turned towards observer or intruder; hunts flycatcher-style or flits among taller branches; flicks tail and bends body when disturbed.

INDIAN ROLLER

Coracias benghalensis Coraciidae

Size 31 cm

Voice Usually silent; occasionally harsh *khak...kak...kak...* notes; exuberant screeching notes and shrieks during courtship display, diving, and screaming wildly

Range Almost entire subcontinent, south of outer Himalayas, where found upto about 1,500 m

Habitat Open country; cultivation; orchards; light forests

affinis

Pale greenish-brown above; pinkish-brown breast; deep blue tail has light blue subterminal band; in flight, bright blue wings and tail, with Cambridge-blue bands distinctive. Sexes alike. Solitary, or in pairs; perches on overhead wires, bare branches, earthen mounds and small bush-tops; either glides and drops on prey or pounces suddenly; batters prey against perch. Elaborate courtship display, performs startling aerobatics including a series of 'rolls'.

EUROPEAN ROLLER

Coracias garrulus Coraciidae

Size 31 cm

Voice Call a loud, harsh *rack...rack*

Range Breeding resident in N Pakistan and Kashmir. Scarce winter visitor

Habitat Open, dry country and cultivation

Crow-sized bird with large head, and crow-like bill. Pale blue head, neck and underparts; orangish-brown upperparts; azure scapulars. Black eye-stripes and black apical tips to tail; cinnamon rump. Juvenile greyer. Feeds on large insects, reptiles and rodents, usually catching them on ground in shrike-like pounce. Solitary. Seen perched on poles or wires.

DOLLARBIRD

Eurystomus orientalis Coraciidae

Size 31 cm

Voice Call a rasping *drak...drak*

Range Scarce breeding resident, partial migrant to NE India, Western Ghats

Habitat Forest edges and clearings, also nearby cultivation

Dark greenish-brown upperparts, washed bluish-green on back and wings. Brown breast; throat and undertail glossy blue; silvery-blue 'coin' on primaries, visible in flight; pale belly and undertail-coverts; stout red bill with black tip; red legs and eye-rings. Perches high in trees on bare branches from where it launches itself to catch large-flying insects. Crepuscular and sociable, groups often hunt after dusk. Nests in tree holes.

STORK-BILLED KINGFISHER

Pelargopsis capensis Halcyonidae

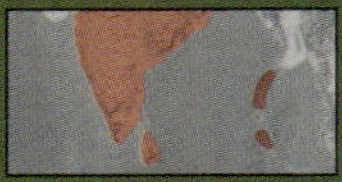

Size 38 cm

Voice Noisy. Call a *kee...kee... kee*, repeated many times

Range Subcontinent, except drier parts of NW India

Habitat Canals, streams, coastal backwaters in well-wooded country

capensis

Large kingfisher with blue-green back, blue wings and blue tail. Enormous red bill diagnostic; red legs. Dark grey-brown head with yellowish and blue collar on back of neck. Brownish-yellow underparts. Sexes alike. Solitary, more heard than seen. Does not normally hover. Laboured flight.

intermedia

WHITE-THROATED KINGFISHER

Halcyon smyrnensis Halcyonidae

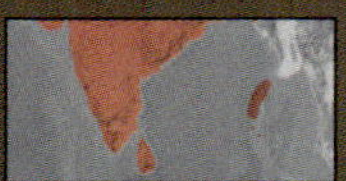

Size 28 cm

Voice Noisy, loud, crackling laugh, often audible over crowded urban areas; song a longish, quivering whistle, sounding *kilililili*...characteristic feature of hot season, in breeding; fascinating courtship display

Range Subcontinent, south of outer Himalayas

Habitat Forests, cultivation, lakes, riversides; also coastal mangroves and estuaries

Chestnut-brown head, neck and underbody below breast; bright turquoise-blue above, often with greenish tinge; black flight feathers with white wing-patch visible in flight; white chin, throat and breast distinctive; coral-red beak and legs. Sexes alike. Solitary, or scattered pairs atop overhead wires, poles and tree-tops; frequently found far from water; drops on to ground to pick up prey.

BLACK-CAPPED KINGFISHER

Halcyon pileata Halcyonidae

Size 30 cm

Voice Call a shrill, fairly loud cackle, quite like the Commoner White-Breasted, but unmistakable once heard

Range The coast, from around Mumbai south along entire W seaboard and all along the E coast, Sri Lanka

Habitat Chiefly coastal areas, mangroves, estuaries; may wander inland, especially along rivers

Black cap, white collar and deep blue upperbody; white throat, upper breast and dull rufous below; in flight conspicuous white wing-patch; deep, dagger-like, coral-red beak. Sexes alike. Mostly solitary; coastal bird; has favoured feeding sites; dives for fish but also takes insects from ground.

COLLARED KINGFISHER

Todiramphus chloris Halcyonidae

Size 24 cm

Voice Call a hard *krerk... krerk... krerk*

Range Scarce breeding resident sporadically along the coast from Bangladesh to Goa. Commoner in NE India and on Andaman and Nicobar Islands

Habitat Tidal creeks, mudflats and mangroves where feeds mainly on small crabs and skippers

Medium-sized, heavy-billed kingfisher with broad, white collar. White underparts, sometimes washed buff; turquoise head, wings and tail. Variable dark and white markings depending on race. Upperparts bright turquoise-green, bluer on wings. Sexes alike. Juvenile has faint buff scaling on upperparts, and indistinct dark scaling on underparts and collar. Solitary, or in pairs.

humii

davisoni

ORIENTAL DWARF KINGFISHER

Ceyx erithaca Alcedinidae

Size 13 cm

Voice Call a sharp, squeaky *chicheee… or chcheee…*

Range Apparently disjunct. From E Garhwal through NE states; Western Ghats south from around Mumbai; Nilgiris. Appears in many areas only with the onset of SW monsoons

Habitat Forest streams; nullahs

Brownish-chestnut crown; iridescent purple back, rump; deep purplish-blue of closed wings often hides the back; deep blue and white spots on neck sides and short, chestnut tail; orangish-yellow underbody and large, bright coral-red beak striking. Sexes alike. Solitary, or in pairs; tiny forest bird, usually overlooked when perched on stumps or tangled roots along nullahs and mud walls, often by forest path or road.

BLUE-EARED KINGFISHER

Alcedo meninting Alcedinidae

Size 17 cm

Voice Call a shrill *chichee…chichee*

Range C Nepal eastwards in lowlands

Habitat Rivers, pools, streams in dense tropical and subtropical evergreen forests, bamboo thickets, or near shady vegetation

juvenile

Small, short-tailed and vividly-coloured kingfisher. Brilliant ultramarine blue upperparts and rufous-red underparts; rufous loral spot; bright blue line down centre of back; stronger blue and black barring on crown; blue ear-coverts; creamy-white throat and neck-patch; wing-coverts spangled lighter blue. Dark wings. Solitary and very shy; sits patiently near pools, bobs head and flicks tail; dives to catch prey.

COMMON KINGFISHER

Alcedo atthis Alcedinidae

Size 18 cm

Voice Call a shrill *chichee…chichee*

Range Subcontinent, south of 2,000 m in the Himalayas; various races differ in shade of blue-green upperbody

Habitat Streams, lakes, canals; also coastal areas

Bright blue above, greenish on wings; top of head finely-banded black-and-blue; ferruginous cheeks, ear-coverts and white patch on neck sides; white chin and throat and deep ferruginous underbody distinctive; coral-red legs and blackish beak. Sexes alike. Solitary, or in scattered pairs; never found away from water; perches on pole or overhanging branch; flies low over water, brilliant blue streak, utters shrill notes; sometimes tame and confiding; dives for fish from perch; occasionally hovers over water before diving.

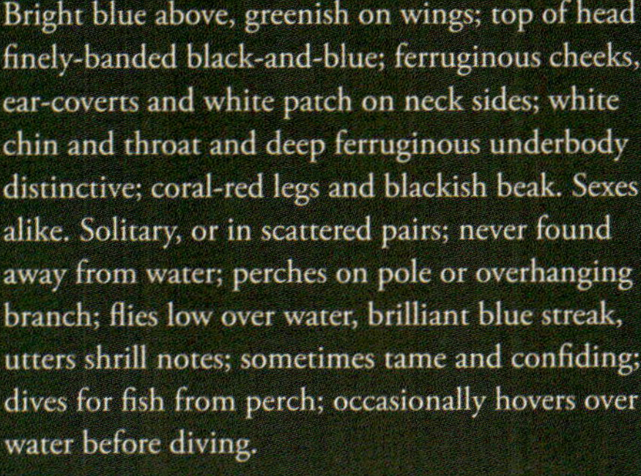

bengalensis

taprobana

PIED KINGFISHER

Ceryle rudis Cerylidae

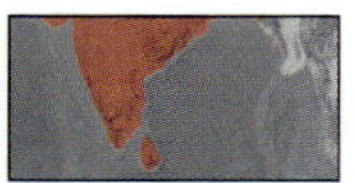

Size 25 cm

Voice Call includes piercing, twittering *chirrruk...chirruk...* cries in flight, sounding as if the bird is complaining

Range Subcontinent, upto about 2,000 m in the Himalayas

Habitat Streams, rivers, ponds; sometimes coastal areas

travancoreensis

Kingfisher with black-and-white plumage; long dagger-like bill; untidy black crest on hindcrown; irregular black eye-band, continuing to back of head; black-and-white speckled underparts; white underwing; double black gorget across breast in male. Female has single, broken breast gorget. Solitary, in pairs or in small groups. Noisy and gregarious; hovers with flayed wings.

lecucomelanura

GREEN BEE-EATER

Merops orientalis Meropidae

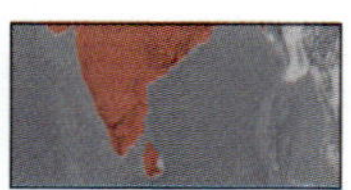

Size 21 cm

Voice Noisy; cheerful trilling notes, chiefly uttered on wing

Range Subcontinent, south of about 1,800 m in outer Himalayas

Habitat Open country and cultivation; light forests

orientalis

Small bee-eater with bright green plumage; red-brown wash on head; pale blue on chin and throat, bordered below by black gorget; slender, curved black beak; rufous wash on black-tipped flight feathers; elongated central tail feathers distinctive. Sexes alike. Small parties; perches freely on bare branches and overhead telegraph wires; attends to grazing cattle, along with drongos, cattle egrets and mynas; also seen in city parks and gardens; launches graceful sorties after winged insects; batters prey against perch before swallowing. Large flocks of upto 300 birds roost communally.

beludschius

BLUE-BEARDED BEE-EATER

Nyctyornis athertoni Meropidae

Size 34 cm

Voice Harsh *korrr…korrr* croaking notes, often followed by softer chuckling call

Range Outer Himalayas to about 1,800 m, from Himachal to extreme E; Western Ghats and Nilgiris; forested parts of Madhya Pradesh, Eastern Ghats through Andhra Pradesh, Odisha, Bihar and West Bengal

Habitat Edges of forests, clearings

Unmarked grass-green above, bluer on forehead; elongated, blue feathers along centre of throat to breast appear beard-like, prominent when bird is calling; buffy-yellow below breast, streaked green; tail lacks long central pins; long sickle-shaped tail. Sexes alike. In pairs, or in groups; arboreal, rarely descending low; makes short aerial sallies after winged insects; batters prey on perch; usually not an easy bird to observe from close.

BLUE-CHEEKED BEE-EATER

Merops persicus Meropidae

Size 27 cm

Voice Noisy. Call a liquid, disyllabic *priit...priit* mainly in high flight

Range Locally common breeding summer visitor: Pakistan, NW India

Habitat Dry, open country near water

Large, emerald green bee-eater with vividly-coloured face. Prominent black eye-stripe with pale blue above and below; yellow throat; rufous upper breast; chestnut underwings; two long central tail pins. Juvenile duller with pointed or square-ended tails. Sexes alike. Nests in colonies in sandy banks. Feeds largely on dragonflies in flight.

BLUE-TAILED BEE-EATER

Merops philippinus Meropidae

Size 30 cm

Voice Musical, ringing notes, chiefly uttered in flight

Range Exact range not correctly known; breeds in parts of NW and N India, and perhaps patchily through E and SC India; spreads wide during the rains and winter

Habitat Open country, light forests, vicinity of water, cultivation; may occasionally be seen in coastal areas

Elongated central tail feathers. Greenish above, with faint blue wash on wings; bluish rump, tail diagnostic; yellow upper throat-patch with chestnut throat and upper breast; slightly curved black beak, broad black stripe through eye. Sexes alike. Usually small flocks, frequently in vicinity of water; launches short, elegant flights from wire or tree perch; characteristic flight, few quick wingbeats and stately glide.

CHESTNUT-HEADED BEE-EATER

Merops leschenaulti Meropidae

Size 21 cm

Voice Musical twittering notes, mostly uttered on wing, and sometimes from perch

Range Disjunct; the Himalayan foothills, from Uttarakhand to extreme NE; Western Ghats south of Goa; also, Sri Lanka. Occasionally may be encountered elsewhere in the peninsula, especially during monsoon

Habitat Vicinity of water in forested areas

Grass-green plumage; chestnut-cinnamon crown, hindneck and upper back; yellow chin and throat; rufous and black gorget. Sexes alike. Small gatherings on telegraph wires or bare upper branches of trees from where it launches short aerial sallies; fast, graceful flight; noisy when converging at roosting trees.

EUROPEAN BEE-EATER

Merops apiaster Meropidae

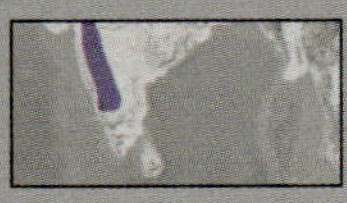

Size 27 cm

Voice Noisy. Call a liquid monosyllabic *prut…prut*, given mostly in flight

Range Common breeding summer visitor: Pakistan, Kashmir. May be encountered elsewhere in the peninsula

Habitat Dry, open country and cultivation

Extremely vividly-coloured, unmistakable bee-eater. Breeding adult has warm chestnut crown merging into golden yellow back; yellow throat bordered with black. Green and chestnut wings; emerald green tail and underparts; red eyes. Adults have short tail pins. Male has chestnut patch in underwing; small or absent in female. Juvenile much duller and blunt-tailed with brown eyes. Pale orange underwings. Sexes alike. Feeds mainly on bees.

COMMON HOOPOE

Upupa epops Upupidae

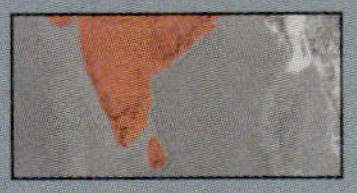

Size 31 cm

Voice Call a pleasant, mellow *hoo...po...po...*

Range Subcontinent, upto about 5,500 m in the Himalayas; several races; spreads considerably in winter

Habitat Meadows, open country, garden lawns, open-light forests

Fawn-coloured plumage; black-and-white markings on wings, back and tail; black-and-white-tipped crest; longish, gently curved beak. Sexes alike. Solitary, or in scattered pairs; small, loose flocks in winter; probes ground with long beak, sometimes feeding along with other birds; flits among tree branches; crest often fanned open.

MALABAR GREY HORNBILL

Ocyceros griseus Bucerotidae

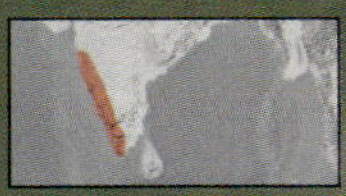

Size 45 cm

Voice Noisy, with squealing, laughing cry

Range Local endemic breeding resident in Western Ghats

Habitat Restricted to open, broadleaved Western Ghat forests

Medium-sized hornbill with dark grey upperparts and paler grey, streaked underparts. Distinct, very pale grey supercilium; blackish crown and eye-stripes; rufous bill graduating to yellow tip. Greyish-brown wings; white carpal-patch; white-tipped primaries and tail; cinnamon vent. Female has black bill base. Immature has more brown upperparts and yellow bill. Similar to Indian Grey but distinguished by darker grey and no casque on bill. Feeds high in trees on fruits and small invertebrates. Nests in tree holes.

INDIAN GREY HORNBILL

Ocyceros birostris Bucerotidae

Size 50 cm

Voice Noisy; normal call a shrill squealing note, also other squeals and screams

Range Almost throughout India, upto about 1,500 m in the Himalayas; absent in arid NW regions and heavy rainfall areas of S Western Ghats

Habitat Forests; orchards; tree-covered avenues; vicinity of habitation

Smallest of the Indian hornbills. Overall grey-brown plumage; large, curved beak with casque diagnostic; long, graduated tail, tipped black-and-white. Male has reddish-brown eyes and black orbital skin. Female has dark brown eyes and red-brown orbital skin. Casque smaller in female. In pairs, or small parties; sometimes large gatherings; mostly arboreal, but descends to pick fallen fruits or lizards; feeds along with frugivorous birds on fruiting trees; noisy, undulating flight.

MALABAR PIED HORNBILL

Anthracoceros coronatus Bucerotidae

Size 65 cm

Voice Call a loud *kek…kek…kek…*

Range Scarce endemic breeding resident in foothills of Western and Eastern Ghats and Sri Lanka, where commoner. Probably overlaps in NC India with the Oriental Pied

Habitat Open forests and groves, particularly ficus and other fruiting trees on hillsides

Striking, medium-sized, with large creamish bill and very prominent black and yellow casque. Black head and neck; black orbital skin; white eye-ring; black white-tipped wings; white underparts. Female smaller with pale blue orbital skin that turns pinkish in breeding. Very similar to Oriental Pied but distinguished by broad white outer-tail feathers and broader wing-tips.

ORIENTAL PIED HORNBILL

Anthracoceros albirostris Bucerotidae

Size 60 cm

Voice Calls include loud cackles and screams; also rapid *pak...pak...pak*

Range Haryana and Uttarakhand to extreme NE; Eastern Ghats, south to Bastar and N Andhra Pradesh

Habitat Forests; orchards; groves

Similar to Malabar Pied, but tail much black; white face-patch, wing-tips (seen in flight) and tips to outer-tail feathers; black throat and breast; white below. Black and yellow beak with large casque. Sexes alike, female slightly smaller. Small parties, occasionally collecting into several dozen birds on favourite fruiting trees; associates with other birds; arboreal but often feeds on ground, hopping about.

GREAT HORNBILL

Buceros bicornis Bucerotidae

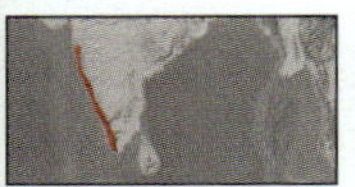

Size 100 cm

Voice Calls include loud and deep barking; loud *tokk* at feeding sites, audible from considerable distance

Range Lower Himalayas east of Uttarakhand, upto about 1,800 m; another population exists in Western Ghats

Habitat Forests

Black face, back and underbody; two white-bars on black wings; white neck, lower abdomen and tail; broad black tail-band; huge black and yellow beak with enormous concave-topped casque distinctive. Female slightly smaller. Sexes alike. In pairs, or small parties; occasionally large flocks; mostly arboreal, feeding on fruiting trees, plucking fruits with tip of bill, tossing it up, catching it in the throat and swallowing; may settle on ground to pick up fallen fruits; noisy flight; alternation of flapping and gliding, less undulating than in other hornbills.

WHITE-CHEEKED BARBET

Megalaima viridis Megalaimidae

Size 23 cm

Voice Call a start-up *burring* followed by repeated, penetrating, rather high-pitched *putruk… putruk*

Range Common endemic breeding resident in SW foothill forests north to Gujarat

Habitat Hill forests; groves; gardens

Medium-sized, green and brown barbet with short white supercilium and broad stripe below eye. Brown head and paler brown upper breast, darker crown and nape; pale pink bill; white throat; heavy white streaking on breast. Rest of body unmarked grass-green. Sexes alike. Strictly arboreal feeding on fruits. Well camouflaged and often difficult to spot. Nests in tree holes.

BROWN-HEADED BARBET

Megalaima zeylanica Megalaimidae

Size 28 cm

Voice Noisy; *kutroo…kutroo or pukrook…pukrook* calls one of the most familiar sounds of the Indian forests; call often begins with a guttural *kurrrr*

Range Most of India, south of the Himalayan foothills (Himachal Pradesh to Nepal)

Habitat Forests, groves; also city gardens

Overall green bird with brownish head, neck and upper back, streaked white; bare yellowish-orange patch around eye; thick reddish-pink bill; short, green tail with brown-black shafts; wing-coverts tipped whitish; uniform green underparts. Sexes alike. Solitary, or in pairs; occasionally small parties; strictly arboreal; keeps to fruiting trees, often with other frugivorous birds; difficult to spot in canopy; noisy in hot season; strong, undulating flight.

COPPERSMITH BARBET

Megalaima haemacephala Megalaimidae

Size 17 cm

Voice Noisy between December and end of April; monotonous *tuk…tuk…* one of the best-known bird calls of India, likened to a coppersmith working on his metal

Range All over India, upto about 1,800 m in the outer Himalayas

Habitat Light forests; groves; city gardens; roadside trees

Small, vividly-coloured bird. Grass-green plumage; yellow throat; crimson breast and forehead; dumpy appearance. Sexes alike. Solitary, in pairs or small parties; strictly arboreal; feeds on fruiting trees, often with other birds; visits flowering *Erythrina* and *Bombax* trees for flower nectar; often spends early morning sunning itself on bare branches.

juvenile

CRIMSON-FRONTED BARBET

Megalaima rubricapillus Megalaimidae

Size 17 cm

Voice Call a slow, repeated *pop…pop…pop…* and rapidly repeated *popo…popo…popo…pop*

Range Sri Lanka

Habitat Similar to Coppersmith's. Open wooded country

Small barbet with bright orange supercilium, cheeks, throat and upper breast; small distinct red patch on breast; unstreaked green belly and flanks; sides of neck and head blue; black crescent marking behind eye; heavy bill, fringed with bristles. Gregarious; lives in large, loose flocks outside breeding season; extremely vocal.

EURASIAN WRYNECK

Jynx torquilla Picidae

Size 17 cm

Voice Call a high-pitched *pee… pee… pee*. Hisses in nest

Range Breeds in Kashmir. Scarce but widespread winter visitor mainly to N areas

Habitat Breeds in edges of forests in N mountains. Elsewhere in scrubs and cultivation

Small, rather reptilian-looking woodpecker, the colour of tree bark. Basically grey-and-brown with dark eye-stripes and dark stripe running from crown to rump. Underparts barred and throat warm buff. Tail long and barred, making it look rather shrike-like in flight. Bill short and pointed. Twists neck round and often raises crown feathers. Unobtrusively feeds with long tongue on ants on ground and tree branches. Does not drill holes or use tail as support. Nests in tree holes.

SPECKLED PICULET

Picumnus innominatus Picidae

Size 10 cm

Voice Call a sharp, rapid *tsip... tsip...*; also loud drumming sound

Range The Himalayas, W to E, foothills to at least 2,500 m

Habitat Mixed forests, fondness for bamboo jungles

Sexes alike. Olive-green above (male has some orange-and-black on forecrown); two white stripes on head sides, upper one longer; dark-olive band through eyes, moustachial stripe; creamy-white below, boldly spotted with black. Usually in pairs; moves around thin branches, or clings upside-down; taps with beak, probes crevices; exhibits typical woodpecker behaviour.

BROWN-CAPPED PYGMY WOODPECKER

Dendrocopos nanus Picidae

Size 13 cm

Voice Call a faint but shrill squeak, sounds like *clicck...rrr*

Range Almost all over India, including some of the drier regions of N India

Habitat Light forests, cultivation, bamboos, orchards; also vicinity of habitation

Small woodpecker. Male barred brown-and-white above; paler crown with short, scarlet streak (occipital); prominent white band from just above eyes extends to neck; pale dirty brown-white below, streaked black. Female similar to male but lacks scarlet streaks on crown sides. Mostly in pairs; often part of mixed bird parties in forests; seen more on smaller trees, branches and twigs, close to ground and also high in canopy; quite active.

FULVOUS-BREASTED WOODPECKER

Dendrocopos macei Picidae

Size 18 cm

Voice Call a hard *tik*, sometimes extended into chatter

Range Common breeding resident in N hills, NE India, Bangladesh and Eastern Ghats

Habitat Open, broadleaved and coniferous forests; edges of forests

Medium-sized, pied woodpecker with heavily barred black-and-white underparts. Male has distinct red crown, orange forehead, while black in female. Buff belly with light barring and streaking on flank; red undertail; whitish cheeks partially bordered black. Feeds on invertebrates. Often props itself on tail. Can be seen with other species in mixed flocks. Locally common. Nests in self-made tree holes.

♀

YELLOW-CROWNED WOODPECKER

Dendrocopos mahrattensis Picidae

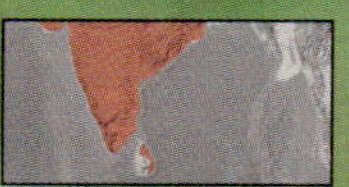

Size 17 cm

Voice Call a soft but sharp *clic…click…clickrrr…*; drums when breeding

Range Common and widespread; subcontinent, from the Himalayan foothills south; uncommon in NE regions

Habitat Open forests; scrubs; cultivation; vicinity of habitation; gardens

Male brownish-black above, spotted all over with white golden-brown forehead and crown; small scarlet crest; pale fulvous below throat, streaked brown; scarlet patch in centre of abdomen distinctive. Female lacks scarlet crest. Solitary or in pairs; sometimes small bands of upto six birds; occasionally seen with mixed hunting parties; moves in jerks along tree stems and branches; hunts in typical woodpecker manner; rather confiding in some areas; birds keep in touch with faint, creaking sounds.

RUFOUS WOODPECKER

Micropternus brachyurus Picidae

Size 25 cm

Voice Rather vocal between January and April; call a loud, high-pitched 3- or 4-noted *ke…ke…kr…ke…*; drums when breeding

Range Subcontinent, south of outer Himalayas, found upto 1,500 m

Habitat Mixed forests

Plumage mixture of different shades of brown; fine black cross-bars on upperbody, including wings and tail; paler edges to throat feathers; crimson patch under eye in male, absent in female. Sexes alike. Usually in pairs; sometimes four or five scattered birds close by; mostly seen around ball-shaped nests of tree ants; clings to outside of nests and digs for ants; plumage often smeared with gummy substance.

WHITE-BELLIED WOODPECKER

Dryocopus javensis Picidae

Size 48 cm

Voice Call a loud, metallic *chiank* note, often while clinging onto tree stems; loud drumming sound during December-March

Range Forested areas of Western Ghats, south of Tapti River; present range reduced due to habitat destruction and the bird, perhaps, no longer exists in N parts of Western Ghats; also Bastar and perhaps across C Indian hills

Habitat Tall evergreen forests

♀

Male has black head, upperbody, breast; white rump and underparts below breast; bright, crimson crown (including forehead), crest and cheeks. Crimson restricted to nape in female. Pairs, sometimes four or five birds in tall forests; moves up along tree stems, jerkily and slowly, inspecting bark-crevices for lurking insects; strong, lazy flight; chuckling note in flight.

LESSER YELLOWNAPE

Picus chlorolophus Picidae

Size 27 cm

Voice Noisy. Call a loud, sad *pee…oo* and descending *ke…ke…ke…ke*

Range Locally common breeding resident in N foothills from Himachal Pradesh to Myanmar border and peninsular hills, Sri Lanka and Bangladesh

Habitat All types of open forests and plantations

chlorigaster

chlorolophus

Medium-sized woodpecker with green upperparts; bright yellow, tufted nape. Olive-green neck and breast; whitish belly, finely barred green; black rump and tail. Adult male has green head and white throat; red markings above eye and nape; red moustachial stripe. Female has red patch above ear-coverts. Juvenile similar to female, but duller. Feeds on invertebrates at lower levels, including ground, and often in mixed hunting groups.

GREATER YELLOWNAPE

Picus flavinucha Picidae

Similar to Lesser, but larger. Lesser has smaller, dark bill, red markings on head, red stripe on whitish chin, smaller crest and barred underparts; prominent yellow-crested nape and throat. Underparts dark olive-green and grey. Brownish crown; flight feathers chestnut-barred black. Feeds on invertebrates from ground to canopy often with mixed-species parties. Shy, flushes readily if disturbed. Uses tail as prop. Nests in tree holes.

Size 33 cm

Voice Calls include loud, plaintive *keeyu* and hard *chep* note. Also, an accelerating trill *quee… quee…quee*

Range Fairly common breeding resident of N foothills, NE India, Bangladesh and Eastern Ghats

Habitat Upland broadleaved forests

STREAK-THROATED WOODPECKER

Picus xanthopygaeus Picidae

Size 30 cm

Voice Call an occasional faint *pick*... mostly silent; also drums on branches

Range Subcontinent; found upto 1,500 m in outer Himalayas

Habitat Mixed forests; plantations

Male grass-green above; crimson crown and crest; orange and black on nape; white supercilium and malar stripe; yellow rump; bold, black scaly streaks on whitish underbody, with tawny-green wash on breast; throat greyer, also streaked. Female has black crown and crest. Solitary, or in pairs; works up along tree stems; moves either straight up or in spirals; taps with beak for insects hiding in bark; also settles on ground.

HIMALAYAN GOLDENBACK

Dinopium shorii Picidae

Size 30-32cm

Voice Call a rapid repeated *klok…klok…klak…klok…klak*

Range The Himalayas; locally in hills of peninsula and Bangladesh

Habitat Mature forests

♀

Largish woodpecker with golden upperparts. Male has black hindneck; brownish-buff throat centre with irregular border of black spots; indistinctly divided moustachial stripe; brownish-buff centre, with small red patch; reddish or brown eyes; blackish bill; greenish-brown feet. Underparts boldly streaked and scalloped black, and on some, almost unmarked. Three-toed. Female has black crest, streaked white. Confiding. Often seen in mixed feeding flocks. Locally common.

COMMON GOLDENBACK

Dinopium javanense Picidae

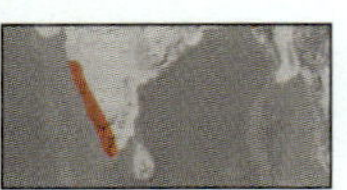

Size 30 cm

Voice Similar to, but higher-pitched than Black-rumped's

Range Locally common breeding resident in foothills of Western Ghats and hills of NE India

Habitat Damp woodlands; mangroves

Medium-sized woodpecker with golden mantle and wings; white face with two malar stripes; black hindneck; red lower back and rump. Male has red crown, while female has black crown. White underparts with strong black scaling; black tail; small bill and only three toes. In pairs, foraging in tree trunks. Very vocal.

LESSER GOLDENBACK

Dinopium benghalense Picidae

Size 30 cm

Voice Noisy. Call a loud, high-pitched cackle, like laughter; drums often

Range Subcontinent, upto about 1,800 m in outer Himalayas; also found in drier areas of NW India

Habitat Forests, both dry and mixed deciduous; orchards; gardens; also neighbourhood of villages and other habitation

Male has shining golden-yellow and black above; crimson crown and crest; black throat and sides of head, with fine white streaks; white underbody, streaked black, boldly on breast. Female has black crown spotted with white; crimson crest. In pairs, sometimes half a dozen together; widespread and common; moves jerkily up and around tree stems or clings on undersides of branches; taps out insects; often associates in mixed hunting parties; may descend to ground, picking off ants and other insects.

♀

psarodes

GREATER GOLDENBACK

Chrysocolaptes lucidus Picidae

Size 33 cm

Voice Noisy. Loud, grating scream; calls mostly in flight

Range Uttarakhand to NE India; parts of Eastern Ghats, SE Madhya Pradesh; Western Ghats, Kerala to Tapti River; plains to about 1,500 m

Habitat Forests

Male has crimson crown and crest; golden-olive above; white and black sides of face and throat; whitish-buff below, profusely spotted with black on foreneck, and speckled over rest of underbody; extensive crimson rump and black tail and flight feathers distinctive. Female has white-spotted black crown and crest.

WHITE-NAPED WOODPECKER

Chrysocolaptes festivus Picidae

Size 29 cm

Voice Call a thin, repeated *tee… tee…tee*

Range Scarce breeding endemic resident mainly restricted to peninsular India, dry zone Sri Lanka and far-W Nepal

Habitat Dry open woodlands, plantations and scrubs

Diagnostic black V-shape surrounds conspicuous white nape and mantle. Striped head and face; broad, bold white supercilium extending to nape; broad black ocular-stripe running across ear-coverts to neck sides; prominent, white moustachial and malar stripes. Male has red, peaked crest, yellow in female. Feeds on lower parts of tree trunks and ground.

HEART-SPOTTED WOODPECKER

Hemicircus canente Picidae

Size 16 cm

Voice Quite vocal, especially in flight; call a somewhat harsh *chur…* note; other sharp clicking and squeaky notes

Range Western Ghats from N Kerala to Tapti River; across E Satpura to SE Madhya Pradesh, Odisha, NE states

Habitat Forests

Male has black forehead (speckled white), crown and crest; black back; broad, pale buff wing-patch (inner secondaries and wing-coverts) with heart-shaped spots; black flight feathers; whitish-buff, olive-and-black below. Female has extensive buff-white on forehead, otherwise like male. Pairs, or small parties; active and arboreal; perches across branches and calls often as it flies from one tree to another.

INDIAN PITTA

Pitta brachyura Pittidae

Size 19 cm

Voice Call a loud, lively whistle, *wheeet...peu;* very vocal when breeding (during rains); also longish single-note whistle

Range Almost entire subcontinent, with considerable seasonal movement

Habitat Forests, orchards; also cultivated country

Multicoloured, stub-tailed, stoutly built bird; bright blue, green, black, white, yellowish-brown and crimson; white chin, throat and patch on wing-tips and crimson vent distinctive. Sexes alike. Solitary, or pairs; spends much time on ground, hopping about, hunting for insects amidst leaf litter and low herbage; quietly flies into tree branch if disturbed; shows fondness for shaded, semi-damp areas.

LARGE WOODSHRIKE

Tephrodornis virgatus Tephrodornithidae

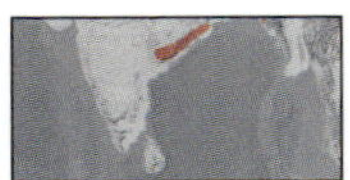

Size 23 cm

Voice Call a tuneful *kew... kew... kew*

Range Lowlands; E Nepal

Habitat Moist evergreen, broadleaved forests; glades

Plain, thickset, shrike-like bird with drab plumage; heavy, black bill; distinct nasal tufts. The Himalayan and eastern race *pelvicus* have grey crown and nape; brown mantle, upperparts; fairly broad, dark mask; black bill; usually, yellow eyes; breast, flanks have pale pink-grey wash. Female duller, with brown upperparts and ill-defined mask; paler bill. Juvenile has spotted, scaly crown. Fairly confiding, but quiet and inconspicuous.

COMMON WOODSHRIKE

Tephrodornis pondicerianus Tephrodornithidae

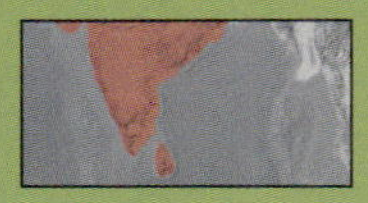

Size 16 cm

Voice Calls include whistling *wheet... wheet...* and interrogative, quick-repeated *whi... whi... whi... whee* afterwards; other trilling, pleasant notes when breeding

Range Across the country, S Himalayan foothills; most common in low country

Habitat Light forests; edges of forests; cultivation; gardens in and around habitation

Sri Lanka Woodshrike

Greyish-brown plumage; broad whitish supercilium and dark stripe below eye distinctive; grey-brown lores; white outer-tail feathers seen when bird flies. Dark stripe may be slightly paler in female. Sexes alike. In pairs, or small parties; quiet for greater part of year, vocal when breeding (February–May); keeps to middle levels of trees, hopping about, sometimes coming to ground. Nest is a small cup of moss and lichen.

ASHY WOODSWALLOW

Artamus fuscus Artamidae

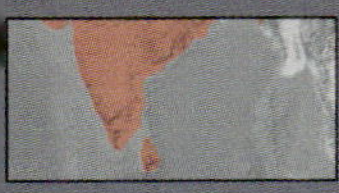

Size 19 cm

Voice Call a harsh *chey…chey…* or *chaek…chaek…*, often uttered in flight; short song occasionally when breeding, mix of harsh and melodious notes

Range Roughly towards east and south from W Gujarat to Shimla; widespread but not continuously distributed; upto about 1,800 m in outer Himalayas

Habitat Open country; edges of forests

Slaty-grey plumage, greyer on head; paler on rump, underbody; short square tail, tipped white; white undertail-coverts; somewhat heavy-looking bird, rather swallow-like in appearance, but wings much shorter and broader. Sexes alike. Small numbers in open country; perches on leaf stalks, overhead wires or flies characteristically, few wingbeats and glide; hunts flying insects; quiet during hot hours, feeds mostly in mornings and evenings.

COMMON IORA

Aegithina tiphia Aegithinidae

Male greenish above (rich black above, with yellowish rump, in some races); black wings and tail; two white wing-bars; bright yellow underbody. Female has yellow-green plumage; white wing-bars; greenish-brown wings. Pairs keep to leafy branches, often with other small birds; moves energetically amidst branches in hunt for insects, caterpillars; rich call notes often a giveaway of its presence in an area.

Size 14 cm

Voice Renowned vocalist; wide range of rich, whistling notes; common call a single or 2-note long-drawn *wheeeeeee* or *wheeeeeee…chu*; another common call a 3-note whistle

Range Subcontinent, upto about 1,800 m in the Himalayas; absent in arid NW India, desert regions of Rajasthan, Kutch

Habitat Forests; gardens; orchards; tree-dotted cultivation; habitation

multicolor

humei

tiphia

LARGE CUCKOOSHRIKE

Coracina macei Campepagidae

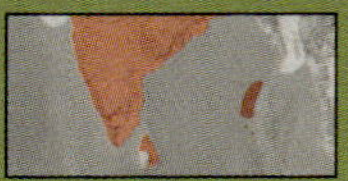

Size 28 cm

Voice Noisy. Call a 2-noted ringing whistle, *ti…treee…* second note long-drawn and higher; somewhat like Blossom-headed Parakeet's call

Range Most of India, from about 2,200 m in the Himalayas; absent in the drier, semi-desert regions of Kutch, C and N Rajasthan and much of NW India

Habitat Forests; gardens; tree-dotted cultivation

Male grey above; broad, dark stripe through eyes to ear-coverts; black wings, tail; greyish breast, whitish below. Female barred grey-and-white below; paler stripe through eyes. In pairs, or small bands of four to six birds; characteristic flight over forest, few wingbeats and glide, often calls in flight; flicks wings on perching; keeps to upper branches, but may descend into bushes; very active and noisy when breeding (March-June).

macei

nipalensis

♀

BLACK-WINGED CUCKOOSHRIKE

Coracina melaschistos Campephagidae

Size 22 cm

Voice Calls include loud, descending *twit...twit to...we* and *peeo...peeo...peeo*

Range Local breeding resident in N mountains from N Pakistan, east to Myanmar border. Winters lower down in foothills and plains mainly in Bangladesh and NE India south to Odisha. Scattered winter records throughout peninsular India

Habitat Open forests; edges of forests, groves

Medium-sized, dark cuckooshrike with unbarred, grey underparts. Male dark grey above with contrasting black wings and tail. Underside of tail shows broad white feather-tips. Female paler with very faint barring on underparts. Feeds on invertebrates in canopy and undergrowth; singly or in pairs. Joins mixed hunting groups. Undulating flight. Nests in trees.

BLACK-HEADED CUCKOOSHRIKE

Coracina melanoptera Campephagidae

Size 20 cm

Voice Silent for most of the year; breeding male has a whistling song, upto a dozen notes, frequently uttered

Range Across E and S India from Mt. Abu to W Uttar Pradesh; a Himalayan race is found in parts of Punjab, Himachal and hill regions of Uttar Pradesh, to about 2,000 m. Undergoes considerable seasonal migration

Habitat Forests; gardens; groves

Male grey plumage; black head, wings, tail, latter white-tipped, except on middle feathers; pale grey below breast, whiter on abdomen, vent. Female has brown plumage; whitish-buff below barred dark brown till abdomen; lacks black head. Solitary, or in pairs, only occasionally several together; often part of mixed hunting bands; keeps for most part to leafy, upper branches, probes foliage for insects; methodically checks foliage before flying off.

♀

ROSY MINIVET

Pericrocotus roseus Campephagidae

Size 18 cm

Voice Not well-known. Squeaky, trilling note recorded

Range Scarce and very local breeding resident, summer visitor: N mountains from N Pakistan, east to Myanmar border. Winter in Bangladesh and India south to Kerala but records very sporadic. Most frequently recorded in NE India and Eastern Ghats

Habitat Poorly known species. Forests; woodlands; gardens

Has grey-brown upperparts. Male has pinkish-red patch on wings and tail; reddish rump; silvery-white face; pale grey crown and nape; blackish-brown wings and long tail. Pale buffy-pink underparts. Female has yellow underparts with yellow-olive rump. Behaviour similar to other minivets. Feeds in canopy on invertebrates. In small parties and less active than other minivets. Nests in trees in open broadleaved forests.

♀

ASHY MINIVET

Pericrocotus divaricatus Campephagidae

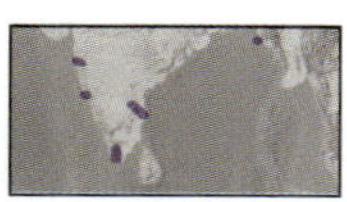

Size 20 cm

Voice Call a somewhat hesitant, *tchue...de...tchue-dee-dee... tchue...dee...dee*, slightly ascending

Range Winter visitor; regular but scarce near Madras, Tamil Nadu, rarely recorded in Maharashtra, Andhra Pradesh, Goa, Kerala and Andaman Islands

Habitat Canopy of light forests

Grey-and-white bird. Male has black head; white forehead and forecrown; black ear-coverts; whitish underparts and dark grey tail; whitish crown and forehead. Whitish wing-bar, visible in flight. Female similarly coloured as male, unlike other minivets with dark slaty-grey stripe across forehead.

Swinhoe's Minivet

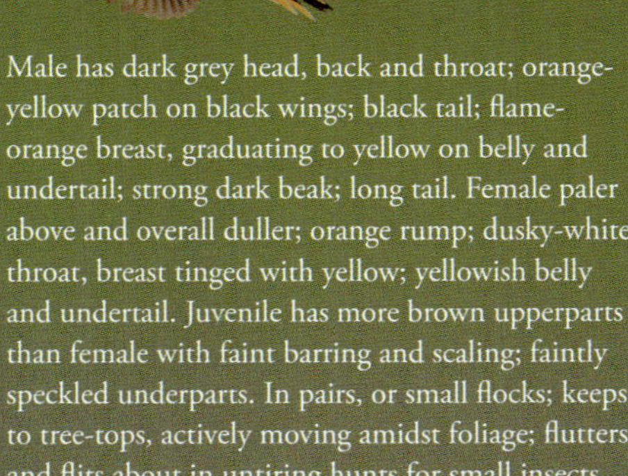

SMALL MINIVET

Pericrocotus cinnamomeus Campephagidae

Size 15 cm

Voice Call a soft, low *swee... swee...* notes uttered as birds hunt in foliage

Range Most of India, upto about 900 m in outer Himalayas; absent in arid parts of Rajasthan

Habitat Forests; groves; gardens; tree-dotted cultivation

Male has dark grey head, back and throat; orange-yellow patch on black wings; black tail; flame-orange breast, graduating to yellow on belly and undertail; strong dark beak; long tail. Female paler above and overall duller; orange rump; dusky-white throat, breast tinged with yellow; yellowish belly and undertail. Juvenile has more brown upperparts than female with faint barring and scaling; faintly speckled underparts. In pairs, or small flocks; keeps to tree-tops, actively moving amidst foliage; flutters and flits about in untiring hunts for small insects, often in association with other small birds; also hunts flycatcher-style.

♀

pallidus

cinnamomeus

WHITE-BELLIED MINIVET

Pericrocotus erythropygius Campephagidae

Size 15 cm

Voice Calls *tseep…tseep* in flight

Range Rare breeding resident of NC Indian lowlands and Gujarat

Habitat Open dry woodlands, thorn scrub

♀

Small minivet, mostly black above with white markings on wing. White underparts with orange on breast and rump; long tail. Female greyish-brown above, with white underparts and grey breast. Juvenile similar to female but has some scaling and barring, particularly on crown and some mottling on breast and white tips on wing-coverts.

SCARLET MINIVET

Pericrocrotus (flammeus) speciosus Campephagidae

Size 20 cm

Voice Call a pleasant, 2-note whistle; also longer, whistling warble

Range Disjunct; several isolated races

Habitat Forests; gardens; groves

♀

Male has glossy bluish-black head and upper back; deep scarlet lower back and rump; black-and-scarlet wings and tail; black throat, scarlet below. Female has rich yellow forehead, supercilium; grey-yellow above; yellow-and-black wings and tail; bright yellow underbody. In pairs, or small parties; sometimes several dozens together; keeps to canopy of tall trees; actively flits about to hunt for insects; also launches aerial sallies after winged insects; often seen in mixed hunting parties of birds; spectacular sight of black, scarlet and yellow as flock flies over forests.

BAR-WINGED FLYCATCHER-SHRIKE

Hemipus picatus Tephrodornithidae

Size 14 cm

Voice Noisy. Calls include persistent *tsit...it... it...tsit...it...it...,si...* and short *chip*

Range Fairly common breeding resident in foothills from E Himachal Pradesh to Myanmar border, Eastern and Western Ghats and Sri Lanka. Makes altitudinal and other local movements

Habitat Open forests, edges of forests including adjoining scrubs

picatus

capitalis

Pied shrike with distinct black cap and hindneck. Brown mantle in the Himalayan race. Black in southern races. Long white patches on black wings showing V in rear views. Tail black with white borders. Throat white, contrasting with pinkish-grey underparts. Female more brown. Feeds on insects in noisy, active flocks, often in mixed hunting groups in canopy and lower down. Often flycatches. Nests high in trees.

BROWN SHRIKE

Lanius cristatus Laniidae

juvenile

Size 19 cm

Voice Calls include harsh chattering, grating; sometimes sings in low chirruping tone with bill closed

Range Winter visitor to peninsular India

Habitat Open country; cultivation; edges of forests; scrubs; gardens

Adult male has uniform rufous-brown upperparts and darkish-brown crown; Broad, black 'bandit-mask' through eye; white brow over. Pale creamy underparts, washed buff; rufous flanks; rufous tail; brown wings. Female has less contrast and faint scalloping on underside. Immature has stronger scalloping on underparts. Solitary; perches in open or tree stumps and returns to same perch repeatedly; territorial.

ISABELLINE SHRIKE

Lanius isabellinus Laniidae

Size 17 cm

Voice Can be noisy. Call a grating *kerishk…kerishk*

Range Breeds in W Pakistan. Common winter visitor to Pakistan and NW India, vagrant further south and east

Habitat Dry thorn scrub and edges of fields, often near water

Small shrike, with rather plain sandy-brown plumage. Adult male has rufous lower rump and tail; dark face-patch; fine white supercilium; white patch on primaries; buff underparts. Adult male of *L. i. phoenicuroides* darker. *L. i. isabellinus* paler. White wing-patch absent in female and juvenile. Sits on prominent perch, in open. Catches insects, small reptiles, mammals and birds from perch. Sometimes, impales prey on thorns.

BAY-BACKED SHRIKE

Lanius vittatus Laniidae

Size 18 cm

Voice Call a harsh *churr*; lively warble of breeding male; sometimes imitates other bird calls

Range Subcontinent, upto about 1,800 m in the Himalayas; absent in the NE

Habitat Open country; light forests; scrubs

Deep chestnut-maroon back; broad black forehead-band, continuing through eyes to ear-coverts; grey crown and neck, separated from black by small white patch; white rump distinctive; black wings with white in outer flight feathers; white underbody, fulvous on breast and flanks. Sexes alike. Solitary, or in scattered pairs in open terrain; keeps lookout from perch on some tree stumps, overhead wires or bush-tops, usually under 4 m off ground; pounces once potential prey sighted; usually devours prey on ground, tearing it; sometimes carries it to perch; keeps to fixed territories, defends aggressively.

juvenile

LONG-TAILED SHRIKE

Lanius schach Laniidae

Size 25 cm

Voice Noisy. Calls include a harsh mix of scolding notes, shrieks and yelps; excellent mimic. Rather musical song of breeding male

Range Three races undergo considerable seasonal movement; subcontinent, from about 2,700 m in the Himalayas

Habitat Open country, cultivation, edges of forests, vicinity of habitation, gardens; prefers neighbourhood of water

Pale grey from crown to middle of back; then bright rufous till rump; black forehead, band through eye; white 'mirror' in black wings; whitish underbody, tinged pale rufous on lower breast and flanks. Sexes alike. Mostly solitary; boldly defends feeding territory; keeps lookout from conspicuous perch; pounces onto ground on sighting prey; said to store surplus in 'larder', impaling prey on thorns; nicknamed Butcher-bird.

erythronotus

tricolor

caniceps

SOUTHERN GREY SHRIKE

Lanius meridionalis Laniidae

Size 25 cm

Voice Call a harsh, grating *khreck...*; mix of other harsh notes and chuckles; pleasant, ringing song of breeding male

Range Drier areas of NW, W and C India, across Gangetic plains to West Bengal; south to Tamil Nadu

Habitat Open country; semi-desert; scrubs; edges of cultivation

Bluish-grey above; broad black stripe from beak through eye; black wings with white 'mirrors'; black-and-white tail; unmarked white underbody. Sexes alike. Mostly in pairs, in open areas; remains perched upright on bush-tops or overhead wires or flies low, uttering harsh scream; surveys neighbourhood from perch and pounces on prey; batters and tears prey before swallowing it; said to maintain 'larder', impaling surplus prey on thorns; keeps feeding territories year round; wild and wary bird.

INDIAN GOLDEN ORIOLE

Oriolus (oriolus) kundoo Oriolidae

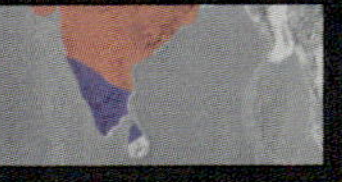

Size 25 cm

Voice Call includes a fluty whistle of 2- or 3-notes, interpreted *pee…lo…lo*

Range Summer visitor to the Himalayan foothills, spreads in winter to plains; breeds in many parts of peninsula

Habitat Forests; orchards; gardens around habitation

Male has bright golden-yellow plumage; black stripe through eye; black wings and centre of tail. Female yellow-green above; has brownish-green wings; dirty-white below, streaked brown. Juvenile similar to female. Solitary, or in pairs; arboreal, sometimes moving with other birds in upper branches; regularly visits fruiting and flowering trees; hunts insects in leafy branches; usually heard, surprisingly not often seen, despite bright colour; seen only when emerges on bare branch or flies across.

juvenile

BLACK-NAPED ORIOLE

Oriolus chinensis Oriolidae

Size 25 cm

Voice Call similar to Indian's but less musical

Range Breeds on Andaman and Nicobar Islands. Scarce winter visitor to Kerala and SE Bangladesh. Scattered records elsewhere in peninsula

Habitat Rubber plantations

Easily differentiated from Golden by broad black eye-stripe continuing to join on nape (and much stouter bill). Female more greenish or olive on mantle. Overall yellow with black in-flight feathers and black tail with yellow patches. Female more greenish-yellow. Juvenile has some streaking on underparts and more diffused eye-stripe. Indulges in high-speed aerial chases. Raids nests of other birds, taking their eggs and chicks.

BLACK-HOODED ORIOLE

Oriolus xanthornus Oriolidae

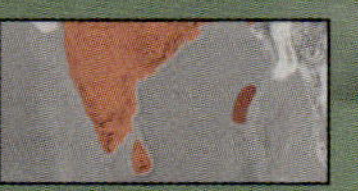

Size 25 cm

Voice Assortment of melodious and harsh calls; fluty 2- or 3-noted *tu...hee or tll...yow...yow...*more common; also single, mellow note

Range Subcontinent, upto about 1,000 m in the Himalayan foothills

Habitat Forests, orchards, gardens, often amidst habitation

Golden-yellow plumage; black head diagnostic; black-and-yellow wings and tail; deep pink-red beak seen at close quarters. Sexes alike. In pairs, or small parties; strictly arboreal, only rarely descending into lower bushes or to ground; active and lively; moves a lot in forests and birds chase one another, rich colours striking against green or brown of forests; very vocal; associates with other birds in mixed parties, frequently joins mixed hunting groups; visits fruiting and flowering trees.

BLACK DRONGO

Dicrurus macrocercus Dicruridae

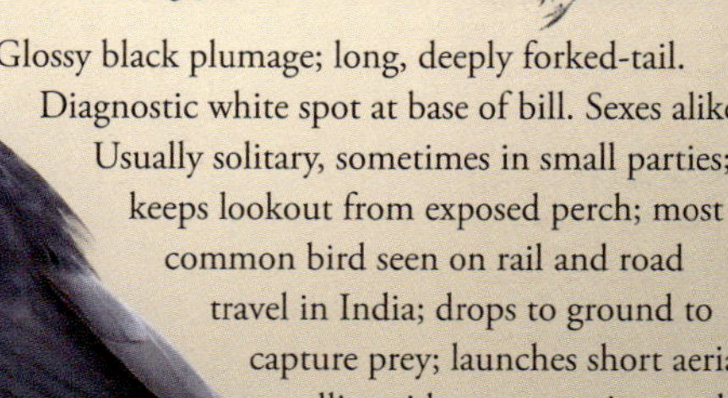

Glossy black plumage; long, deeply forked-tail. Diagnostic white spot at base of bill. Sexes alike. Usually solitary, sometimes in small parties; keeps lookout from exposed perch; most common bird seen on rail and road travel in India; drops to ground to capture prey; launches short aerial sallies; rides atop grazing cattle; follows cattle, tractors, grass-cutters, fires; consumes vast numbers of insects; bold and aggressive species, with several birds nesting in same tree.

Size 31 cm

Voice Call a harsh *tiu...tiu*; also *cheece...cheece*

Range Subcontinent, upto about 1,800 m in the outer Himalayas

Habitat Open country; orchards; cultivation

ASHY DRONGO

Dicrurus leucophaeus Dicruridae

Size 30 cm

Voice Noisy and varied. Calls include *cha...ke wip...kit...whew* and *cheece...cheece...chichuk...*

Range Fairly common breeding summer visitor to N foothills from Pakistan, east to Myanmar border. Winters in plains and peninsula, including Sri Lanka

Habitat Forests and more open woodlands in winter

Adult has ash-grey upperparts; slightly lighter underparts, paler towards belly; red or reddish-brown iris; black legs and bill; black chin. Juvenile more brown than adult, with white edge on underside of tail and brown iris. Sexes similar, but male slightly larger. Agile flier, executing remarkable twists and turns in air with skill and speed. Mimics calls of other birds. Forages near edges of forests; perches on high, open branch to detect prey; swoops down to catch insects on ground or in mid-flight.

WHITE-BELLIED DRONGO

Dicrurus caerulescens Dicruridae

Size 24 cm

Voice Assortment of pleasant, whistling calls and some grating notes

Range Most of S India and east of a line from SE Punjab to around Kutch; east to Bengal; occurs to about 1,500 m

Habitat Open forests and well-wooded habitats

Adult has bluish-black upperparts; long, deeply forked-tail; greyish-brown throat and breast; white belly and undertail-coverts; short legs. Sexes alike. In pairs, or small groups of four birds, sometimes with other birds. Noisy; makes short flights; often hunts till very late in evenings; sits upright while perched prominently in shrike-like pose.

BRONZED DRONGO

Dicrurus aeneus Dicruridae

Size 24 cm

Voice Noisy. Varied whistles and grating calls. Also *cheet… chi… chew*

Range Fairly common breeding resident in foothills from E Punjab to NE India, including Bangladesh, then south through Eastern Ghats and throughout the length of Western Ghats. Makes some local movements

Habitat Clearings in thick forests, usually near streams

Smallish drongo with glossy, black plumage, and bluish-green/purple iridescence. Relatively short, spade-shaped tail with shallow fork, splayed at tips; short and heavy black bill; spiky rictal feathers give whisker-like appearance. Dark underparts, with more gloss over breast. Sexes alike. Perches high on exposed branch, hawking for insects. Very vocal and conspicuous; territorial. Pairs perform noisy displays.

SPANGLED DRONGO

Dicrurus hottentottus Dicruridae

Size 32 cm

Voice Noisy; mix of whistling, metallic calls and harsh screams

Range Lower Himalayan foothills, east of Uttarakhand; down through NE India, along Eastern Ghats, Odisha, Bastar through to Western Ghats, up north to Mumbai, occasionally even further north

Habitat Forests

Glistening blue-black plumage, fine hair-like feathers on forehead; longish, downcurved, pointed beak; diagnostic tail, square-cut and inwardly bent (curling) towards outer ends. Sexes alike. Solitary, or scattered pairs, strictly arboreal forest bird; small numbers may gather on favourite flowering trees; rather aggressive; often seen in mixed hunting parties of birds. Selects exposed branch and flies out to prey.

GREATER RACKET-TAILED DRONGO

Dicrurus paradiseus Dicruridae

Size 32 cm (plus 30 cm streamers)

Voice Noisiest forest bird; amazing mimic; calls include wide variety of whistles and screams, perfect imitations

Range Forested parts of India, roughly east and south of line from S Gujarat to Uttarakhand; upto about 1,400 m

Habitat Forests; edges of forests; orchards

Glossy blue-black plumage; prominent crest of longish feathers, curving backwards; elongated, wire-like outer-tail feathers, ending in 'rackets' diagnostic. Distinguished from Lesser by larger size and wider rackets. Sexes alike. Solitary, or in pairs, sometimes small gatherings; arboreal, but often descends into low bushes; moves a lot in forests; confirmed exhibitionist, both by sight and sound; extremely noisy, often vocal long before sunrise; bold and aggressive, seen mobbing bigger birds 100 m over forests.

nicobarensis

WHITE-THROATED FANTAIL

Rhipidura albicollis Rhipiduridae

Size 17 cm

Voice Call a harsh *chukrrr…* note

Range Fairly common breeding resident of foothills from extreme NE Pakistan to Myanmar border, throughout NE India

Habitat Shaded forests, scrubs and gardens, favouring well-wooded ravines

Distinguished by dark fan-shaped tail edged with white. Overall brown-and-white bird with broad, white tip to tail (except to two central tail feathers); white throat and supercilium. Himalayan *R. a. canescans* has slaty-grey upperparts and underparts, and black eye mask, while *R. a. albogularis,* found in peninsular India, has dark grey upperparts, whitish underparts, and grey breast-band. Sexes alike.

INDIAN PARADISE-FLYCATCHER

Terpsiphone paradisi Monarchidae

intermediate phase

Size 20 cm (male's tail 30 cm more)

Voice Call a sharp, grating *chwae* or *chchwae*…; melodious warbling song and display of breeding male

Range The Himalayas, foothills to about 1,800 m, rarely 2,500 m; N India, south to Bharatpur; absent in broad belt across Gangetic plains; widespread in peninsular India

Habitat Light forests; gardens; open country

Glossy blue-black head, crest and throat; black in wings; silvery-white body, long tail-streamers. Male occurs in two morphs: rufous phase has white parts replaced by rufous-chestnut with white underparts. White phase more variable, but has predominantly white plumage. Female and juvenile have no tail-streamers; shorter crest; rufous above; ash-grey throat and nuchal-collar; whitish below. Short legs; tends to sit upright on perch. Solitary, or in pairs; makes short sallies; flits through trees, tail-streamers floating; strictly arboreal, sometimes descending into taller bushes; cheerful disposition.

♀

rufous phase

white phase

BLACK-NAPED MONARCH

Hypothymis azurea Monarchidae

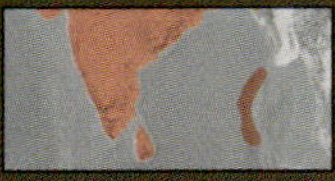

Size 16 cm

Voice Common call a sharp, grating, high-pitched *chwich… chweech* or *chwae…chweech*, slightly interrogative in tone, two notes quickly uttered; has short, rambling notes when breeding

Range India, south of outer Himalayas, to about 1,200 m, east of W Uttarakhand; absent in arid NW and N India

Habitat Forests; bamboos; gardens

Male has lilac-blue plumage; black patch on nape, gorget on breast; slight black scaly markings on crown; sooty on wings and tail; white below breast. Female ash-blue, duller; lacks black on nape and breast. Solitary, or in pairs in forests, often amidst mixed hunting parties; extremely active and fidgety, flits and flutters about, often fans tail slightly; calls often as it moves about, calls are often first indication of its presence.

♀

RUFOUS TREEPIE

Dendrocitta vagabunda Corvidae

Size 50 cm

Voice Common call a fluty 3-note *goo…ge…lay or ko…ki…la;* harsh, guttural notes often uttered

Range Almost all over India, upto about 1,500 m in outer Himalayas

Habitat Forests; gardens; cultivation; habitation

Sexes alike. Rufous above; sooty grey-brown head and neck; black, white and grey on wings, best seen in flight; black-tipped, grey tail, long and graduated. In pairs, or small parties; feeds up in trees, but also descends low into bushes and onto ground to pick up termites.

vagabunda

pallida

GREY TREEPIE

Dendrocitta formosae Corvidae

Size 40 cm

Voice Noisy and variable. Call a loud, clanking *klok…ti…klok…ti…ti*

Range Locally common breeding resident in N hills from extreme NE Pakistan to Myanmar border; Eastern Ghats

Habitat Forests; secondary growth

Duller and less rufous than the Rufous; long tail; grey-and-brown plumage; dusky grey face and grey head, neck and underparts; rufous vent; radiated grey tail black-edged and tipped; brownish back; black wings with small white patch. Sexes alike. Less often near human habitation than Rufous. Behaviour and food as Rufous but shyer. Arboreal, often in groups or mixed hunting groups. Seems to seek company of drongos.

WHITE-BELLIED TREEPIE

Dendrocitta leucogastra Corvidae

Size 50 cm

Voice Noisy. Calls include various loud, harsh and metallic notes, including *tikituk…tikituk* and *kreah…kreah*

Range Local breeding endemic resident in S Western Ghats

Habitat Evergreen hill forests; thick scrub; plantations

White, grey and chestnut crow with very long, black-tipped and pale grey-edged tail. Black face contrasts with white head and underparts. Chestnut mantle and black wings with white patches. Sexes alike. Sociable, often with Greater Racket-tailed Drongos, which they imitate freely as well as other forest species. Feeds mainly on invertebrates at lower and middle levels. Nests in shrubs.

HOUSE CROW

Corvus splendens Corvidae

Size 43 cm

Voice Call a familiar *caw*; occasionally pleasant *kurrrrr* note; several other notes

Range Subcontinent, reaching about 2,500 m in the Himalayas

Habitat Rural and urban habitation; cultivation, edges of forests; wide range of habitats

Sleek-looking crow with glossy black plumage; grey collar, upper back and breast; glossy black on forehead, crown and throat; long, prominent, arched bill; black feet; brown eyes. Sexes alike. Mobs other birds, even large raptors; performs important scavenging services; occasionally flies very high into skies, either when flying long distance, or simply for fun; roosts communally.

zugmayeri

splendens

protegatus

LARGE-BILLED CROW

Corvus macrorhynchos Corvidae

Size 48 cm

Voice Call a harsh *khaa…khaa*; several variations among various races

Range The Himalayas

Habitat Forests, rural habitations; small numbers in towns and cities

Glossy black plumage; heavy beak, with noticeable culmen-curve. Relatively broad wings, particularly primaries; long tail, slightly wedged, obvious only in flight; nasal tufts; black bill and legs; dark iris. Sexes alike. Solitary, or in groups of two to six; most common around villages and only small numbers in urban areas; overall not as 'enterprising' as familiar House; in forested areas, behaviour often indicates presence of carnivore kills. Large nest, untidy assembly of twigs.

CINEREOUS TIT

Parus major Paridae

Size 13 cm

Voice Call a loud, clear whistling *whee...chi...chee...*; other whistling and harsh notes

Range Widespread in the Himalayas, foothills to about 3,500 m; peninsular India

Habitat Open forests; gardens; habitation

Adult has grey back; black crown continuing along neck sides to broad black band from chin along centre of underbody; white cheeks, nape-patch, wing-bar and outer feathers of black tail; ashy-white sides. Sexes alike. In pairs or small bands, often with other small birds; restless, clings upside down, and indulges in acrobatic displays while hunting among leaves and branches; holds food fast between feet and pecks at it noisily; tame and confiding.

BLACK-LORED TIT

Parus xanthogenys Paridae

Size 14 cm

Voice Cheerful, musical notes. Call a loud tailorbird-like *towit...towit* near nest; other 2- to 4-noted whistling calls; whistling song. Also, harsh *charrr* and some chattering notes

Range The Himalayas to E Nepal; 1,200-2,500 m, widespread in parts of C, E and W India

Habitat Forests; gardens

Large tit with diagnostic bushy, black crest. Olive-green back; black crest, faintly-tipped yellow; stripe behind eye, broad central band from chin to vent; bright yellow nape-patch, supercilium and sides of underbody. Sexes alike. In pairs or small flocks, often with other small birds; arboreal, active; feeds in foliage; sometimes enters gardens. Female and juvenile like male, but may have black replaced by olive.

WHITE-NAPED TIT

Parus nuchalis Paridae

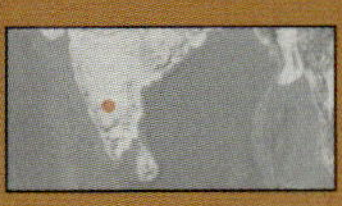

Size 12 cm

Voice Vocabulary very similar to Great's

Range Gujarat, Rajasthan. Isolated records from S India

Habitat Thorn-scrub forests. Globally threatened

Black-and-white tit with large white nuchal-patch. Male has glossy black mantle and wing-coverts; extensive white on wing; white cheeks. Underparts white, with strong black ventral-band from throat to vent. Sexes similar, but female has bluish gloss to black parts and small, white tips to primaries. Juvenile duller and lacks gloss, smaller white nuchal-patch and less white in tail and wings. In pairs, or family parties; shy; restless. More heard than seen; located through musical call. Feeds in canopy and shrub level.

PLAIN MARTIN

Riparia paludicola Hirundinidae

Size 12 cm

Voice Calls *brret*..., rather harsh in tone, usually on the wing around nest colony. Twittering song

Range NW and N India, from the outer Himalayas, south at least to line from vicinity of Mumbai-Nasik to C Odisha; moves considerably locally

Habitat Vicinity of water, sandbanks, sandy cliffsides

Long wings and slightly forked-tail. Grey-brown above, slightly darker on crown; dark brown wings and tail; dull grey below, whiter towards abdomen. Sexes alike. Gregarious species, always in flocks, flying around sandbanks along water courses; individual birds occasionally stray far and high; hawks small insects in flight; flocks perch on telegraph wires.

SAND MARTIN

Riparia riparia Hirundinidae

Size 13 cm

Voice Call a dry, quiet *trass*

Range Scarce breeding resident in Assam. Local winter visitor to Bangladesh. Scarce and irregular passage migrant, perhaps winter visitor in NW India

Habitat Vicinity of water

Adult has greyish-brown upperparts; darker tail and wings; long wings; slightly notched tail; dark underwings, white throat and underparts; contrasting brown chest-band sometimes extending to centre of belly; small, black beak; blackish or dark brown legs and feet. Sexes similar. Juvenile has buff or cream wash on belly, pale rust wash on face, neck, chin and breast. Gliding swallow-like flight. Northwestern Pale similar in flight but much paler. Feeds on aerial insects close to surface of water. Sociable. Nests in tunnels in sandbanks.

PALE MARTIN

Riparia diluta Hirundinidae

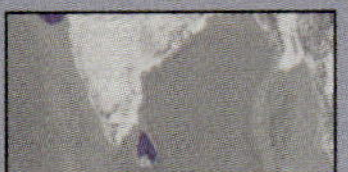

Size 13 cm

Voice Undocumented

Range Breeds in the Himalayas; winters in Pakistan and probably farther E

Habitat Large waterbodies

Treated as conspecific with Pale Sand. However, smaller and slimmer with shallower tail-fork; paler upperparts; greyish-brown; breast-band paler, more greyish-brown and less distinct with diffuse lower border. In some, the breast-band only slightly darker than rest of underparts, gives impression of broken breast-band with paler centre merging to darker sides; paler head, particularly crown and ear-coverts, contrasting with dark eye and darker lores; pale (often almost pure white, or buffish) throat.

BARN SWALLOW

Hirundo rustica Hirundinidae

Size 18 cm

Voice Calls vary with object of alarm. Hard *vit* in flight and twittering rambling song

Range Common breeding resident to N mountains from W Pakistan east to Myanmar border. Common winter visitor throughout rest of the region

Habitat Cultivation, towns and villages usually near or over water

Slender bird with long, narrow, pointed wings, and deeply forked-tail with long streamers; spends most of its life on wing. Steel bluish-black upperparts; black wings and tail; pale underparts; red throat; steel-blue breast-band. Sexes alike, but male may have longer streamers. Juvenile has paler underparts and less deeply forked-tail. Agile flier; low, fast, powerful in flight. Constructs nest under eaves of buildings. Gregarious.

PACIFIC SWALLOW

Hirundo tahitica Hirundinidae

Size 13 cm

Voice Call a hard *qwik…qwik*

Range Resident in Andaman Islands

Habitat Open country and along coasts and rivers

Distinguished from Barn by lack of blue breast-band and streamers. Blue-black upperparts; short, forked-tail. Rufous from forehead to breast; greyish-white belly; dark grey vent with white scalloping; grey underwing-coverts. Hunts alongside Barn, but does not associate with them otherwise. Feeds sociably on aerial insects. Flight less sweeping than Barn. Often perches on wires and bare branches. Nests against wall in building or against bank or culvert.

WIRE-TAILED SWALLOW

Hirundo smithii Hirundinidae

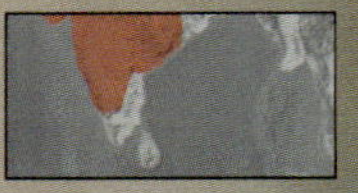

Size 14 cm

Voice Call a soft twittering note; pleasant song of breeding male

Range Common breeding (summer) visitor to N India, to about 1,800 m in the Himalayas; breeds in many other parts of India; widespread over the area, except arid zones

Habitat Open areas; cultivation; habitation, mostly in vicinity of canals, lakes, rivers

Glistening steel-blue above; chestnut cap; unmarked, pure white underbody distinctive; two long, wire-like projections (tail-wires) from outer-tail feathers diagnostic. Sexes alike. In solitary, or small parties; almost always seen around water, either perched on overhead wires or hawking insects in graceful, acrobatic flight, swooping and banking; often flies very low, drinks from surface; roosts in reed beds and other vegetation, often with warblers and wagtails.

EURASIAN CRAG MARTIN

Ptyonoprogne rupestris Hirundinidae

Size 15 cm

Voice Calls include short *plee*, musical *weeeh* and harsh *tshrr*

Range Fairly common but local breeding resident and summer visitor in W Pakistan and N mountains from N Pakistan to Bhutan. Winter visitor to Western Ghats

Habitat Rocky gorges; cliffs; old hill forts

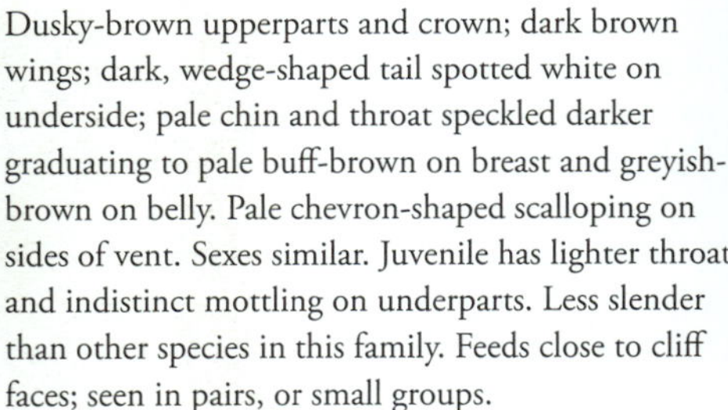

Dusky-brown upperparts and crown; dark brown wings; dark, wedge-shaped tail spotted white on underside; pale chin and throat speckled darker graduating to pale buff-brown on breast and greyish-brown on belly. Pale chevron-shaped scalloping on sides of vent. Sexes similar. Juvenile has lighter throat and indistinct mottling on underparts. Less slender than other species in this family. Feeds close to cliff faces; seen in pairs, or small groups.

DUSKY CRAG MARTIN

Ptyonoprogne concolor Hirundinidae

Size 13 cm

Voice Call a faint *chip…*, uncommonly uttered

Range Nearly, all over India, south of the Himalayan foothills, to about 1,500 m

Habitat Vicinity of ruins; old stone buildings in towns

Dark sooty-brown above; square-cut, short tail, with white spot on all but outermost and central tail feathers; paler underbody; faintly rufous chin and throat, with indistinct black streaking. Sexes alike. In small parties; flies around ruins, crags and old buildings, hawking insects in flight; acrobatic, swallow-like flight and appearance; rests during hot hours on rocky ledges or some corner.

RED-RUMPED SWALLOW

Cecropis daurica Hirundinidae

Size 18 cm

Voice Call a mournful chirping note. Pleasant twittering song of breeding male

Range Six races over the subcontinent, including Sri Lanka; resident, migratory

Habitat Cultivation; vicinity of human habitation; town centres; rocky hilly areas

Glossy steel-blue above; chestnut supercilium, head sides, neck-collar and rump; dull rufous-white below, streaked brown; deeply forked-tail diagnostic. Sexes alike. Small parties spend much of day on wing; migrant, winter-visiting race *nipalensis* highly gregarious; hawks insects along with other birds; freely perches on overhead wires, thin branches of bushes and trees; hunts insects amongst most-crowded areas of towns, over markets and refuse heaps, flying with amazing agility, wheeling, banking and stooping with remarkable mastery.

STREAK-THROATED SWALLOW

Petrochelidon fluvicola Hirundinidae

Size 12 cm

Voice Calls include *chrrp* and *trr…trr*

Range Locally common breeding resident in Indo-Gangetic plains from E Pakistan to Uttar Pradesh and south through W peninsula to Karnataka. Mainly summer visitor to N areas

Habitat Open country, cultivation near water

Glossy black upperparts; some whitish edges to dorsal feathers; dark-rufous crown; brownish rump; white underparts with black mesial streaks to feathers from throat to breast; pale brown underwing; tail slightly furcate, small whitish spot towards tip of inner web of each feather. Upto 200 birds nest communally on cliff faces.

juvenile

COMMON HOUSE MARTIN

Delichon urbicum Hirundinidae

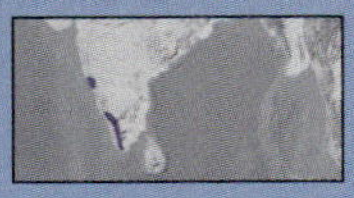

Size 14 cm

Voice Noisy. Calls include soft twittering chirps and short *prrit…prrit*

Range Local breeding summer visitor to N mountains from N Pakistan east to Himachal Pradesh. Scarce passage migrant throughout India, but perhaps overlooked because it flies so high. Some winter in Western Ghats

Habitat Mountain valleys with cultivation, cliffs and gorges

Adult has steel-blue upperparts and white underparts. Glossy bluish-black head; white rump and underwings conspicuous in flight; short legs with downy feathers; brown eyes; small black bill; deeply forked-tail. Sexes alike. Juvenile sooty-black, and wing-coverts, quills edged and tipped white. Sociable. In groups of several hundreds or even thousands of individuals. Spends time in open country. Cup-shaped nest made of mud and grass.

JERDON'S BUSH LARK

Mirafra affinis Alaudidae

Size 14 cm

Voice Call a short, high-pitched trill. Dry, metallic rattle delivered from perch or during short song flight

Range Peninsular India and Sri Lanka

Habitat Dry open areas with bushes and trees

Stocky lark with large bill, short tail and wings, and relatively long legs. Narrow supercilium; buffish-grey-brown crown and nape with dark streaking; distinct yellow nape-band; pale grey ear-coverts, also streaked darker; rufous-buff upperparts; paler underparts, heavily spotted breast, rufous patch on wing; rufous-buff outer webs to outer-tail feathers, and dark-centered-coverts and tertials.

SINGING BUSH LARK

Mirafra cantillans Alaudidae

Size 14 cm

Voice High-pitched, Skylark-like song in air or from perch

Range Very local and patchily distributed breeding resident mainly in N and C peninsular India and parts of Pakistan and Bangladesh

Habitat Dry, open scrub, fallow and grasslands

Smallish lark with relatively short, stubby bill; prominent, pale supercilium and slight crest. Overall buff-brown; heavily streaked upperparts; brownish-buff ear-coverts; long tail with white outer-tail feathers; light rufous wing edgings. Buff underparts; white throat; fine streaks on breast sides; relatively long tail. Rufous wing-patches visible in flight. Sexes alike. Feeds singly, or in pairs. Flies rapidly into cover when flushed. Often perches on top of low bushes if disturbed, or to sing. Nests on ground.

INDIAN BUSH LARK

Mirafra erythroptera Alaudidae

The word erythroptera i.e. red-winged in its Latin name, is for its prominent rufous-coloured primaries. Overall brown lark with prominent dark streaks and heavily spotted breast; cheek-patch bounded by white supercilium; dark buff outer-tail feathers; whitish, unstreaked belly; stout bill and shortish tail. Sexes alike. Feeds on invertebrates and seeds on ground; in pairs, or small groups, when disturbed. Nests on ground.

Size 14 cm

Voice Calls include *sweee* and *trrr…weet*. Song a whistling *tit…tit…tit tsweeh…tsweeh…tsweeh*, starts from top of bush and continues in parachuting song flight. Often sings at night

Range Locally common endemic breeding resident in plains of N and C India from S Punjab to Odisha and in W, N Tamil Nadu. Also in parts of Pakistan. Absent from SE, NE, Nepal, Bangladesh and Sri Lanka

Habitat Sparse rocky scrub and barren flats

RUFOUS-TAILED LARK

Ammomanes phoenicura Alaudidae

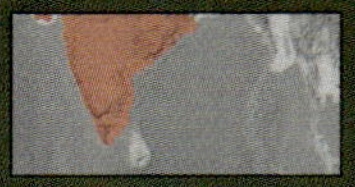

Size 16 cm

Voice Song a mix of rich whistling notes and chirps; sings on wing and from perch on earth mounds, stones or low bush

Range Commoner east from Kutch to around Delhi; east to West Bengal and south to N Andhra Pradesh

Habitat Cultivation; fallow ground; open riversides

Dark brown upperparts; rufous-brown underparts, with brown streaks on throat, breast; rich rufous tail with black band across tip diagnostic. Sexes alike. Pairs when breeding in small flocks during winter, occasionally with other larks; difficult to locate because of dull colouration; mostly keeps to ground, running about erratically; flies short distance if disturbed; as with several other larks, sudden appearance and disappearance of this species in many localities.

GREATER SHORT-TOED LARK

Calandrella brachydactyla Alaudidae

Size 15 cm

Voice Soft, dry rippling *chirp* and *dyu* often combined. Flocks call constantly in flight

Range Locally common, often numerous, winter visitor to lowlands of Pakistan, Nepal, Bangladesh and India south to Madhya Pradesh

Habitat Dry pasture; stubble; fallow; semi-desert; dry mudflats

Medium-sized, heavily streaked lark, without crest. Sandy-brown and sometimes brownish-black upperparts. Fine streaks on forehead; flattish head; dark cap; pale lores; short, pointed, pale pinkish bill; two black breast-patches. Whitish underparts; short dark tail. Sexes alike. Juvenile has dark brown feathers edged buff. Bold, undulating flight. Imitates calls of other birds.

CRESTED LARK

Galerida cristata Alaudidae

Size 18 cm

Voice Ordinary call note a pleasant *tee…ur…*. Short song of male during soaring display flight

Range N, NW India, Gangetic plains; Rajasthan, Saurashtra, N Madhya Pradesh

Habitat Semi-desert; cultivation; dry grassy areas

Similar to Eurasian, but paler and weaker streaking on plumage. Sandy-brown above, streaked blackish; pointed, upstanding crest distinctive; brown tail has dull rufous outer feathers; whitish and dull yellowish-brown below, breast streaked dark brown. Sexes alike. In small flocks, breaking into pairs when breeding; runs briskly on ground, pointed crest carried upstanding; also settles on bush-tops, stumps, wire fences and overhead wires.

MALABAR LARK

Galerida malabarica Alaudidae

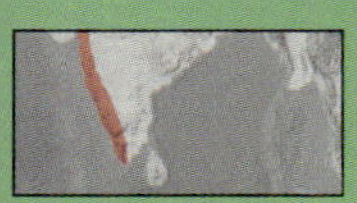

Size 15 cm

Voice Calls *chew…chew…yu.* Song similar to Crested's

Range Locally common endemic breeding resident in plains and hills of Western Ghats and W coast from Gujarat south to Kerala

Habitat Dry open habitats, preferably with some scrubs and rocks; cultivation; grassy hillsides and open scrub

Sturdy, medium-sized lark with prominent, long, spiky crest and short tail. Similar to Sykes's, but smaller. Reddish-brown upperparts boldly streaked black. Underparts pale rufous-buff with black streaking on breast. Pale rufous outer-tail feathers and large bill. Sexes similar. Very confiding, usually crouching if alarmed. Sings from perch or in short song flight. Nests on ground. Feeds on seeds and invertebrates on ground. In pairs, solitary or in small flocks.

SYKES'S LARK

Galerida deva Alaudidae

Size 14 cm

Voice Call a nasal *dwezee.* Song similar to Indian Busk Lark's

Range Local endemic breeding resident in Deccan from Gujarat and S Uttar Pradesh south to N Karnataka and Andhra Pradesh

Habitat Dry stony grasslands; open scrub, arable cultivation. Often on dark soils

Small lark with spiky crest, inconspicuous when folded. Overall buff plumage, heavily streaked with black; pale buff supercilium. Underparts tawny brown with some streaking on breast; rufous-buff outer feathers; short bill. Sexes alike. Feeds on invertebrates and seeds singly, in pairs or small parties. Fairly approachable. Nests on ground.

ORIENTAL SKYLARK

Alauda gulgula Alaudidae

Size 16 cm

Voice Longish, pleasant warble of male, often imitations of other bird calls thrown in. Sings usually when soaring high

Range All over India

Habitat Grasslands; cultivation; mudflats; fallow lands

Similar to Eurasian; brownish above, feathers edged yellow-brown with black centres; short, indistinct crest, not often visible; dark brown tail with pale-buff outer feathers; dull-buff below; more yellowish-brown on breast, faintly streaked and spotted darker. Sexes alike. Pairs, or small parties on ground, runs in short spurts; squats when approached and flies low at the last moment.

ASHY-CROWNED SPARROW LARK

Eremopterix griseus Alaudidae

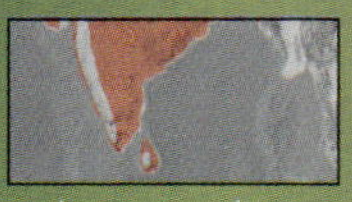

Size 12 cm

Voice Pleasant, monotonous trilling song by male; sings on wing and on ground

Range Almost across India, south of the Himalayan foothills; moves during rains; uncommon in heavy rainfall areas

Habitat Open scrub; semi-cultivation; fallow river basins; tidal mudflats

♀

Adult male has pale greyish-brown forehead and crown; sandy-brown upperparts; white cheeks and breast sides; dark chocolate-brown sides of face and most of underbody; dark brown tail with whitish outer feathers. Female sandy-brown overall; dull rufous sides of face and underbody. Mostly loose flocks, scattered over area; pairs, or small parties when breeding. Feeds on ground; fond of dusty areas, where large numbers may squat about. Sandy colouration makes it impossible to spot birds, but when disturbed, large numbers suddenly take wing; striking display flight of male.

ZITTING CISTICOLA

Cisticola juncidis Cisticolidae

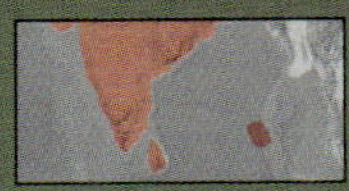

Size 10 cm

Voice Call a sharp, clicking *zit… zit*, continuous during display in air

Range Subcontinent, south of the Himalayan foothills; absent in extreme NW Rajasthan

Habitat Open country; grass; cultivation; reed beds; also coastal lagoons

Rufous-brown upperparts, prominently streaked darker; rufous-buff, unstreaked rump; white tips to fan-shaped tail diagnostic; buffy-white underbody, more rufous on flanks. Diagnostic calls. Sexes alike. Seen in pairs, or several birds over open expanse; great skulker, lurking in low growth; usually seen during short, jerky flights, low over ground; soon dives into cover; most active when breeding, during rains; striking display of male, soaring erratically, falling and rising, incessantly uttering sharp, creaking note; adult arrives on nest in similar fashion.

non-breeding

RUFOUS-FRONTED PRINIA

Prinia buchanani Cisticolidae

Size 12 cm

Voice Song a *chid-le-weest* followed by repetitive *chidle…ee…chidle…ee*

Range Pakistan and NW, C India

Habitat Scrubs in semi-desert

Medium to small-sized, overall pale-looking prinia with short, rounded wings. Long, dark brown, graduated tail with broad, white tips to outer feathers, conspicuous in flight. Greyish-brown upperparts (greyer in non-breeding); rufous-washed forehead and crown; dark brown flight feathers. Underparts almost completely white with slight rufescent wash on flanks, undertail-coverts and vent. Juvenile similar to adult, but rufous on crown absent.

RUFESCENT PRINIA

Prinia rufescens Cisticolidae

Size 11 cm

Voice Call a buzzing *peez…eez…eez…eez*. Song a rhythmic *chewp…chewp…chewp*

Range The Himalayas in Nepal and from Sikkim east to Arunachal Pradesh; hills of NE India and Bangladesh; Simlipal hills, Odisha and Andhra Pradesh

Habitat Tall grasslands; grass under deciduous forests; bushes around terraced cultivation; open wooded areas; secondary growth and edges of forests

Rather plain-looking, dull-coloured prinia. Short, rounded wings; white lores and supercilium; medium-sized, graduated tail with buffish-white tips and subterminal band on outer feathers; uppertail more chestnut brown. Breeding adult has rufous brown upperparts; greyish-brown nape and ear-coverts. Underparts dirty-white with yellowish-beige wash on belly, undertail-coverts and flanks. Thin, longish, decurved bill. Non-breeding adult has rufous-brown crown, ear-coverts and longer tail.

GREY-BREASTED PRINIA

Prinia hodgsonii Cisticolidae

Size 11 cm

Voice Noisy when breeding. Longish, squeaky song; contact calls, almost continuous squeaking

Range All over India, S Himalayan foothills upto about 1,800 m; absent in arid W Rajasthan

Habitat Edges of forests; cultivation; gardens; scrub, often in and around habitation

Grey-brown, with some rufous above; long grey tail, tipped black-and-white; white underbody; when breeding, soft grey breast-band diagnostic. Sexes alike. Small bands always on the move; keeps to low growth but often clambers into middle levels; singing male may climb to tops of trees; few nearly always present in mixed hunting parties. Confiding.

JUNGLE PRINIA

Prinia sylvatica Cisticolidae

Size 15 cm

Voice Song a loud, rhythmic *zee…tu…zee…tu*

Range Locally common endemic breeding resident in lowlands and hills throughout most of India and Sri Lanka. Rare in NW India

Habitat Dry scrub and grass, often in rocky areas

Medium to large-sized, plain-looking prinia with long, graduated tail and a long, stout bill. Short supercilium; red iris. Breeding adult has dark grey-brown upperparts and creamy white underparts. Prominent white tips and whitish outer feathers on tail. More rufous-brown in non-breeding plumage. Sexes similar. Short supercilium and voice distinguish it from similar, but smaller, Plain. In pairs, or small parties. Feeds on insects low down but sings from high perch. Secretive but will appear in open briefly. Nests low down. Often seen with other prinias and babblers.

ASHY PRINIA

Prinia socialis Cisticolidae

Size 13 cm

Voice Nasal *pee…pee…pee…* song. Loud and lively *jivee…jivee…jivee…* or *jimmy…jimmy…*, rather like Common Tailorbird's in quality, but easily identifiable once heard

Range Subcontinent south of the Himalayan foothills, upto about 1,400 m; absent in W Rajasthan

Habitat Cultivation; edges of forests; scrubs; parks; vicinity of habitation

Adult has rich, ashy-grey upperparts and rufous wings. Long, graduated, white-tipped tail with black subterminal spots; short, black bill; whitish lores; grey crown. Underparts dull rufous. In winter, less ashy, more rufous-brown; longer tail; whitish chin and throat. Sexes alike. Solitary, or in pairs. Common and familiar as Common Tailorbird in some areas; actively moves in undergrowth; hops on ground foraging for insects. Often flicks and erects tail; typical jerky flight when flying from bush to bush; noisy and excited when breeding. Delivers song from perch on bush. Nests close to ground, on shrubs or tall grass.

PLAIN PRINIA

Prinia inornata Cisticolidae

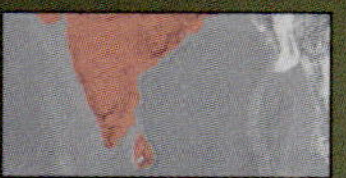

Size 13 cm

Voice Call a plaintive *tee…tee;* also *krrik…krrik* sound. Wheezy song, very insect-like in quality

Range Subcontinent, from Terai and Gangetic plains southwards; absent in W Rajasthan

Habitat Tall cultivation; grass; scrubs; prefers damp areas

Pale brown upperparts; whitish supercilium and lores; dark wings and tail; long, graduated tail, with buff tips and white outer feathers; buff-white underbody; tawny flanks and belly. In winter, more rufous above. Sexes alike. Pairs, or several, move about in low growth; skulker, difficult to see; jerky, low flight, soon vanishing into bush; tail often flicked. Similar to Jungle but smaller and with shorter tail.

COMMON TAILORBIRD

Orthotomus sutorius Cisticolidae

Size 13 cm

Voice Very vocal. Call a loud, familiar *towit…towit.* Song a rapid version of call, with slight change, loud *chuvee…chuvee… chuvee,* uttered for upto seven minutes at a stretch; male sings on exposed perch

Range Subcontinent to about 2,000 m in outer Himalayas

Habitat Forests; cultivation; habitation

breeding

Olive-green above; rust-red forecrown; buffy-white underbody; dark spot on throat sides, best seen in calling male; long, pointed tail, often held erect; central tail feathers about 5 cm longer and pointed in breeding male. Sexes alike. One of India's best-known birds; found usually in pairs; rather common amidst habitation, but keeps to bushes in gardens; remains unseen even when at arm's length, but very vocal; tail often cocked, carried almost to back; clambers up into trees more than other related warblers.

GREY-HEADED BULBUL

Pycnonotus priocephalus Pycnonotidae

Size 19 cm

Voice Calls include *chalk*, a buzzing *dzee* and high *tweep*

Range Locally common endemic breeding resident of forests of SW India from Goa southwards

Habitat Moist broadleaved evergreen forests with bamboo and dense undergrowth

Overall olive-green bulbul with bluish-grey head and pale yellow bill. Grey forehead; yellow wash on grey cheeks; dark greyish-black chin; similar coloured barring on lower back and rump with broad, pale yellow tips; bluish-grey uppertail-coverts and middle tail feathers; outer-tail feathers broadly edged with grey. Underparts more olive-yellow; grey undertail-coverts. Sexes alike. Juvenile has duller yellow on forehead and dark olive head.

BLACK-CRESTED BULBUL

Pycnonotus (melanicterus) flaviventris Pycnonotidae

Size 18 cm

Voice Cheerful whistles; also harsh *cburrr* call; 4- to 8-note song

Range The Himalayas, from Himachal Pradesh eastwards; NE India; foothills to about 2,000 m

Habitat Forests; bamboos; clearings; orchards; forest and dense scrub

Distinctive-looking bird with glossy black head, tall, erect crest and black throat; olive-yellow nape and back, graduating to brown on tail; yellow below throat. Sexes alike. In pairs or small parties, sometimes with other birds; arboreal. Sits conspicuously on open perch and calls. Feeds on fruit and insects.

RED-WHISKERED BULBUL

Pycnonotus jocosus Pycnonotidae

emeria

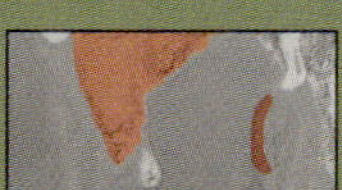

Size 20 cm

Voice Calls include cheerful whistling notes; also harsh, grating alarm notes

Range From Uttarakhand east along the Himalayan foothills to about 1,500 m; most common in south of Satpura mountains in peninsular India; disjunct population in hilly areas of S, SE Rajasthan and N Gujarat

Habitat Forests, clearings, gardens and orchards; vicinity of human habitation

Slim bulbul with prominent, black crest; black crown and nape; black moustachial stripe; prominent white cheeks with red patch behind eye. Mostly dark brown above. Whitish underparts; buff flanks with white tail-tips and underparts; sometimes broken dark, chest-band; long, brown tail, tipped white; red vent. Sexes alike.

fuscicaudatus

YELLOW-THROATED BULBUL

Pycnonotus xantholaemus Pycnonotidae

Size 20 cm

Voice Call a lively *whichit woo… ichit wee…wee*

Range Extremely local endemic breeding resident restricted to few hills in S Andhra Pradesh, E Karnataka and Tamil Nadu

Habitat Rocky, scrub-covered hills

One of India's rarest bulbuls with limited distribution. No crest; greenish-grey upperparts; bright yellow throat, vent and tail tip; yellowish-green head and wing edgings; dark greenish-grey tail; dirty-white breast, washed grey; greyish belly and flanks. Sexes alike. Feeds on fruits, insects; usually in pairs, or small groups. Shy, usually hides in scrub, but sometimes perches in open. Nest not well known.

WHITE-BROWED BULBUL

Pycnonotus luteolus Pycnonotidae

Size 20 cm

Voice Calls include loud, explosive chatter; assortment of bubbling, whistling notes and chuckles

Range Peninsular India, south of line from C Gujarat to S West Bengal; avoids heavy-rainfall hill zones of Western Ghats

Habitat Dry scrub; village habitation; light forests

Sexes alike. Olive plumage, brighter above; whitish forehead and supercilium, explosive calls confirm identity. In pairs, or small parties; not an easy bird to see; skulks in dense, low growth, from where its chattering calls suddenly explode; seen only momentarily when emerges on bush-tops, or flies low from one bush-patch to another; usually does not associate with other birds.

bengalensis

RED-VENTED BULBUL

Pycnonotus cafer Pycnonotidae

Size 20 cm

Voice Cheerful whistling calls; alarm calls on sighting snake, owl or some other intrusion, serving to alert other birds

Range Subcontinent, to about 1,800 m in the Himalayas

Habitat Light forests; gardens; haunts of man

Dark sooty-brown upperparts; pale edges of feathers on back and breast give scaly appearance; glossy, black head, with slight crest; almost black throat; white rump and bright red vent distinctive; dark tail tipped white; brown breast graduated to white belly. Sexes alike. In pairs or small flocks, but large numbers gather to feed; arboreal, keeps to middle levels of trees and bushes; well-known Indian bird, rather attached to human habitation; pleasantly noisy and cheerful, aggressive and quarrelsome; indulges in dust-bathing; also hunts flycatcher-style.

humayuni

YELLOW-BROWED BULBUL

Acritillas indica Pycnonotidae

Size 20 cm

Voice Noisy. Call a fluty *whit… wee* which is extended into song. Also, harsh *churrs*

Range Common endemic breeding resident in Western Ghats and associated hills south from Maharashtra

Habitat Forest and secondary cover

Overall bright olive-green and bright yellow bulbul. Black bill and eyes; yellow face and throat; slightly decurved bill; bright yellow orbital-patch; Upperparts bright olive-green; and underparts bright yellow. Sexes alike. Juvenile duller with rufous in wings. Feeds on berries and invertebrates, often in mixed hunting groups, and usually at middle or lower levels. Lively and not shy. Nests in bushes.

BLACK BULBUL

Hypsipetes leucocephalus Pycnonotidae

Ashy-grey plumage; black, loose-looking crest; coral-red beak and legs diagnostic; whitish below abdomen. Sexes alike. Flocks in forest, often dozens together; strictly arboreal, keeps to topmost branches of tall forest trees, rarely comes down into undergrowth; noisy and restless, hardly staying on trees for few minutes; feeds on berries, fruits, but also hunts insects in flycatcher manner.

white-headed

Size 23 cm

Voice Very noisy. Calls include an assortment of whistles and screeches

Range Several races; resident in the Himalayas and NE India. Southern race *H.l. ganeesa* darker with squared-tail and is found in Western Ghats and Sri Lanka. White-headed races are vagrants to the NE of the region

Habitat Tall forests; hill-station gardens

forked-tailed

squared-tailed

BRISTLED GRASSBIRD

Chaetornis striata Locustellidae

Size 22 cm

Voice Call a soft whistle followed by loud weee…*choo*

Range Globally threatened; endemic breeding resident; very erratically recorded

Habitat Tall, wet, grasslands; reed beds

Large buff-brown warbler, with strong black streaks on upperparts; unmarked underparts; stout blackish bill; no obvious supercilium; indistinct necklace of dark, stiffened feathers on breast; slight streaking on lower throat; prominent rictal bristles; cross-barring on undertail. Similar to Striated, but smaller and less streaked with shorter, graduated tail with pale tips. Sexes alike. Exceptionally furtive. Feeds on invertebrates low in grass.

STRIATED GRASSBIRD

Megalurus palustris Locustellidae

Size 25 cm

Voice Call a metallic, long-drawn whistle, ending in a loud weee…*choo*

Range Locally common to rare resident; NE and C India

Habitat Tall grass; scrubs; reed beds near water

Large warbler with a long, graduated tail and upright posture. Mainly buff upperparts; blackish streaking from crown to rump; some rufous on crown; heavily streaked above; long whitish supercilium; whitish lores; light streaking on whitish-buff underparts; long pale bill and pale legs. In worn plumage, greyer than buff. Sexes alike, but female slightly smaller. Often confused with Striated Babbler. Singly or in pairs. Frequently seen perched on tall grass or reeds. Easier to see during breeding; secretive otherwise. Feeds and nests low down in vegetation, close to ground.

PALE-FOOTED BUSH WARBLER

Cettia pallidipes Cettiidae

Size 11 cm

Voice Call a series of sharp chirps. Song a loud, explosive *zip…zip…tschuk…o…tschuk*

Range Resident, altitudinal migrant in the lower Himalayas, NE India and S Andaman Islands

Habitat Tall grass and bushes on forest edges

Small, plain-looking bush warbler with short tail; large, rounded head; olivish-brown forehead, crown and nape; whitish supercilium; white chin, throat and middle belly and undertail-coverts; brown tail with indistinct greenish-brown fringe. Distinguished from Brown-flanked by smaller size, paler underparts; brownish-olive breast sides and flanks; more rufescent upperparts; shorter, square-ended tail; pale pinkish legs and feet. The Andaman race *osmastoni* has a bigger bill, with richer brown upperparts.

GRASSHOPPER WARBLER

Locustella naevia Locustellidae

Size 13 cm

Voice Call a sharp *pstt*. Song a rhythmic, insect-like churring. Unlikely to be heard in our region

Range Widespread and much overlooked winter visitor throughout region; most regularly seen in SW India

Habitat Damp grasslands; reed beds and paddy fields

Uniformly olive-brown warbler with short rounded wings. Upperparts streaked darker; head rather plain; whitish or yellowish underparts usually unstreaked; olive-brown crown and mantle; hint of pale supercilium; undertail-coverts long and streaked; long, graduated and rounded tail; pink legs. Sexes alike. Creeps low down feeding on insects. Reluctant flier. Rarely seen unless flushed, then flies low into cover. Crepuscular.

THICK-BILLED WARBLER

Phragamaticola aedon Acrocephalidae

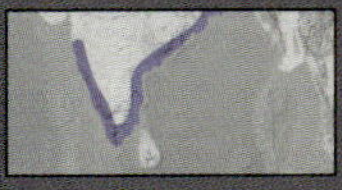

Size 18 cm

Voice Calls include loud *tschack* and *chack*

Range Scarce and local winter visitor mainly to plains of S Nepal, NE, S India, Bangladesh

Habitat All types of low scrubs and grass often, but not exclusively, in wetlands

Large grey-brown warbler. Unstreaked, brown upperparts; buff underparts; short, heavy, pointed bill; small, black eyes; plain face with pale lores and supercilium; rusty rump; long, rounded and graduated tail; short wings. Juvenile a richer buff. Sexes alike. Feeds on invertebrates low down in vegetation, hopping through in a crouched, rather babbler-like fashion with tail held low. Secretive and usually singly.

CLAMOROUS REED WARBLER

Acrocephalus stentoreus Acrocephalidae

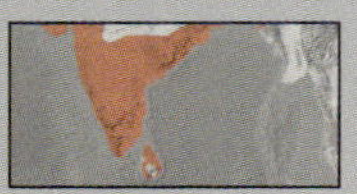

Size 19 cm

Voice Highly vocal. Calls include loud *chack*, *chakrrr* and *khe* notes; distinctive, loud warbling. Loud, lively song

Range From Kashmir valley, south through country; sporadically breeds in many areas, migrant in others

Habitat Reed beds; mangroves

Upperparts plain uniform brown; distinct pale supercilium; whitish throat, dull buffy-white below; short, rounded wings; at close range, salmon-coloured inside of mouth can be seen; call diagnostic. Sexes alike. Solitary or in pairs; difficult to see but easily heard; keeps low in dense reeds, mangrove and low growth, always around water; does not associate with other species; flies low, immediately vanishes into the vegetation; occasionally emerges on reed or bush-tops, warbling with throat puffed out.

PADDYFIELD WARBLER

Acrocephalus agricola Acrocephalidae

Size 13 cm

Voice Call a rather harsh *chrr... chuck* or single *chack* note

Range Winter visitor; common over most of India, south of and including the Terai

Habitat Damp areas; reed beds; tall cultivation

Medium-sized warbler with rufescent-brown upperparts; brighter on rump; whitish throat and belly; rich buff underparts; short, rounded wings; darker tertials with darker centres and pale edges; short, stubby bill; long cream-coloured supercilium. Sexes alike. Solitary, hopping amidst low growth; rarely seen along with other birds; damp areas, especially reed growth and cultivation are favourite haunts; flies low, but soon vanishes into growth.

BLYTH'S REED WARBLER

Acrocephalus dumetorum Acrocephalidae

Size 13 cm

Voice Call a loud quick *tchik...* or *tchi...* Rarely, a warbling song

Range Common winter visitor to plains of S India, Bangladesh, NE India. Common passage migrant in N India

Habitat Well-wooded, often quite dry country

Medium-sized warbler with olive, brown-and-grey upperparts and whitish underparts with greyish flanks; long sloping forehead; longish bill; grey legs. Sexes alike. Juvenile more rust above. Feeds on invertebrates at all levels, including canopies, bushes and ground. Rarely in reed beds. Flicks wings and fans tail. Usually singly or in loose groups.

BOOTED WARBLER

Iduna caligata Acrocephalidae

Size 13.5 cm

Voice Call a strong, but low *chak…chak…churrr*

Range Winters over peninsula, south from Punjab to West Bengal

Habitat Open country with acacias and scrub; occasionally light forests

Very small warbler with dull olive-brown upperparts; short, pale white supercilium; pale buffy-white below. Dark toes give it a 'booted' look, hence its name. Confused with Blyth's Reed which is brighter olive-brown and mostly frequents bushes. Sexes alike. Solitary or two to four birds, sometimes in mixed bands of small birds; very active and agile; hunts amongst leaves and upper branches; overall behaviour very Leaf Warbler-like, but calls diagnostic.

COMMON CHIFFCHAFF

Phylloscopus collybita Phylloscopidae

Size 11 cm

Voice Mostly silent but sometimes utters a soft *wheep, zit* or *peeu*

Range Common winter visitor throughout N plains

Habitat All types of wooded country, preferably near water; reed beds and crops

Small, plain dull greyish-brown warbler often with olive wash. Creamish throat, breast and belly; dark eye-stripe; short, whitish supercilium; short rounded wings; long, square-ended tail; tail and flight feathers more brownish, edged olive-yellow; black bill and legs. Sometimes shows very slight wing-bars and, more often, yellow at shoulder. Sexes alike. Feeds actively at all levels foraging in foliage for insects. Approachable and easy to observe.

DUSKY WARBLER

Phylloscopus fuscatus Phylloscopidae

Size 11 cm

Voice Call a strong *chock…chock*

Range Winter visitor; Himalayan foothills; NE India and Bangladesh

Habitat Bushes; long grass

Upperparts, wings and tail vary between dark and pale brownish-grey; whitish underparts with touches of buff on breast sides and flanks; slender, dark legs; broad, dark eye-stripe; whitish-grey eye-ring; greyish lores. Sexes alike. Northeast wintering *P. f weigoldi* darker above, and duskier below, and with touch of yellow on underparts in fresh plumage. Skulking; keeps low in undergrowth, often on ground.

TICKELL'S LEAF WARBLER

Phylloscopus affinis Phylloscopidae

Size 11 cm

Voice Call a strong *chip* or *tsip*

Range Not uncommon breeding summer visitor to N mountains. Winters mainly in Bangladesh, hills of NE and SW India

Habitat Summers in montane scrub. Winters in edges of forests, scrubs and gardens

Small roundish warbler with dark olive-green upperparts; underparts yellow, graduating to buff on sides; no wing-bar; distinct yellow supercilium extends behind crown; pale yellow eye-ring; chin, throat and belly paler buff-yellow; prominent dark eye-stripe; pale legs and lower mandible; long wings; slightly forked tail. Sexes alike. Feeds on invertebrates, close to the ground; flits through the foliage singly or in small parties. Confiding and conspicuous. Nests close to ground.

SULPHUR-BELLIED WARBLER

Phylloscopus griseolus Phylloscopidae

Size 11 cm

Voice Call a soft *dip* or *pik*

Range Locally common breeding summer visitor mainly to N and C India in plains

Habitat Rocky areas with scrubs and scattered trees. Winters in old ruins and open woodland

Small, dark, rotund warbler with prominent bright yellow supercilium that is orangish towards crown; upperparts dark brownish-grey; no wing-bars; underparts pale yellow, with pale green wash, turning olivish towards rump; thin, pale legs; longish wings; short tail. Sexes alike. Sulphur-bellied not as dark above as Smoky or Dusky. Characteristically forages between rocks and tree trunks in wren-like manner for invertebrates, on or close to ground. Singly, or in pairs. Confiding but unobtrusive. Nests in low vegetation.

HUME'S LEAF WARBLER

Phylloscopus humei Phylloscopidae

Size 10-11 cm

Voice Calls include disyllabic *whit-hoot* and sparrow-like *chwee*. Song a repeated *wesoo*, often followed by descending high-pitched *zweeeeeeeoooo*

Range Breeds in the Himalayas. Winters in plains

Habitat Breeds in subalpine forests. Winters in forest and secondary growth

Small, fairly bright warbler. Overall greyish-olive upperparts; yellowish-green mantle and back; brownish crown; indistinct beige supercilium, beige ear-coverts; greyish-green lores and eye-stripe; creamish underparts; short, rounded wings; dark brown tail with greenish edges; poorly-defined median-covert bar but two wing-bars much more obvious; greater-covert wing-bars buffish-white; dark bill and legs. Colours brighter when fresh, duller when worn. Very similar to Yellow-browed, but paler grey above. Singly, or in pairs but often found in mixed feeding parties outside breeding season. Very shy. Arboreal. Feeds in canopy at all levels.

LARGE-BILLED LEAF WARBLER

Phylloscopus magnirostris Phylloscopidae

Size 13 cm

Voice Call a distinctive *dir…tee*, the first note slightly lower. Loud, ringing song

Range Breeds in the Himalayas. Spends winters over most of the peninsula, though exact range uncertain

Habitat Forests; groves

Medium-sized, brightly-coloured leaf warbler. Upperparts brown-olive; greenish-grey wash on breast sides and flanks; yellowish supercilium, dark eye-stripe distinctive; one or two faint wing-bars, not always easily seen. Underparts dull-yellow below. Sexes alike. Usually solitary, sometimes in mixed parties of small birds; quite active; spends most time in leafy upper branches of medium-sized trees; not easy to sight, but characteristic call notes help in confirming presence.

TYTLER'S LEAF WARBLER

Phylloscopus tytleri Phylloscopidae

Size 10 cm

Voice Call a long *sooeeet*; also a harsh *huweest*

Range Rare endemic breeding summer visitor restricted to N Pakistan and Kashmir. Winters mainly in Western Ghats; passage records elsewhere

Habitat Forest undergrowth; coniferous forests

Slim, small warbler with plain, unmarked upperparts; a long, thin black bill. Underparts whitish, sometimes with pale yellow wash; long, whitish supercilium; dusky cheeks; short tail; flanks olive-tinged; dark lores and eye-stripe; mottled cheeks and ear-coverts; dark legs. Sexes alike. Arboreal. Feeds very actively on invertebrates on leaves and stems and sometimes flycatches. Not confiding, but difficult to see. Nests in trees. Winter habits little known.

WESTERN CROWNED WARBLER

Phylloscopus occipitalis Phylloscopidae

Size 11 cm

Voice Mostly silent. Though sometimes *chit…weei*

Range Summer breeding visitor to N hills upto E Uttarakhand. Winters mainly in Eastern and Western Ghats. Scattered records elsewhere and more widespread in India on passage

Habitat Forests

Stocky warbler with pale central crown-stripe, pale lower mandibles and dark legs. Upperparts greyish-green, with more green on wings and tail; two yellowish wing-bars on each wing; striking yellowish supercilium; underparts white. Sexes alike. Feeds on invertebrates actively in canopy and also in shrub layers. Seen in small parties and mixed hunting groups. Alternately flicks wings half-open. Confiding. Nests low down.

GREENISH WARBLER

Phylloscopus trochiloides Phylloscopidae

Size 11 cm

Voice Call a loud *tis...lee*

Range Breeding resident in the Himalayas. Winters widely in penisular lowlands and Sri Lanka. Common passage migrant elsewhere

Habitat All types of wooded country, including gardens

Dull greenish-brown bird with cream underparts. Medium-sized; slim; prominent, long, sweeping supercilium; whitish eye-ring; broad eye-stripe; mottled ear-coverts; strong patterning on head; one wing usually visible; brown legs. Sexes alike. Arboreal. Feeds on invertebrates, mainly in the canopy but also lower down. Active and restless. Frequently flycatches. Usually in scattered parties or mixed hunting groups. Nests low down.

GREEN-CROWNED WARBLER

Seicercus burkii Phylloscopidae

Size 11 cm

Voice Fairly noisy. Calls include sharp *chip...chip* or *cheup... cheup* notes

Range Breeds in the Himalayas. Winters in foothills, parts of C and E peninsula, N Maharashtra, S Madhya Pradesh, NE Andhra Pradesh

Habitat Forest undergrowth

Brightly-coloured warbler with a distinctive yellow eye-ring. Olive-green upperparts; greenish or grey-green eyebrow bordered above with prominent black coronal bands; greyish-green nape and crown; greenish sides of face; completely yellow below; greyish-brown wing-coverts edged with green; orange lower mandible; brownish-yellow legs. Sexes alike. Small, restless flocks, often in association with other small birds; keeps to low bushes and lower branches of trees.

ORPHEAN WARBLER

Sylvia hortensis Sylviidae

Size 15 cm

Voice Loud warbling song

Range Summer visitor to Pakistan. Winters mainly in India

Habitat Bush-covered hills; winters in scrub, orchards and groves

Medium-sized, dull-coloured warbler with strong markings. Large dark grey head; upperparts mostly grey; pale grey mantle; blackish crown; dark forehead, forecrown and even darker ear-coverts; underparts whitish, tinged pink; dark uppertail with greyish centres; blackish tail with pale fringes to undertail-coverts; long, pointed wings; square-ended tail; pale iris and dark legs. Female overall more brown with a dark brown head; underparts tinged buff rather than pink and more creamy-brown, speckled iris. Mostly singly or in pairs. Very confiding and mostly hidden in thick cover in breeding season. Seen calling from bush-tops or shrubs.

LESSER WHITETHROAT

Sylvia curruca Sylviidac

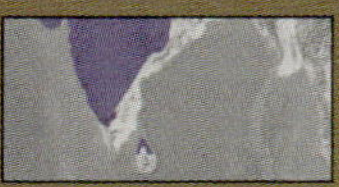

Size 13 cm

Voice Noisy. Call a clicking *tek*; also churrs. Song a flourished rattle

Range Common winter visitor to Pakistan, W peninsula and N India; south to N Tamil Nadu and N Sri Lanka. Absent or rare from most of E and NE India, Bangladesh

Habitat Open woodlands; scrubs

Dull ash-brown warbler with dark cheek-patches; grey head; brown mantle and wings; short brown tail with white outer-tail feathers; underparts creamy-white; throat white; grey breast and belly; brownish flanks. Recently split Desert Whitethroat is smaller and paler. Often in loose groups. Horizontal carriage. Confident direct flight. Rather shy. Feeds on insects and nectar, usually high in trees but also in bushes.

PUFF-THROATED BABBLER

Pellorneum ruficeps Timaliidae

Size 15 cm

Voice Best-known call a 4-noted whistle, interpreted as *he...will... beat...you.* Noisy when breeding; mellow whistle, 2, 3, or 4-noted

Range Hilly-forest areas; the Himalayas, to about 1,500 m, east of SE Himachal Pradesh; NE states; S Bihar, Odisha, Satpura Range across C India, Eastern and Western Ghats

Habitat Forest undergrowth; bamboos; overgrown ravines; nullahs

Small bird with olive-brown upperparts; dark rufous cap; whitish-buff stripe over eye; white throat; dull fulvous-white underbody, boldly streaked blackish-brown on breast and sides. Sexes alike. Solitary, or in pairs; shy, secretive bird of undergrowth; mostly heard, extremely difficult to see; rummages on ground, amidst leaf litter; hops about, rarely ascends into upper branches.

ruficeps

mandellii

ABBOTT'S BABBLER

Malacocincla abbotti Timaliidae

Size 17 cm

Voice Calls include trills, churrs, mews. Whistled song *tchwee… tchu…tchwee*; occasionally, duets

Range Nepal, Bhutan, Assam and Arunachal Pradesh

Habitat Thick undergrowth in moist broadleaved evergreen forests; thickets; streams; tree ferns

Plain, drab, brownish babbler with short tail, thick bill, stocky appearance; light-grey supercilium and lores; greyish or greyish-white throat and breast; olive-brown above; unmarked throat and breast; rufous breast sides; olive-brown flanks; rufous tail, uppertail-coverts; brighter rufous vent and undertail-coverts. Solitary, or in pairs; territorial and site-loyal; terrestrial; forages on or near ground; shy and secretive; stays close to dense cover; rarely flies. Juvenile has dark rufescent-brown crown and upperparts.

INDIAN SCIMITAR BABBLER

Pomatorhinus horsfieldii Timaliidae

Size 22 cm

Voice Fluty, musical whistle, often followed by bubbling note; often calls in duet

Range Hilly forest regions of peninsular India, with four races

Habitat Mixed forests; scrub; bamboos

Deep olive-brown above; long, white supercilium; broad, black band through eye; white throat, breast and belly centre; diagnostic long, curved yellow 'scimitar' beak with blackish base to upper mandible. Tail long, broad and graduated; short, rounded wings. Sexes alike. Juvenile overall darker, lacks black lateral crown-stripes and has paler bill. In pairs, or small, loose bands in forests; keeps to undergrowth, more often heard than seen. Hops on jungle floors, vigorously rummages through leaf litter, digs with long beak; hops into leafy branches, but not for long; scattered birds keep in touch through calls. Rarely seen flying in open.

RUFOUS-FRONTED BABBLER

Stachyridopsis rufifrons Timaliidae

Size 12 cm

Voice Same as Rufous-capped's

Range E Nepal to Myanmar

Habitat Undergrowth in moist broadleaved evergreen forests; secondary growth; bamboos

Often confused with the very similar Rufous-capped. Has white throat, streaked faintly with black. Grey supercilium a good distinguishing feature.

TAWNY-BELLIED BABBLER

Dumetia hyperythra Timaliidae

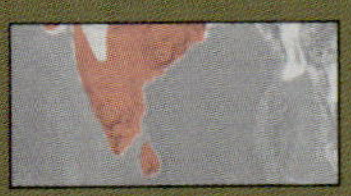

Size 13 cm

Voice Calls include faint *cheep… cheep* contact notes; also, mix of other whistling and chattering notes

Range From SE Himachal Pradesh, east along foothills into peninsular India; absent in arid NW, Punjab plains, extreme NE states

Habitat Scrubs and bamboos, in and around forests

Olivish-brown above; front part of crown reddish-brown; white throat in western and southern races; nominate race has underbody entirely fulvous. Sexes alike. Small, noisy parties in undergrowth; rummages on floor, hopping about, always wary; hardly associates with other birds; great skulkers, difficult to see; any sign of danger and flock disperses amidst noisy chorus of alarm notes but soon reunites.

PIN-STRIPED TIT BABBLER

Macronous gularis Timaliidae

Size 11 cm

Voice Very noisy. Call a loud, regular and repeated barbet-like *chunk… chunk…chunk*. Also, *chrrr*

Range Common breeding resident in N foothills from Uttarakhand east through Nepal to Arunachal Pradesh, NE India and Eastern Ghats

Habitat Forest undergrowth and bamboos, often feeding fairly high but also on ground

Small, brownish babbler; underparts yellow-brown, streaked finely with black; rusty-brown crown; pale yellow lores; plain, rufous-brown wings and tail; mantle more olive; yellowish supercilium; pale iris; dark eye-stripe. Sexes alike. Feeds on invertebrates; in pairs or small parties, often in mixed flocks. Active but furtive, creeping on ground. Nests in undergrowth.

DARK-FRONTED BABBLER

Rhopocichla atriceps Timaliidae

Smallish, rich rufous-brown babbler with black head. Creamy-white breast, throat and belly. Yellow eyes. Square-tipped tail. The typical form with black head is found along Western Ghats from Belgaum to Nilgiris, being replaced in Cochin and Travancore Hills by another race *R. a. bourdilloni* which has the black largely replaced by sooty-brown. A third race *R. a. nigrifrons* is found in Ceylon. Has top of head the same colour as back and black confined to broad band through each eye joining across forehead. All three races occur from sea-level upto 6,000 feet and strictly resident.

Size 13 cm

Voice Calls include unobtrusive *tup*, scolding *churr* and plaintive nasal *mewing*. Also loud, throaty grating

Range Endemic to the subcontinent. Western Ghats in Goa, Karnataka, Kerala, W Tamil Nadu

Habitat Evergreen biotope in dense undergrowth, thickets near streams, reed beds, bamboos, and cardamom cultivation

nigrifons

atriceps

YELLOW-EYED BABBLER

Chrysomma sinense Timaliidae

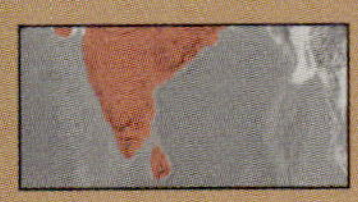

Size 18 cm

Voice Call a mournful *cheep… cheep*. Noisy when breeding (mostly monsoons); melodious, whistling notes

Range Subcontinent, from the Himalayan foothills south; absent in arid parts of Rajasthan

Habitat Scrub; tall grass; cultivation; edges of forests

Sexes alike. Rufous-brown above; whitish lores, short supercilium; yellow iris and orange-yellow eye-rim distinctive at close range; cinnamon wings; long, graduated tail; white below, tinged pale-fulvous on flanks and abdomen. In pairs, or small bands in tall grass and undergrowth; noisy but skulking, suddenly clambers into view for few seconds, before vanishing once again; works its way along stems and leaves, hunts insects; short, jerky flight.

COMMON BABBLER

Turdoides caudata Timaliidae

Size 22 cm

Voice Noisy. Calls include pleasant, warbling whistles, often in chorus; squeaky alarm notes. Calls on ground and in low flight

Range Most of N, NW, W and peninsular India, south of outer Himalayas to about 2,000 m; east to West Bengal

Habitat Thorn scrub; open cultivation; grass

Dull brown above, profusely streaked; brown wings; olivish-brown tail, long and graduated, cross-rayed darker; dull white throat; pale fulvous underbody, streaked on breast sides. Sexes alike. Pairs, or small bands in open scrub; skulker, working its way low in bushes or on ground; moves with peculiar bouncing hop on ground, its long, loose-looking tail cocked up; extremely wary, vanishes into scrubs at slightest alarm; weak flight, evident when flock moves from one scrub patch to another, in ones and twos.

LARGE GREY BABBLER

Turdoides malcolmi Timaliidae

Size 28 cm

Voice Very noisy. Calls include a chorus of squeaking chatter, short alarm note

Range From around E Uttar Pradesh, south through most of peninsula; east to Bihar; abundant in the Deccan

Habitat Scrubs; open country; gardens; vicinity of habitation

Upperparts ash-brown; dark centres to feathers on back give streaked look; greyer forehead; long graduated tail cross-rayed with white outer feathers, conspicuous in flight; fulvous-grey below. Sexes alike. Gregarious; flocks in open country, sometimes seen in dozens; extremely noisy; moves on ground and in medium-sized trees; hops about, turning over leaves on ground; weak flight, never for long; at any sign of danger, flock comes together.

RUFOUS BABBLER

Turdoides subrufa Timaliidae

Size 25 cm

Voice Calls include high-pitched shrill, sometimes frenzied squabbling or scolding squeaks

Range Endemic to SW India from C Maharashtra south throughout Western Ghats and east to NC Tamil Nadu

Habitat Thick cover, edges of forest clearings and plantations in broadleaved evergreen, moist deciduous biotope; favours habitats intermixed with tall grass and bamboos

Largish chestnut-brown, unstreaked babbler with rufous underparts. Light grey forehead and forecrown; dark lores; white eyes; upper breast and belly lighter rufous. Black upper mandible and yellow lower mandible. Some show no grey on forehead or forecrown. Juvenile has dark grey iris.

JUNGLE BABBLER

Turdoides striata Timaliidae

Size 25 cm

Voice Very noisy. Calls include harsh *ke…ke…ke* and hysterical chattering and squeaking in chorus

Range Common endemic breeding resident throughout lowlands and foothills except parts of NE India and Sri Lanka

Habitat Open woodlands; scrub; cultivation; gardens; villages

Overall grey-brown babbler. Light-brown head; whitish iris; stout, yellow bill; short, dark eyebrow; pale lores; dark brown tail. Underparts paler with some greyish streaking on breast. Western race *somervillei* may be separate species, with chestnut tail and dark brown primaries. Extremely noisy. Feeds in groups on insects and seeds, mainly on ground. Confiding and inquisitive. Breeds throughout the year. Nests in bushes.

somervillei

orientalis

sindiana

YELLOW-BILLED BABBLER

Turdoides affinis Timaliidae

Size 23 cm

Voice Noisy. More musical chatter than the more common Jungle

Range S peninsular India; Karnataka, Andhra Pradesh, Tamil Nadu, Kerala; also Sri Lanka

Habitat Forests; dense growth; neighbourhood of cultivation and habitation; orchards

Rather drab-looking babbler with creamy-white crown; dull brown above, appearing scaly on centre of back; darker wings; ash-brown ear-coverts; cross-barring along tail centre; dark brown throat and breast. Pale blue-grey eyes; pale grey edges to feathers give scaled appearance; yellowish-buff below breast. Sexes alike. In small noisy parties; feeds on ground, turning leaves; if disturbed, moves about in series of short, hopping flights; hops amongst tree branches towards the top, from where travels to adjoining tree after short flight. Similar to Jungle, but has more white on lores, forehead and crown.

WYNAAD LAUGHINGTHRUSH

Garrrulax delesserti Timaliidae

Size 23 cm

Voice Calls include particularly frenzied, discordant series of screeches, squeals and cracked rattles from flock

Range Endemic to Western Ghats, from N Karnataka south to S Kerala and east to W Tamil Nadu

Habitat Humid broadleaved evergreen forests; also cardamom *sholas*; favours patches of dense Strobilanthes undergrowth

Large, ash-brown laughingthrush. Crown and nape lighter grey; black mask; chestnut wing-coverts and back, white throat, greyish breast, blackish tail. Diagnostic yellowish-pink lower mandible. Breast light grey-brown; rufous-wash on belly and darker rufous vent. Skulking. Seen in flocks.

BLACK-CHINNED LAUGHINGTHRUSH

Garrrulax cachinnans Timaliidae

Size 20 cm

Voice Very noisy. Calls include squealing 'laughter' often in chorus; *pee…ko…ko and kee…kee…kee*

Range Globally threatened. Very local but, in places, common endemic breeding resident in Nilgiri Hills of W Tamil Nadu and nearby parts of Kerala

Habitat Forest undergrowth, secondary growth and gardens

Medium-sized, plain, dark brown babbler. Distinctive white feathery eyebrows; dark grey crown; black chin and forehead; broad eye-stripe. Underparts rusty-ochre. Sexes alike. Small parties feed mainly on invertebrates on ground under cover.

jerdoni

cachinnans

BROWN-CHEEKED FULVETTA

Alcippe poioicephala Timaliidae

Size 15 cm

Voice Best-known call 4- to 8-syllabled, interpreted as *daddy...give...me...chocolate*; harsh *churrr* notes serve as contact calls

Range Peninsular India, south from S Rajasthan across Pachmarhi (Satpura) to S Bihar and Odisha

Habitat Forests, undergrowth, bamboos; also hill-station gardens in Western Ghats

Sexes alike. Olive-brown above; grey crown and nape distinctive; thin black stripe through eye; rufescent-brown wings and tail; dull fulvous underbody. In pairs or small parties, often along with other birds; moves actively in undergrowth and leafy branches, clinging sideways or springing from perch; rather shy in most areas, but occasionally emerges into open areas.

ORIENTAL WHITE-EYE

Zosterops palpebrosus Zosteropidae

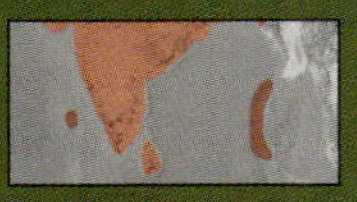

Size 10 cm

Voice Calls include soft, plaintive *tsee* and *tseer* notes. Short jingling song

Range All over India, from the Himalayan foothills to 2,000 m; absent in arid parts of W Rajasthan

Habitat Forests; gardens; groves; secondary growth

Sexes alike. Olive-yellow above; short, blackish stripe through eye; white eye-ring distinctive; bright yellow throat and undertail; whitish breast and belly. Small parties, occasionally upto 40 birds, either by themselves or in association with other small birds; keeps to foliage and bushes; actively moves amongst leafy branches, clinging sideways and upside-down; checks through leaves and sprigs for insects and also spends considerable time at flowers; calls often, both when in branches and when flying in small bands from tree to tree.

ASIAN FAIRY BLUEBIRD

Irena puella Irenidae

Size 25 cm

Voice Common call a 2-noted *wit…weet…*; also a *whi…chu*; besides, some harsh notes, occasionally heard

Range Disjunct distribution; one population in Western Ghats and associated hills south of Ratnagiri; another in E Himalayas, east of extreme SE Nepal; Uttarakhand foothills; Andaman and Nicobar Islands

Habitat Dense, evergreen forests; *sholas*

Male glistening blue above; deep velvet-black sides of face, underbody and wings; blue undertail-coverts. Female has verditer-blue plumage; dull black lores and flight feathers. In pairs, or small, loose bands; spends day in leafy tall branches; often descends into undergrowth to feed on berries or hunt insects; utters 2-noted calls while flitting amongst trees; seen along with other birds.

♀

CHESTNUT-BELLIED NUTHATCH

Sitta castanea Sittidae

Size 12 cm

Voice Calls include loud *tzsib...*; faint twitter; loud whistle during breeding season

Range Lower Himalayas east of Uttarakhand; to about 1,800 m. Also in hills of peninsular India (race *cinnamoventris*.)

Habitat Forests; groves; roadside trees; habitation

Male blue-grey above; black stripe from lores to nape; whitish cheeks and upper throat; all but central tail feathers black, with white markings; chestnut below. Female duller chestnut below. In pairs or several, often with other small birds; restless climber; clings to bark and usually works up the tree stem, hammering with beak; also moves upside-down and sideways; may visit the ground.

♀

VELVET-FRONTED NUTHATCH

Sitta frontalis Sittidae

Small nuthatch. Male has violet-blue upperparts; jet-black forehead; stripe through eye; white chin and throat, merging into vinous-grey below; coral-red beak. Underparts variable from beige to pinkish-buff. Female lacks black stripe through eye. In pairs, or several in mixed hunting parties; creeps about on stems and branches; fond of moss-covered trees; also clings upside-down; active and agile, quickly moving from tree to tree; calls often, till long after sunset; also checks fallen logs and felled branches.

Size 10 cm

Voice Calls include fairly loud, rapidly repeated, sharp, trilling *chweet…chwit…chwit* whistles

Range From around W Uttarakhand east along lower Himalayas; widespread over hilly, forested areas of C, S and E India; absent in flat and arid regions

Habitat Forests; also tea and coffee plantations

SPOTTED CREEPER

Salpornis spilonotus Certhiidae

Size 13 cm

Voice Calls include thin see… ee and deep *kek…kek…kek*. Whistling song

Range Strangely rare and very local breeding resident in N peninsula from Haryana, Uttar Pradesh and Bihar south to Maharashtra and Andhra Pradesh. Also occurs in Africa, where very local

Habitat Open woodlands and groves, favouring trees with deep-fissured bark such as mangoes and babul

Plump, brown and buff bird with long, curved bill. Broad, white supercilium; dark wings; short, squarish tail, broadly-barred white. Upperparts streaked black-and-white; white throat, fulvous breast, barred and mottled brown. Sexes alike. Feeds usually singly, on invertebrates in bark at all levels in trees. Climbs rapidly up and under tree trunks and branches, often fluttering down to change position. Does not spiral. Nest made of leaves, bark and lichen, usually in branch fork.

LESSER HILL MYNA

Gracula (religiosa) indica Sturnidae

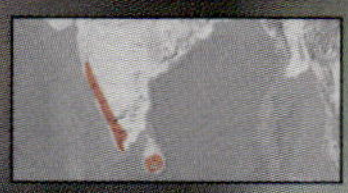

Size 24 cm

Voice Similar to Common Hill's

Range Western Ghats; Sri Lanka

Habitat Moist forests; plantations

Compared with Common, has smaller and finer bill; eye wattles distinctly separated from those on nape (wattles on nape extend upto sides of crown). Bill finer than Sri Lanka Hill, but has no blue at base; wattles on sides of head. Dark eyes, often white in Sri Lanka Hill.

JUNGLE MYNA

Acridotheres fuscus Sturnidae

Size 23 cm

Voice Similar to Common's, but higher, more liquid

Range Hills of Pakistan to Arunachal Pradesh

Habitat Edges of forests; wooded areas near cultivation and settlements; plantations; scrubs

Ash-brown myna with small crest at base of bill. Black head; no orbital-patch; chin, throat and breast slaty-grey graduating to buffish-white belly; dark blue base to yellow-orange bill; yellow legs and bill; white wing-patch and white-tipped tail. Superficially similar to Common and Bank, but distinguished by greyer colour, darker cap not as defined; pale yellow eye, rather than red of Bank; also, white wing-patch and tail-tip; gregarious; in pairs, or small groups; larger flocks when not breeding; shyer, less confiding than Common, and less associated with humans; more arboreal. *Mahrattensis* is found in peninsular India while the nominate *fuscus* is found in N and NE India.

mahrattensis

fuscus

COMMON MYNA

Acridotheres tristis Sturnidae

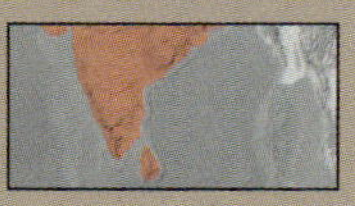

Size 23 cm

Voice Noisy. Calls include a great mix of chattering notes. One of India's most familiar bird sounds

Range Subcontinent, upto about 3,500 m in the Himalayas

Habitat Human habitation; cultivation; light forests

Medium-sized bird with rich vinous-brown plumage; black head, neck and upper breast; yellow beak, legs and naked wattle around eyes distinctive; large white spot in dark brown flight feathers, best visible in flight; blackish tail, with broad, white tips to all but central feathers; whitish abdomen. Sexes alike. Seen in solitary, or in scattered pairs or small, loose bands. India's most common and familiar bird; hardly ever strays far from human habitation; rather haughty and confident in looks; aggressive, curious and noisy; struts about on ground, picks out worms; attends to grazing cattle and refuse dumps; enters verandahs and kitchens, sometimes even helping itself on dining tables.

juvenile

BANK MYNA

Acridotheres ginginianus Sturnidae

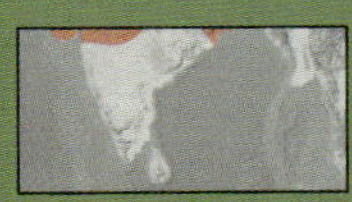

Size 21 cm

Voice Similar to Common's but softer

Range Widespread resident in N and C India

Habitat Human habitation; cultivation; grasslands

Similar to Common but smaller; has bluish-grey neck, mantle and underparts; black head with orange-red wattle around eye; orange-yellow bill, legs and feet yellow; black wings; buff-orange tail-tips and wing-patch; grey flanks have cinnamon-brown tinge. Sexes alike. Usually observed in small, scattered groups around human habitation; bold and confiding; often seen along roadside restaurants picking out scraps.

CHESTNUT-TAILED STARLING

Sturnia malabarica Sturnidae

Size 21 cm

Voice Noisy. Metallic, whistling call, becoming a chatter when in flock. Warbling song when breeding

Range India, roughly east and south from S Rajasthan to around W Uttarakhand; upto about 1,800 m in the Himalayan foothills

Habitat Light forests; open country; gardens

Slim bird with silvery-grey upperparts, with faint brownish wash. Dull rufous till breast; brighter below; black-and-grey in wings. Sexes alike. Juvenile more greyish-brown. Sociable; noisy parties in upper branches of trees, frequently along with other birds; incessantly squabbles and moves about, indulging in all manners of acrobatic positions to obtain nectar or reach out to fruits; descends to ground to pick up insects.

ASIAN PIED STARLING

Gracupica contra Sturnidae

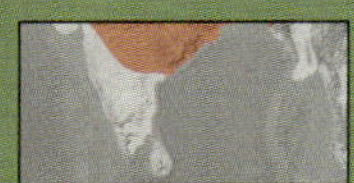

Size 23 cm

Voice Noisy. Calls include a mix of pleasant whistling and screaming notes

Range NC, C and E India, south and east of line roughly from E Punjab, through E Rajasthan, W Madhya Pradesh to Krishna Delta; escaped cage birds have established themselves in several areas out of original range in and around Mumbai

Habitat Open cultivation; orchards; vicinity of habitation

Sexes alike. Black-and-white (pied) plumage distinctive; orange-red beak and orbital skin in front of eyes confirm identity. Sociable; small parties either move on their own or associate with other birds, notably other mynas and drongos; rather common and familiar over its range but keeps distance from human; may make its ungainly nest in garden trees, but never inside houses, nor does it enter houses; bird of open, cultivated areas, preferably where water; attends to grazing cattle; occasionally raids standing crops.

juvenile

BRAHMINY STARLING

Sturnia pagodarum Sturnidae

Size 20 cm

Voice Quite noisy. Calls include a pleasant mix of chirping notes and whistles, sounds as conversational chatter. Good mimic. Pleasant warbling song of breeding male

Range Subcontinent, to about 2,000 m in W and C Himalayas

Habitat Light forests; gardens; cultivation; vicinity of habitation

Grey, black-and-rufous myna; black crown, nape and forehead, extending to long, black crest; grey back; rich buff sides of head, neck and underbody; black wings and brown tail with white sides and tip distinctive in flight. Sexes similar. Female has slightly smaller crest. Seen in small parties, occasionally collecting into flocks of 20 birds; associates with other birds on flowering trees or on open lands; walks typical myna-style, head held straight up, confident in looks; roosts communally, with other birds.

juvenile

ROSY STARLING

Pastor roseus Sturnidae

Size 22 cm

Voice Extremely noisy. Calls include a mix of guttural screams, chattering sounds and melodious whistles

Range Winter visitor to India, most common in W and S India and Sri Lanka. Mainly passage migrant in N India. Arrives end of July and departs mid April to early May

Habitat Open areas; cultivation; orchards; flowering trees amidst habitation

Medium-sized starling with rose-pink and black plumage; glossy black head, crest, neck, throat, upper breast, wings and tail; rest of plumage rose-pink, turns brighter with approach of spring migration. Gregarious; flocks often contain juveniles, crestless, dull brown and sooty; often along with other mynas on flowering Erythrina and Bombax trees; causes enormous damage to standing crops; seen also around grazing cattle and damp, open lands; overall aggressive; in huge roosting colonies, resulting in deafening clamour before settling.

juvenile

COMMON STARLING

Sturnus vulgaris Sturnidae

Size 20 cm

Voice Mix of squeaking, clicking notes; other chuckling calls

Range The race *indicus* breeds in Kashmir to about 2,000 m; this including three other races winter over NW and N India, occasionally straying to S Gujarat

Habitat Meadows; orchards; vicinity of habitation; open, fallow lands

Glossy black plumage, with iridescent purple-and-green; plumage spotted with buff-and-white; hackled feathers on head, neck and breast; blackish bill and red-brown legs. Summer (breeding) plumage mostly blackish with yellow bill. Several races winter in N India, with head purple or bronze-green, but field identification of races not very easy in winter. Gregarious, restless; feeds on ground, moves hurriedly, digs with beak in soil; entire flock may often take off from ground; flies around erratically or in circles, but soon settles on trees, or returns to ground.

MALABAR WHISTLING THRUSH

Myophonus horsfieldii Turdidae

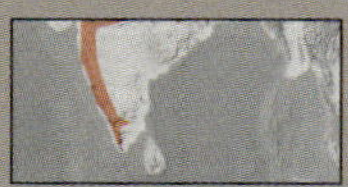

Size 25 cm

Voice Renowned vocalist; especially vocal during rains. Call a harsh, high-pitched *kreeee*; begins to call very early morning. Rich, whistling song, very human in quality, nicknamed 'whistling schoolboy'; fluty notes float over the roar of water

Range Hills of W India, from S Rajasthan, south all along Western Ghats, to about 2,200 m; also, parts of Satpura

Habitat Forest streams; waterfalls; gardens

Large, whistling thrush with deep blue-black plumage, more glistening on wings and tail; bright, cobalt-blue forehead and shoulder-patch; black bill and black legs. Sexes alike. Solitary, or in pairs; lively bird of hilly, forested countries; keeps to forest streams and waterfalls; also perches on trees; peculiar stretching of legs and raising of tail; often encountered on roadside culverts, from where it bolts into nullahs or valleys.

PIED THRUSH

Zoothera wardii Turdidae

Size 22 cm

Voice Alarm call a spitting *ptz…ptz…ptz…ptz*

Range Breeds in the Himalayas, from E Himachal Pradesh to Arunachal Pradesh, and NE India. Migrates through India to winter in Sri Lanka and Tamil Nadu

Habitat Open broadleaved forests; edges of forests; secondary scrub with scattered trees; thickly-vegetated ravines; undergrowth alongside streams; well-wooded gardens

Adult male mainly black-and-white above, with white supercilium, white wing-bars and white tips to tertials and secondaries; rump has white barring; white belly and flanks, barred with black. Female olive-brown above with buff supercilium, buff wing-bars and tail-tips; spotted olive-brown breast, white belly and flanks, darkly scaled. Juvenile like female, but has streaked mantle and breast.

♀

ORANGE-HEADED THRUSH

Zoothera citrina Turdidae

Size 21 cm

Voice Call a shrill, screechy *kreeee*. Loud, rich song, often with mix of other birds' calls thrown in. Noisy in early mornings and late evenings

Range *Cyanotus* peninsular India south of line from S Gujarat across to Odisha; the nominate race *Citrina* breeds in the Himalayas, NE India; winters in foothills, the Terai, parts of E India, Gangetic plains and south along Eastern Ghats. *Albogularis* restricted to Andamans and Nicobar

Habitat Shaded forests; bamboo groves; gardens

citrina

Blue-grey above; orangish-rufous head, nape and underparts; white ear-coverts with two dark brown vertical stripes; white throat and shoulder-patch; vent and undertail-coverts white. Orange-headed nominate race has entire head rufous-orange. Usually in pairs; feeds on ground, rummages in leaf litter and under thick growth; flies into leafy branches if disturbed; occasionally associates with laughingthrushes and babblers; vocal and restless when breeding. Feeds on invertebrates in leaf litter. Crepuscular.

cyanotus

SCALY THRUSH

Zoothera dauma Turdidae

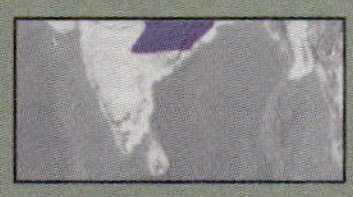

Size 26 cm

Voice Normally silent. Harsh *tchik*; varied, thrush-like song

Range Breeds Kashmir to Myanmar. Winters south to Odisha

Habitat Mixed broadleaved and coniferous forests; *sal* and bamboos

Distinctive scaled thrush; distinguished from other thrushes by prominent black or buff-tipped feathers; scales on olive-buff upperparts; black patch behind ear-coverts; whitish lores; indistinct malar stripe; dark scaling on whitish underparts, heavier on breast, flanks; sturdy bill and legs. Solitary, or in pairs. Mainly terrestrial feeder, forages in leaf litter. Shy and reclusive; flies to low branches or bushes when disturbed; dips and flares tail like most thrushes.

juvenile

TICKELL'S THRUSH

Turdus unicolor Turdidae

Size 21 cm

Voice A 2-noted alarm call; also some chattering calls. Rich song

Range Breeds in the Himalayas, 1,500-2,500 m, east to C Nepal, and Sikkim; winters along foothills east of Kangra, NE, parts of C and E peninsular India

Habitat Open forests, groves

Light ash-grey bird; duller breast and whiter on belly; rufous underwing-coverts in flight. Female olive-brown above; white throat, streaked on sides; tawny flanks and white belly. Small flocks on ground, sometimes along with other thrushes; hops fast on ground, stopping abruptly, as if to check some underground activity; digs worms from under soil; flies into trees when approached too close.

♀

COMMON BLACKBIRD

Turdus merula Turdidae

Size 25-28 cm

Voice Calls *chack...chack*. Song not very melodious

Range Breeding visitor to NW Pakistan

Habitat High-altitude rocky slopes, grassy alpine meadows, dwarf juniper scrub, rhododendron scrub

Large, glossy brown-black thrush with prominent yellow bill. Dark crown; narrow, golden-yellow eye-ring. Similar to White-collared but lacks collar. Distinguished from Grey-winged by lack of wing-patch. Female dark brown, with lightly streaked throat and darker bill. Juvenile has paler brown head, rufous underparts; streaked, spotted, barred above and below. In pairs, or small groups when breeding; in small winter flocks with other thrushes; largely, terrestrial feeder.

♀

BLUETHROAT

Luscinia svecica Muscicapidae

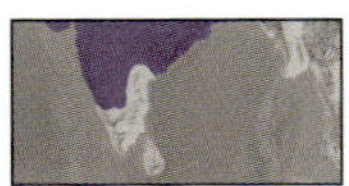

Size 15 cm

Voice Calls *tshik…tshik*. Long, varied song

Range Kashmir to Arunachal Pradesh

Habitat Damp scrub, reed beds and cultivation near water

Adult breeding male has greyish-brown upperparts; whitish underparts; bright blue bib with rufous patch in middle, bordered below by narrow black-and-white band and broad rufous band. Non-breeding male similar, but has markings on chin, diffused by pale feather-tips. Female has creamy white throat; bordered below by neck-band of darker streaking and mottling; white moustachial stripe. Juvenile more blackish with buffish spots on back; buff underparts mottled dark brown, giving scaly appearance.

pallidogularis

♀

svecica

cyanecula

abbotti

SIBERIAN RUBYTHROAT

Luscinia calliope Muscicapidae

Size 15 cm

Voice Call a *shuk; ee… lu*, etc.

Range Uttarakhand to Myanmar

Habitat Dense undergrowth; tall grass, cane, reeds; edges of cultivation

Plumpish, heavy-bodied bird. Breeding male overall olive-brown. Bold, white supercilium and sub-moustachial stripe, edged black; black lores and malar stripe; plain brown rump and tail; ruby-red throat, bordered by thin, black band, varying amounts of grey on breast; greyish-brown underparts; short, unmarked tail. Female uniform brown; buff supercilium, whitish throat, washed grey; grey-brown breast-band. Skulks in dense vegetation; mainly terrestrial; feeds on ground or in low bushes; cocks tail. Feeds singly.

♀

INDIAN BLUE ROBIN

Luscinia brunnea Muscicapidae

Size 15 cm

Voice Calls include high-pitched *churr* and harsh *tack*... in winter. Trilling song of breeding male, sometimes singing from exposed perch

Range Breeds in the Himalayas, 1,500-3,300 m. Winters in S Western Ghats, Ashambu Hills, and Sri Lanka

Habitat Dense rhododendron, ringal bamboo undergrowth in summer. Evergreen forest undergrowth, coffee estates in winter

Male deep slaty-blue above; white supercilium; blackish lores and cheeks; rich chestnut throat, breast and flanks; white belly centre and undertail. Female brown above; white throat and belly. Solitary, rarely in pairs; great skulker, very difficult to observe; moves amidst dense growth and hops on ground.

ORIENTAL MAGPIE ROBIN

Copsychus saularis Muscicapidae

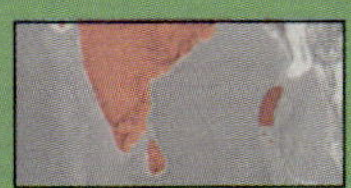

Size 20 cm

Voice Common call a plaintive *sweee. . .* . One of India's finest songsters; rich, clear song of varying notes and tones; male sings from exposed perches, most frequently between March and June, intermittently year round; also, has harsh *churr* and *chhekh* notes

Range Subcontinent, upto about 1,500 m in the outer Himalayas; absent in extreme W Rajasthan

Habitat Forests; parks; towns

Familiar bird of India. Male glossy blue-black and white; white wing-patch and white in outer-tail distinctive; glossy blue-black throat and breast; white below. Female rich slaty-grey, male black. Solitary, or in pairs, sometimes with other birds in mixed parties; hops on ground, prefers shaded areas. Common about human habitation; when perched, often cocks tail; flicks tail often, especially when making short sallies; active at dusk.

♀

WHITE-RUMPED SHAMA

Copsychus malabaricus Muscicapidae

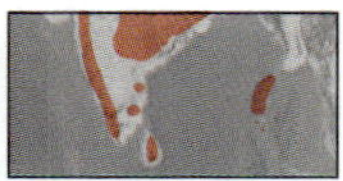

Size 25 cm

Voice Rich songster; melodious, 3- or 4-whistling notes very characteristic. Variety of call notes, including a mix of some harsh notes

Range The Himalayan foothills, the Terai, east of Uttarakhand; NE India; hill forests of Bihar, Odisha, SE Madhya Pradesh, E Maharashtra, south along Eastern Ghats to about Cauvery river; entire Western Ghats

Habitat Forests; bamboos; hill station gardens

Male has glossy black head and back; white rump and sides of graduated tail distinctive; black throat and breast; orange-rufous below. Female grey, male black with shorter tail and duller rufous breast. Arboreal; keeps to shaded areas and foliage, only occasionally emerging in open; launches short sallies.

INDIAN ROBIN

Saxicoloides fulicatus Muscicapidae

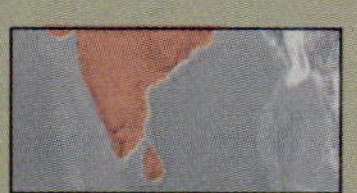

Size 16 cm

Voice Call a long-drawn *sweeeech* or *weeeech*. Warbling song when breeding; also, guttural *charrr*... note

Range Subcontinent, S Himalayan foothills; absent in extreme NE India

Habitat Open country; edges of forests; vicinity of habitation; scrubs

♀

Several races in India. Male has dark brown, blackish-brown or glossy blue-back upperbody. Male has white wing-patch glossy blue-black below; chestnut vent and undertail. Female lacks white in wings; duller grey-brown below. Solitary, or in pairs in open country, and often in and around habitation. Rather suspicious and maintains safe distance between man and itself; hunts on ground, hops or runs in short spurts; when on ground, holds head high and often cocks tail, right upto back, flashing chestnut vent and undertail.

BLACK REDSTART

Phoenicurus ochruros Muscicapidae

Size 15 cm

Voice Call a squeaking *tictitic*…, often beginning with faint *tsip*… note. Trilling song of breeding male

Range Breeds in the Himalayas, 2,400-5,200 m; winters over much of the subcontinent

Habitat Open country; cultivation

♀

Male black above (marked with grey in winter); grey crown and lower back; rufous rump and tail sides; black throat and breast; rufous below. Female duller brown above; tail similar to male's; dull tawny-brown below. Eastern race *rufiventris* has black crown; common wintering bird of India. Mostly solitary in winter, when common all over India; easy to observe. Perches on overhead wires, poles, rocks and stumps; characteristic shivering of tail and jerky body movements; makes short dashes to ground, soon returning to perch with catch; rather confiding in summer, breeds in houses, under roofs and in wall crevices.

COMMON STONECHAT

Saxicola torquatus Muscicapidae

Size 13 cm

Voice Call a double-noted *wheet chat*. Soft, trilling song of breeding male in the Himalayas, occasionally in winter grounds

Range Breeds in the Himalayas, 1,500-3,000 m; all over India in winter, except Kerala and much of Tamil Nadu

Habitat Dry, open areas; cultivation; tidal creeks

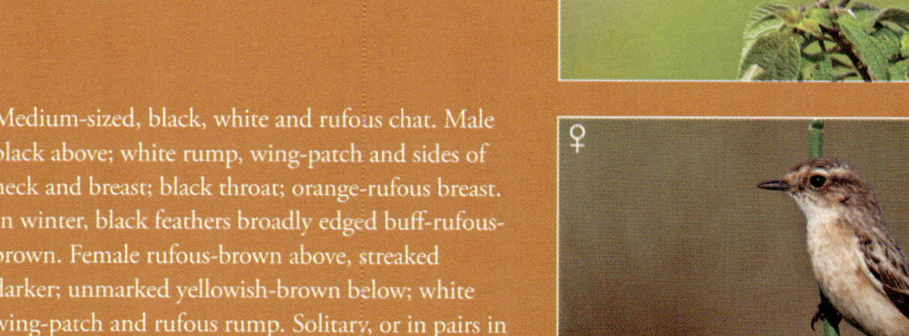

Medium-sized, black, white and rufous chat. Male black above; white rump, wing-patch and sides of neck and breast; black throat; orange-rufous breast. In winter, black feathers broadly edged buff-rufous-brown. Female rufous-brown above, streaked darker; unmarked yellowish-brown below; white wing-patch and rufous rump. Solitary, or in pairs in open country; perches on small bushes, fence posts and boulders; restless, makes short forays to capture insects, soon returning to perch.

breeding

PIED BUSHCHAT

Saxicola caprata Muscicapidae

Size 13 cm

Voice Harsh, 2-noted call serves as contact and alarm. Short, trilling song of breeding male

Range Subcontinent, from outer Himalayas to about 1,500 m

Habitat Open country; scrubs; cultivation; ravines

breeding

♀

Breeding male has glossy metallic black plumage; white in wing, rump and belly. Female brown above, paler on lores; darker tail; dull yellow-brown below with rusty wash on breast and belly. Juvenile more grey-brown with yellowish spots and buffy underparts with dark spotting. Solitary, or in pairs; perches on bushes, overhead wires; makes short sallies to prey on ground or carries it to perch; active, sometimes guards feeding territories in winter; flicks and spreads wings.

ISABELLINE WHEATEAR

Oenanthe isabellina Muscicapidae

Size 17 cm

Voice Calls include *chak…chak* and *tew*

Range Locally common breeding summer visitor to Balochistan. Fairly common winter visitor to Pakistan and NW India south to Gujarat with scattered records south to Maldives and Sri Lanka and E Sikkim

Habitat Mainly sandy semi-desert and overgrazed pasture

'Isabelline' refers to its pale greyish-yellow or pale fawn overall colouration. Wings slightly darker than body; long, strong, slightly hooked bill; relatively short tail; long body usually held upright; black-and-white tail. Sexes similar. White basal patches on black tail. Looks long-legged because of very upright stance. Paler than female Northern and Desert. More terrestrial than other wheatears, mainly catches prey on ground. Solitary and territorial. Shy. Breeds in rocky gulleys and plateaux. Nests in deep, rodent holes.

DESERT WHEATEAR

Oenanthe deserti Muscicapidae

Size 15 cm

Voice Call an occasional *ch…chett* alarm note in winter. Reportedly utters short, plaintive song in winter too

Range Winter visitor over N, C, W India, almost absent south of S Maharashtra and Andhra Pradesh. Tibetan race *oreophila* breeds in Kashmir, Ladakh, Lahaul and Spiti, at about 3,000-5,000 m

Habitat Open, rocky, barren country; sandy areas; fallow lands

Male sandy above, with whitish rump and black tail; black wings; white in coverts; black throat and head sides; creamy-white below. Female has black wings and tail; lacks black throat. Winter male has throat feathers fringed white. Keeps to ground or perches on low bushes or small rocks; has favoured haunts; colouration makes it difficult to spot; makes short sallies to capture insects.

♀

BROWN ROCK-CHAT

Cercomela fusca Muscicapidae

Size 17cm

Voice Calls include harsh *chaeck* and whistling *cheee*. Short, melodious song with mimicry

Range Locally common endemic breeding resident in plains and foothills of NW India from Punjab south to Maharashtra and east to Bihar. Rare in N Pakistan and S Nepal

Habitat Buildings in towns and villages, ruins, quarries, rocky hills and cliffs

Largish chat with brown upperparts and rufous-brown underparts; darker brown wings; dark grey-brown vent; blackish tail. Sexes alike. In pairs; confiding; captures insects on ground; territorial when breeding. Nests in rock clefts. Flicks open wings and tail. Also, slowly raises and fans tail and bobs head. Feeds mainly on insects on ground. Melodious song in breeding season.

BLUE ROCK THRUSH

Monticola solitarius Muscicapidae

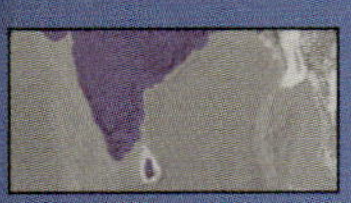

Size 23 cm

Voice Silent in winter. Short, whistling song of breeding male

Range Breeds in the Himalayas, from extreme W to E Nepal; winters from N foothills, NE, S India, throughout the peninsula

Habitat Open, rocky country; cliffs; ravines; ruins; habitation

Male has deep blue plumage; black wings and tail; pale fulvous and black scales more conspicuous in winter; belly whiter in winter. Female duller, grey-brown above; dark shaft-streaks; black barring on rump; dull white below, barred brown. Solitary; has favoured sites, often around habitation; perches on rocks, stumps, rooftops; has rather upright posture; flies on to ground to feed, but sometimes launches short aerial sallies.

BLUE-CAPPED ROCK THRUSH

Monticola cinclorhynchus Muscicapidae

Size 17 cm

Voice Mostly silent in winter, except for occasional harsh single or 2-noted call. Rich song of breeding male

Range Breeds in the Himalayas, 1,000–2,500 m, sometimes higher; winters in Western Ghats, from Narmada river

Habitat Shaded forests, groves

Male has blue crown and nape; black back; broad stripe through eyes to ear-coverts; blue throat and shoulder-patch; white wing-patch and chestnut rump distinctive; chestnut below throat. Back feathers edged fulvous in winter. Female unmarked olive-brown above; buffy-white below, thickly speckled with dark brown. Female Blue Rock *M. solitarius* grey-brown above, has yellow-brown vent and dull wing-bar. Solitary, or in pairs.

ASIAN BROWN FLYCATCHER

Muscicapa dauurica Muscicapidae

Size 13 cm

Voice Call a thin *tzee*. Whistling song

Range Breeding resident of the Himalayan foothills, with several small disjunct populations resident in the hills of C and peninsular India. Widespread winter visitor in the peninsula

Habitat Open forests; groves; gardens; plantations

Nondescript-looking, ashy-brown flycatcher; greyish wash on dirty white breast; short tail; large head with huge eye and prominent eye-ring; pale lores; basal half of lower mandible pale and fleshy; black legs. Sexes alike. Usually solitary; perches upright on lower branches of trees, makes sallies to catch insects and returns to same perch.

juvenile

BROWN-BREASTED FLYCATCHER

Muscicapa muttui Muscicapidae

Size 13 cm

Voice Call a thin *zit*. Pleasant song

Range Assam. Distribution little understood in the NE region. Said to be absent in Nepal and Bhutan

Habitat Overgrown thickets in hill forests

Small, rich brown flycatcher, with largish head and large eyes with white eye-ring; sub-moustachial stripe; darker malar stripe. Crown slightly darker than mantle; whitish lores; lower mandible almost entirely yellowish; yellowish legs. Creamy underparts; warm brown breast-band; white throat; brownish-grey wash on flanks; generally warmer rufous tinge to wings, rump, tail; in some plumages, rufous-orange wing-bar. Solitary; shy and unobtrusive; partly crepuscular; prefers to perch in lower forest storeys; hunts aerially.

RUSTY-TAILED FLYCATCHER

Muscicapa ruficauda Muscicapidae

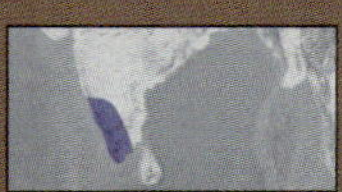

Size 14 cm

Voice Call a plaintive *peu…peu*. Also, churrs

Range Fairly common endemic breeding summer visitor to N mountains from N Pakistan east to E Nepal. Winters mainly in SW India but widespread passage records from elsewhere in India

Habitat Open forests, clearings and edges

Medium to small-sized flycatcher with flattish head. Warm brown upperparts; dark brownish from throat to breast, whitish belly to vent; large eye; ill-defined supercilium and eye-ring. Rump and notched tail bright rufous. Lower mandible pale orange. Sexes alike. Juvenile dark brownish above with buffy streaks and pale buff-brownish-spotted underparts.

KASHMIR FLYCATCHER

Ficedula subrubra Muscicapidae

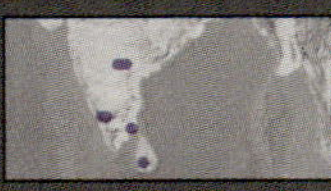

Size 13 cm

Voice Song a short, sweet phrase, *sweet…eat, sweet…eat…didhe*

Range Endemic to the subcontinent. Breeds in NW Himalayas in Neelum valley, Pakistan, Kashmir and Pir Panjal Range, India. Winters in Sri Lanka

Habitat Deciduous forests. Winters in gardens, tea estates and edges of forests

Male has ashy-brown upperparts; deep rufous throat, breast, upper belly and flanks; black-bordered throat and breast; black tail with white panel in outer-tail feathers. Female and first-winter male usually more rufous-orange on throat and breast; grey sides to neck and breast. Juvenile has tail pattern as adult, but has dark brown-spotted upperparts and buffish underparts scaled with dark brown.

RED-BREASTED FLYCATCHER

Ficedula parva Muscicapidae

Size 13 cm

Voice Sharp clicking sound. Call a double *tick…tick*

Range Winter visitor, arrives by early September; all over India, south of the Himalayan foothills

Habitat Forests; gardens

Male dull-brown above with greyish-brown head; bright rufous-orange bib; whitish below. Bold, white basal patches to black tail, diagnostic. Female has pale cinnamon upperparts; white throat; pale buff breast; narrow, white eye-ring; no bib. Shy when breeding. Solitary, or in scattered pairs in shaded areas; may descend to ground, but prefers low and middle branches; launches short aerial sallies; hunts till late in the evening; calls often. Feeds in foliage in warbler-like manner.

ULTRAMARINE FLYCATCHER

Ficedula superciliaris Muscicapidae

Size 10 cm

Voice Call a faint *tick...tick...* in winter; a *chrrr* alarm note. Three-syllabled song in the Himalayas

Range Breeds in the Himalayas, 1,800-3,200 m. Winters in N and C India, south to Karnataka and N Andhra Pradesh

Habitat Forests; groves; orchards; gardens

Male deep blue above; sides of head, neck and breast, forming broken breast-band; long, white eyebrow; white in tail; white below. Female dull-slaty above and grey-white below. Eastern race *aestigma* lacks white over eye and in tail. Solitary, or in pairs; seen in mixed parties during winter; active, hunts in characteristic flycatcher-style; rarely ventures into open.

♀

BLACK-AND-ORANGE FLYCATCHER

Ficedula nigrorufa Muscicapidae

Size 13 cm

Voice Call note a soft, gloomy *pee*…; sharp *zit*…*zit* alarm call. High-pitched, metallic song when breeding

Range Very local; restricted to Nilgiris and associated hills in S Western Ghats, most common above 1,500 m

Habitat Dense evergreen forests; undergrowth; bamboos

Male has rich orangish-rufous plumage; blackish crown, nape, sides of face and wings. Female similar to male, but has deep olive-brown head; pale eye-ring. Usually solitary, but pairs often close by. Keeps to dense, shaded undergrowth, either hopping low or making short flycatcher-like sallies from low perch; in its restricted range, quite tame and confiding once spotted.

VERDITER FLYCATCHER

Eumyias thalassinus Muscicapidae

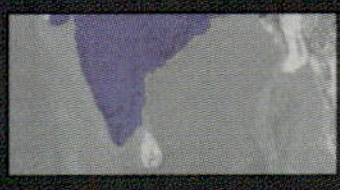

Size 16 cm

Voice Silent in winter, except a rare, faint *chwe…* call. Rich, trilling notes and song during the Himalayan summer

Range The Himalayas, 1,200-3,200 m. Winters in Indian plains, hill forests of C, E and S India

Habitat Open forests; orchards

Male has verditer-blue plumage, darker in wings and tail; black lores. Female duller, greyer overall, has short bill and longish tail. Solitary, or in pairs in winter, sometimes with other birds; restless, flicks tail; rather more noticeable than other flycatchers because of its continuous movement and habit of perching in open-exposed positions, like bare twigs on tree-tops.

juvenile

NILGIRI FLYCATCHER

Eumyias albicaudatus Muscicapidae

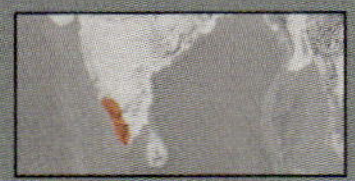

Size 15 cm

Voice Call *tsik…tsik,…chip…chip.* Song a slow, hesitant warble of upto 10 notes

Range Globally near-threatened but fairly common endemic breeding resident restricted to Western Ghats from S Karnataka southwards

Habitat Evergreen forests and edges of forests, often near streams. Also, well-grown plantations

Small to medium-sized, long-tailed flycatcher. Male has slaty-indigo upperparts; forehead and supercilium have faint reddish-purple cast; greyer on belly, with white scaling on vent; small, white basal spots on tail. Female dark greenish-grey. Both much darker than similar species. In pairs; feeds on insects which it catches in aerial sorties, mostly from canopy.

PALE-CHINNED FLYCATCHER

Cyornis poliogenys Muscicapidae

Size 18 cm

Voice Calls include hard clicks and rattles *tick…tick…, etc.* Song a high-pitched series of notes *chee…chee, chit…chit…*, etc.

Range C Nepal to Arunachal Pradesh; S Assam Hills

Habitat Bushes, undergrowth, low trees in open broadleaved forests of foothills; open country in the plains

Medium to large-sized, fairly plain-looking flycatcher. Warm brown upperparts; has varying degrees of grey on crown and face depending on the race; buff lores and eye-ring; buff or creamy-white throat; pale rufous-orange breast and flanks, creamy-white belly with pale rufous wash; rufous rump and tail; mostly arboreal; prefers hunting for insects in forest understoreys, sometimes trees, though will also descend to ground.

WHITE-BELLIED BLUE FLYCATCHER

Cyornis pallipes Muscicapidae

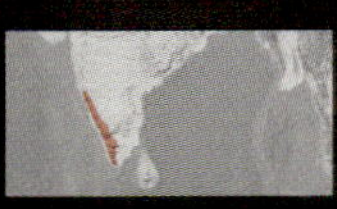

♀

Size 15 cm

Voice Soft 2-noted call. Longish, squeaky song when breeding. Rather silent for most part of the year

Range Western Ghats, south of C Maharashtra, around the latitude of Pune

Habitat Dense forest undergrowth

Male indigo-blue above; black lores; bright blue forehead, supercilium; indigo-blue throat and breast; white lower breast. Female deep olive-brown above; greyish on head; chestnut tail; rufous-orange till breast, whiter below. Juvenile has brown back, scaly head and chest; whitish belly. Solitary, rarely in pairs; sometimes in mixed parties; mostly silent and unobtrusive, hence overlooked; hunts in low growth, often flicks tail.

TICKELL'S BLUE FLYCATCHER

Cyornis tickelliae Muscicapidae

Size 14 cm

Voice Clear, metallic song of 6-notes, sometimes extending to 9 or 10; often uttered in winter too

Range All over India, south roughly of a line from Kutch to W Uttarakhand east along the Terai; absent in extreme N, NW India

Habitat Shaded forests; bamboos; gardens

Male dark indigo-blue above; bright blue on forehead and supercilium; darker, almost appearing black on face sides; rufous-orange throat and breast; whitish below. Female duller overall. Usually in pairs in shaded areas, often in mixed hunting parties; flits about intermittently or launches short sorties; has favourite perches; often breaks into fluty song.

♀

BLUE-THROATED BLUE FLYCATCHER

Cyornis rubeculoides Muscicapidae

Size 14 cm

Voice Calls include harsh *chrr* and hard *tak…tak*. Rapidly delivered warbling song

Range Locally breeding summer visitor to N hills from N Pakistan east to Myanmar border. Winters in foothills

Habitat Damp forests, particularly overgrown ravines

Small flycatcher with blue throat. Male bright blue; has glossy blue forehead; orange upper breast (sometimes extending onto flanks); white belly to vent. Distinguished from Tickell's by blue throat. Female brown above, more rufous on rump and tail with pale orange throat and upper breast. Lores, belly and vent white. Female Tickell's bluish above. Feeds on invertebrates at lower levels.

♀

GREY-HEADED CANARY FLYCATCHER

Culicicapa ceylonensis Muscicapidae

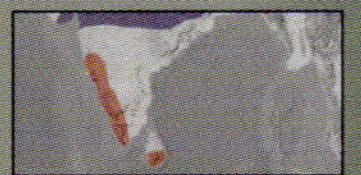

Size 9 cm

Voice Vocal. High-pitched 2- or 3-syllabled calls, *whi…chichee… whi…chichee*. Longer, trilling song; also chattering notes

Range Commonly breeds in the Himalayas, 1,500-3,000 m; possibly in some of the hill forests of C India and Eastern Ghats. Common in winter over much of the subcontinent

Habitat Forests, gardens, orchards

Has ashy-grey hood, throat and breast; darker crown; squarish crest; yellow-green back and yellow rump; yellow in browner wings and tail; bright canary-yellow below breast. Sexes alike. Solitary, or in pairs, occasionally several in vicinity, especially in mixed parties; forest bird, typical flycatcher; excitedly flitting about, launching aerial sallies, calling aloud and generally on the move; wherever this bird is, its cheerful unmistakable calls are heard.

BLUE-WINGED LEAFBIRD

Chloropsis cochinchinensis Chloropseidae

Size 20 cm

Voice Typical song with loud drongo-like chatty phrases, much mimicry plus varied whistles

Range Hills of NE India and Bangladesh

Habitat Edges of forests, groves, open fcrests, gardens, isolated large trees near villages or in cu tivation

Male overall bright green with lighter green head. Turquoise-blue edges to primary coverts and primaries (duller on female and juvenile); blue sides to tail, diagnostic. Black face and throat; blue moustachial stripe. Uniform, green underparts. Strong, black beak with bristles at base. Female greener on head; has turquoise blue throat-patch. Juvenile like female, but no blue on throat.

GOLDEN-FRONTED LEAFBIRD

Chloropsis aurifrons Chloropseidae

Size 19 cm

Voice Most common call a drongo or shikra-like *che…chwe*. Noisy; wide assortment of whistling notes, including imitations of several species

Range Upto about 1,600 m in Uttarakhand Himalayas; east to Bihar, Odisha, south along Eastern Ghats and up the Western Ghats and adjoining areas

Habitat Forests

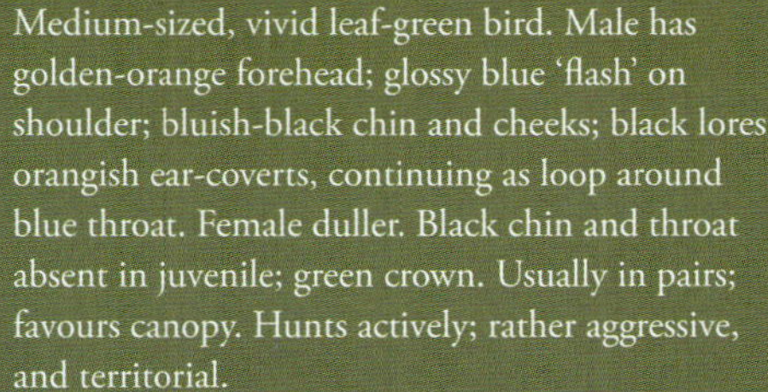

Medium-sized, vivid leaf-green bird. Male has golden-orange forehead; glossy blue 'flash' on shoulder; bluish-black chin and cheeks; black lores; orangish ear-coverts, continuing as loop around blue throat. Female duller. Black chin and throat absent in juvenile; green crown. Usually in pairs; favours canopy. Hunts actively; rather aggressive, and territorial.

THICK-BILLED FLOWERPECKER

Dicaeum agile Dicaeidae

Size 9 cm

Voice Call a loud, sharp *chik…chik*

Range S India, including the Himalayan foothills; absent over arid parts of NW India and large tracts of Tamil Nadu

Habitat Forests, orchards, gardens

Small flowerpecker. Adult has olive-washed brownish-grey upperparts; more olive-brown rump; short, white-tipped tail; whitish spots on undertail-coverts; dull whitish-grey underparts, streaked brown; breast more densely streaked; orangish-red eyes and thick, blue-grey beak. Sexes alike. Juvenile has less streaked underparts. Solitary, or in pairs in canopy foliage; arboreal, restless; flicks tail often while hunting under leaves or along branches; frequents parasitic clumps of *Loranthus* and *Viscum*.

PLAIN FLOWERPECKER

Dicaeum c minullum Dicaeidae

Size 8 cm

Voice Calls include sharp repeated *chik* and *pseep*, particularly in flight. Extended as song

Range Locally common breeding resident in N foothills from C Nepal east to Myanmar border, parts of Bangladesh, Andaman Islands

Habitat Forest canopy, orchards, gardens and mangroves

Tiny, olive-brown arboreal bird with short, dark, decurved bill. Pale supercilium and lores; yellowish-white underparts. Juvenile has paler bill. Southwestern race darker above and whiter below. Andamans' race greener above and yellowish on belly. Sexes similar. Feeds in pairs or small groups, mainly on *Loranthus* berries. Flies strongly and noisily from site to site over large area. Very lively. Nests high in trees.

PALE-BILLED FLOWERPECKER

Dicaeum erythrorynchos Dicaeidae

Size 8 cm

Voice Call a sharp, loud *chik…chik*

Range From E Kangra along foothills to NE India; peninsular India south of a line from W Gujarat to S Bihar

Habitat Light forests, groves

Rather plain-looking flowerpecker with olive-brown upperparts and uniform greyish-white underparts; pinkish flesh and yellow-brown, markedly downcurved beak. Sexes alike. Solitary, or two to three birds in canopy; frequents parasitic *Loranthus* and *Viscum;* flits from clump to clump; strictly arboreal, restless; territorial even when feeding.

RUBY-CHEEKED SUNBIRD

Chalcoparia singalensis Nectariniidae

Size 11 cm

Voice Calls *chwee…eest*

Range Uttarakhand to Arunachal Pradesh; S Assam Hills

Habitat Open broadleaved evergreen forests; secondary growth

Distinctive, medium-sized sunbird with short, rather straight bill, orange throat and breast, yellow over rest of underparts. Male has iridescent emerald green upperparts; deep ruby-red lores and ear-coverts, edged below with purplish moustachial stripe. Female yellowish-olive-green above, with duller orange throat and breast and no ruby cheek; distinguished from other female sunbirds by orange breast, yellow underparts and short bill; more gregarious than other sunbirds; sometimes in small flocks when not breeding; actively forages in foliage in lower half of trees and shrubs.

PURPLE-RUMPED SUNBIRD

Leptocoma zeylonica Nectariniidae

Size 10 cm

Voice Calls *tsiswee… tsiswee…*. Sharp, twittering song of breeding male, much lower in tone and volume than that of Purple Sunbird

Range Peninsular India south of a line from around Mumbai, C Madhya Pradesh, S Bihar and West Bengal

Habitat Open forests, gardens, orchards; common in towns

Male has deep chestnut-crimson back; metallic green crown and shoulder-patch; metallic purple rump and throat; maroon collar below throat; yellow underparts. Female ash-brown above, with rufous in wings; whitish throat; yellow underparts. Usually in pairs; very active, flits from flower to flower; occasionally descends into flowering garden bushes.

CRIMSON-BACKED SUNBIRD

Leptocoma minima Nectariniidae

Size 8 cm

Voice Call a stereotypical *tsee… sit…see…su…tse…sit…swee…*

Range Endemic to the Western Ghats and adjacent hills

Habitat Evergreen biotope, chiefly in foothills; forests, sholas, gardens, and flowering shade trees in tea and coffee plantations

♀

Distinguished from Purple-rumped by smaller size and finer, more downcurved bill, and by flowerpecker-like call. Male similar to Purple-rumped, has metallic green crown, purple rump and purple throat. Distinguished by broad, crimson breast-band restricted to belly, crimson sides of head and mantle, and lack of metallic green shoulder-patch. Eclipse male as female, but has metallic purple rump and crimson scapulars and back. Female distinguished from other female sunbirds by combination of small size, crimson rump, olive-green upperparts and edges to wings, uniformly yellowish underparts. Juvenile male appears to be similar to eclipse male, but with duller greyish underparts.

PURPLE SUNBIRD

Cinnyris asiaticus Nectariniidae

Size 10 cm

Voice Noisier than other sunbirds. Calls include loud *chweet*... notes

Range Subcontinent, south from the Himalayan foothills to about 1,500 m

Habitat Open forests, gardens, groves

Male metallic purple-blue above, and on throat and breast; dark purplish-black belly; narrow, chestnut-maroon band between breast and belly; yellow and scarlet pectoral tufts, normally hidden under wings. Female olive-brown above; pale yellow below (*zeylonica* female has whitish throat). Non-breeding male similar to female but with broad, purple-black stripe down centre of throat to belly. Solitary, or in pairs; important pollinating agent, almost always seen around flowering trees and bushes; displays amazing agility and acrobatic prowess when feeding; sometimes hunts flycatcher-style.

♀

LOTEN'S SUNBIRD

Cinnyris lotenia Nectariniidae

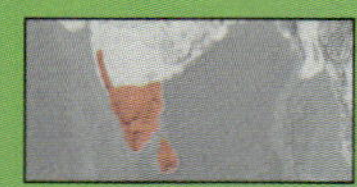

Size 13 cm

Voice Call a hard *tchit… tchit*. Measured song *titti…titu chewit…chewit*

Range Fairly common endemic breeding resident to S peninsular India and Sri Lanka, south of Mumbai and S Andhra Pradesh

Habitat Open wooded country including gardens

Large, dark sunbird with diagnostic, long, steeply-curved bill. Male metallic blackish-purple on head and upperparts with more black wings and tail and sooty brown belly. Maroon breast-band and yellow breast tufts. Eclipse male similar to female but with blackish stripe from chin to belly. Female dark olive-green above and pale yellow below with white tail-tips.

♀

CRIMSON SUNBIRD

Aethopyga siparaja Nectariniidae

Size Male 15 cm; Female 10 cm

Voice Sharp, clicking call notes. Pleasant chirping song of breeding male (June-August)

Range The Himalayas, hills of NE India. Winters in the Himalayan plains

Habitat Forests, gardens

Male has metallic green crown and long tail; deep crimson back and neck sides; yellow rump not commonly seen; bright scarlet chin and breast; olive-yellow belly. Female has olive plumage; yellow underparts. Solitary, or in pairs; active gymnast, hanging upside-down and sideways as it probes flowers; also hovers; moves in forests, between tall bushes and canopy.

♀

LITTLE SPIDERHUNTER

Arachnothera longirostra Nectariniidae

Size 14 cm

Voice Call a high-pitched *chee… chee*. Song a loud *which…which…*, sounding somewhat like tailorbird's

Range Disjunct; found in Western Ghats and Eastern Ghats, foothills from SE Nepal eastwards, E Himalayas and much of NE states

Habitat Forests, secondary growth; nullahs, sholas

Sexes alike. Olive-green above; dark tail, tipped white; greyish-white throat, merging into yellow-white below; orangish pectoral tufts. Very long, curved beak diagnostic. Usually solitary; sometimes two or three birds in vicinity; active, moving considerably between bush and canopy; favours wild banana blossoms, clings upside-down on bracts; long, curved beak especially adapted to nectar diet.

HOUSE SPARROW

Passer domesticus Passeridae

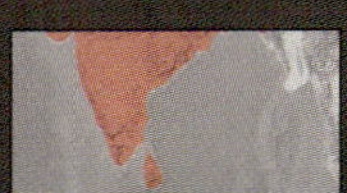

Size 15 cm

Voice Noisy; medley of chirping notes; richer notes of breeding male; double- and triple-brooded

Range Subcontinent, to about 4,000 m in the Himalayas

Habitat Habitation, cultivation

Male has grey crown and rump; chestnut sides of neck and nape; black streaks on chestnut-rufous back; black chin, centre of throat and breast; white ear-coverts. Female dull grey-brown above, streaked darker; dull whitish-brown below. Seen in small parties to large gatherings; mostly commensal on human habitation, feeds and nests in and around habitation, including most crowded localities; also feeds in cultivation; hundreds roost together.

EURASIAN TREE SPARROW

Passer montanus Passeridae

Size 14 cm

Voice Call a *chip…chip; tet…et…et… tsveet*

Range Uttarakhand east to Myanmar; S Assam Hills

Habitat Cities, towns or habitation; cultivation; village groves; orchards

Fairly distinctive sparrow; distinguished from all other *Passer* species by prominent black spots on white ear-coverts, white collar between nape and mantle, cinnamon-chestnut crown; black lores and small throat-patch; darkly streaked, buff-brown upperparts; warm rufous-brown wing panel; two well-defined wing-bars; female slightly paler, with smaller throat and ear-covert patches; buff-washed flanks; racial variations; gregarious.

CHESTNUT-SHOULDERED PETRONIA

Gymnoris xanthocollis Passeridae

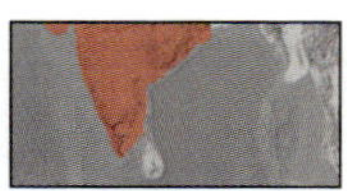

Size 14 cm

Voice Noisy. Calls include *cheellup* and *cheep*. Song a rather high *cheep…cheep*

Range Locally common resident and local migrant throughout most of Indian plains and hills except extreme NW and NE India. Summer visitor to Pakistan. Vagrant to Sri Lanka; unknown in Bangladesh

Habitat Open woodlands, forests and thorn-scrub, often near cultivation

Uniformly grey bird with bold chestnut shoulder-patches. Prominent yellow patch on chin and throat; broad, white tips to median coverts; narrower white tips on greater coverts. Underparts pale buff-grey. Female similar with duller throat-patch. Breeding male has yellow bill, black in non-breeding male. Short, notched tail. Long, slender bill. Feeds on invertebrates, leaves and nectar. Difficult to spot in foliage.

BLACK-BREASTED WEAVER

Ploceus benghalensis Ploceidae

Size 15 cm

Voice Calls *chit...chit.* Song a quiet, repeated *tsik...tsik...tsik*

Range Plains from Punjab to Arunachal Pradesh

Habitat Marshes; reed beds; irrigated fields

juvenile

Mainly yellow, black, brown and whitish weaver, distinguished from other weavers by pale blue-grey bill. Breeding male has bright yellow crown and broad, black breast-band; ear-coverts, throat may be whitish or brownish, irrespective of region; whitish or pale underparts with weak streaking on flanks; upperparts streaked brown. Non-breeding male has black cap, yellow supercilium, throat, under-eye crescent; black eye-stripe and malar stripe; sometimes broken breast-band; female, juvenile somewhat similar; gregarious even when breeding; colonial nester.

BAYA WEAVER

Ploceus philippinus Ploceidae

Size 15 cm

Voice Chirping and high-pitched wheezy notes of breeding male. Very noisy at nesting colony (monsoons)

Range Most of India upto about 1,000 m in outer Himalayas; absent in Kashmir

Habitat Open country, tree- and palm-dotted cultivation

Breeding male has bright yellow crown; dark brown above streaked yellow; dark brown ear-coverts and throat; yellow breast. Female buffy-yellow above streaked darker; pale supercilium and throat, turning buffy-yellow on breast, streaked on sides. Non-breeding male has bolder streaking than female; male of eastern race *burmanicus* has yellow restricted to crown. Gregarious; one of the most familiar and common birds of India, best known for its nest; keeps to cultivated areas, interspersed with trees; feeds on ground and in standing crops.

philippinus

♀

burmanicus

burmanicus

♀

♂
philippinus

STREAKED WEAVER

Ploceus manyar Ploceidae

Size 15 cm

Voice Calls include high-pitched chirping, wheezy notes and chatter; much like Baya's

Range Most of India, south of the Himalayas; absent in parts of Rajasthan and NW regions

Habitat Reed beds, tall grass in well-watered areas, marshes

Male has yellow crown; blackish head sides; fulvous streaks on dark brown back; heavily streaked lower throat and breast. Female and non-breeding male have streaks above; yellow stripe over eye continues to behind ear-coverts; very pale below, boldly streaked on throat and breast. Gregarious; prefers tall grass and reed beds in well-watered areas; often nests close to other weavers. Eastern race *peguensis* darker and much more rufous above.

♀

GREEN AVADAVAT

Amandava formosa Estrildidae

Size 10 cm

Voice Call a quiet *swee…swee*

Range Globally threatened; endemic and rare breeding resident known only from a few sites in NC peninsular India, from Rajasthan east to Odisha, and south to Andhra Pradesh. Scattered records from elsewhere, probably relate to escaped or released cage birds

Habitat Grass, scrubs and sugarcane often near water

Tiny, green weaver with distinct striped flanks. Upperparts green, with black tail; yellow underparts, paler throat. Female has more brown in upperparts. Red bill. Feeds on small seeds or invertebrates on ground. Small flocks. Nests in thick cover.

RED AVADAVAT

Amandava amandava Estrildidae

Size 10 cm

Voice Calls include shrill and high-pitched notes, also uttered in flight

Range Subcontinent, south of the Himalayan foothills

Habitat Tall grass, reeds, sugarcane, scrubs, gardens

Breeding male crimson and brown, spotted white on wings and flanks; white-tipped tail. Female brown above, spotted on wings; crimson rump; dull white throat; buffy-grey breast, yellow brown below. Non-breeding male similar to female, but has greyer throat; upper breast distinctive. In small flocks, often with other weavers; partial to tall grass and scrubs, preferably around well-watered areas; active and vibrant, rather confiding; huge numbers captured for bird markets.

♀

INDIAN SILVERBILL

Euodice malabarica Estrildidae

Size 10 cm

Voice Calls include faint *tee... tee...* notes; also, whistling note sometimes

Range Subcontinent to about 1,500 m in the Himalayas, chiefly the outer ranges

Habitat Prefers dry areas; cultivation, scrub and grass; sometimes light, open forests

Overall rather 'dull' bird, both in colour and demeanour. Sexes alike. Dull-brown above with white rump; very dark, almost black wings; pointed tail; pale buffy-white below with some brown on flanks; thick, grey-blue or slaty beak striking. Gregarious; mostly keeps to scrubs in open country; feeds on ground and on standing crops, especially millet.

SCALY-BREASTED MUNIA

Lonchura punctulata Estrildidae

Size 10 cm

Voice Common call a double-noted *ki...tee...ki...tee*

Range Most of India, to about 1,500 m in parts of the Himalayas; absent in much of Punjab, NW regions and W Rajasthan

Habitat Open scrub, cultivation, especially where interspersed with trees; gardens

Chocolate-brown upperparts; olive-yellow, pointed tail; white bars on rump; chestnut sides of face, chin and throat. Silvery-white underparts, thickly speckled with very dark brown on breast, flanks and part of belly (speckles may be absent during winter and much of summer). Sexes alike. Sociable, moves in flocks of six to several dozen birds, often with other munias and weavers; feeds on ground and low bushes, rests in trees.

WHITE-RUMPED MUNIA

Lonchura striata Estrildidae

Size 10 cm

Voice Call a weak up and down twittering

Range Foothills of Uttarakhand to Arunachal Pradesh; Bangladesh

Habitat Light wooded areas, scrubs, fields, grasslands

Slim, dark munia with short, thick, conical beak; dark brown head, throat, upper breast, mantle, wings, tail, vent, with shaft streaking; white patch on lower back; white belly; short, wedge-shaped tail. *Acuticauda* of the Himalayan foothills of N India, Nepal, Bhutan and NE subcontinent has more rufous brown on face, neck, breast. In small family parties when breeding; otherwise, larger flocks; communal rooster; usually associated with other munias and weavers. Forages on ground or on stalks and stems of seed-bearing grass and crops.

BLACK-THROATED MUNIA

Lonchura kelaarti Estrildidae

Size 12 cm

Voice Calls include *tay* and *chirp*

Range Hills of SW and E India

Habitat Forest clearings; scrub lands

Brown-black head, more brownish on crown, nape and mantle; brown-black rump spotted or finely barred white; blackish face, throat and centre of breast; lower breast, belly, flanks creamy-white spotted with deep brown. Short, stout bill with dark upper mandible and paler lower mandible with dark tip; long, black tail. Gregarious. Feeds mainly on seeds. Sexes alike.

BLACK-HEADED MUNIA

Lonchura malacca Estrildidae

Size 10 cm

Voice Call a faint *pee…pee…*

Range Foothills; the Terai from SE Punjab eastwards; most of NE India, N Odisha; peninsular India south from Mumbai to S Madhya Pradesh

Habitat Reed beds, paddy, grass and scrubs

Male has black head, throat, breast, centre of belly and thighs; rufous-chestnut back, deeper chestnut on rump; white upper belly and sides of underbody. Female similar to male, but has deep brown undertail-coverts. Gregarious, except when breeding; prefers reed beds and cultivation, especially where flooded; during breeding season (monsoons), often seen along with Streaked; feeds on ground.

FOREST WAGTAIL

Dendronanthus indicus Motacillidae

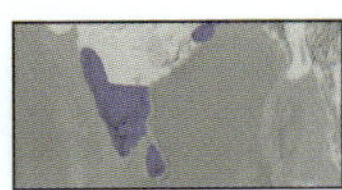

Size 17 cm

Voice Calls *pink; zi…fi zi…fi* or *zi…chu zi…chu*

Range C Nepal to entire NE India

Habitat Paths, clearings in forests

Distinctive wagtail with relatively short tail; olive or grey-brown upperparts; whitish throat, underparts; two broad, black 'half-necklace' breast-bands; white supercilium, patch below ear-coverts. Broad, white median coverts, barred greater wing-coverts; white patches on primaries, secondaries; white-edged grey-brown tail; pale pinkish legs. Solitary, or in pairs when breeding; wags tail, hindquarters from side to side, rather than up and down like other wagtails. Walks, and runs along openings, paths in forests; also walks along horizontal branches.

CITRINE WAGTAIL

Motacilla citreola Motacillidae

Size 17 cm

Voice Ordinary call note a wheezy *tzzeep*

Range Winter visitor over most of India

Habitat Marshes, wet cultivation, edges of jheels

♀

Grey back; diagnostic yellow head, sides of face, complete underbody; white in dark wings. The race *calcarata* has deep black back and rump; yellow of head may be paler in female; plumage of races often confusing. Sociable, often with other wagtails; shows marked preference for damp areas; sometimes moves on floating vegetation on pond surfaces; either walks cautiously or makes short dashes.

♂ *calcarata*

♂ *calcarata*

♂ *citreola*

YELLOW WAGTAIL

Motacilla flava Motacillidae

Size 17 cm

Voice Calls include *swee…ip; zhrreep*

Range Lowlands throughout the region. Said to be absent in Bhutan

Habitat Marshy pastures; flooded fields; edges of waterbodies

Very variable, mainly greenish-and-yellow wagtail; many races and hybrids occur; only wagtail with olive-green or brownish mantle, back, and rump (brownish-backed Forest Wagtail has unmistakable wing, breast pattern). Relatively shorter tail; yellow underparts, vent (Citrine has white vent); two wing-bars. Breeding male has greenish-yellow to dark grey crown and ear-coverts. Non-breeding and female brownish with straight, pale supercilium (Citrine has curved); whitish or yellow-washed underparts; very gregarious in winter; less undulating wagtail flight.

beema

lutea

thunbergi

taivana

feldegg

superciliaris

WHITE WAGTAIL

Motacilla alba Motacillidae

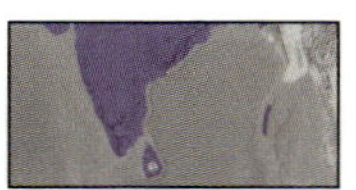

Size 18 cm

Voice Calls include *chee… cheep; cheesik*

Range Throughout the region

Habitat Summers in upland meadows or open areas near streams. Winters in wet fields; often near water

alba

Very variable, black, white and/or grey wagtail; for purposes of ID, races characterised as black-backed or grey-backed; several races of White have white foreheads. Breeding bird has extensive black on throat and/or breast. Non-breeding adult generally has white throat; variable wing pattern. Solitary, or in pairs when breeding; sometimes in loose, scattered flocks; communal rooster. Forages on ground; sits prominently on exposed perches; calls while perched, in flight, or on ground.

baicalensis

alboides

personata

dukhunensis

ocularis

leucopsis

WHITE-BROWED WAGTAIL

Motacilla maderaspatensis Motacillidae

Size 21 cm

Voice Call a sharp *tzizit* or *cheezit*.... Pleasant whistling song of breeding male

Range Most of India; south of the Himalayan foothills to about 1,200 m; only resident wagtail in the Indian plains, breeding upto 2,000 m in peninsula mountains

Habitat Rocky streams, rivers, ponds, tanks; may enter wet cultivation

Black above; prominent white supercilium and large wing-band; black throat and breast; white below. Female usually more brown, male black. Mostly in pairs, though small parties may feed together in winter; bird of flowing waters, especially fond of rock-strewn rivers. Feeds at edges of water, frequently wags tail; also rides on ferry boats plying rivers.

GREY WAGTAIL

Motacilla cinerea Motacillidae

Size 19 cm

Voice Call a sharp *tzitsi*..., uttered on the wing. Pleasant song and display flight of breeding male

Range Breeds in the Himalayas, from N Balochistan east to Nepal, 1,200-4,300 m; winters from foothills south throughout India

Habitat Rocky mountain streams in summer. Open areas, forest clearings, watersides in winter

breeding

Breeding male grey above with white supercilium; brownish wings with yellow-white band; yellow-green at base of tail; blackish tail with white outer-tail feathers; black throat and white malar stripe; yellow below. Wintering male and female have whitish throat (sometimes mottled black in breeding female); paler yellow below. Mostly solitary, or in pairs; typical wagtail, feeds on ground, incessantly wags tail; settles on house roofs and overhead wires.

BLYTH'S PIPIT

Anthus godlewskii Motacillidae

Size 17 cm

Voice Calls include buzzing *spzeeu* and *chup…chup*

Range Probably widespread and fairly common winter visitor to most of Indian plains, but identification problems make status uncertain. Very rare in Pakistan and Sri Lanka; rare in Bangladesh and Nepal

Habitat Short, open grasslands, cultivation, fallow and marshes; similar to Paddyfield's, wetter than Tawny's and drier than Richard's, although all four can occur together

Similar to Richard's, but has shorter bill, tail, legs and hind claws; also, more buff below. Adult has squared centres to median coverts. Penultimate outer-tail feathers have white edges. Powerful flight. Feeds in loose groups, on ground, on insects and seeds. Can be rather furtive.

PADDYFIELD PIPIT

Anthus rufulus Motacillidae

Size 15 cm

Voice Call a thin *tsip, tseep* and *tsip…tseep…* .Trilling song of breeding male

Range Upto about 2,000 m in outer Himalayas, south throughout India

Habitat Grasslands, marshy ground, cultivation

Sexes alike. Fulvous-brown above with dark brown central feathers, giving a distinctive appearance; dark brown tail with white outer-tail feathers, easily seen in flight; dull fulvous below, streaked dark brown on sides of throat, neck and entire breast. In pairs, or several scattered on ground; runs in short spurts; when disturbed, utters feeble note as it takes off; singing male perches on grass tufts and small bushes.

TAWNY PIPIT

Anthus campestris Motacillidae

Size 16 cm

Voice Calls *tseep* or *chulp*

Range Common winter visitor mainly to Pakistan and NW India but scattered records throughout lowlands. Rare in Nepal and Bangladesh

Habitat Dry open country including semi-desert, fallow and plough

Plain, medium-sized sandy pipit with dark lores. Adult plain sandy-brown above with streaking only on crown and breast sides. Juvenile streaked above and spotted on breast and easily confused with other streaked pipits. Long, pale supercilium and indistinct moustache. Obvious white-edged, black median coverts. Outer-tail feathers buff. Hind claws short. Horizontal wagtail-like carriage.

LONG-BILLED PIPIT

Anthus similis Motacillidae

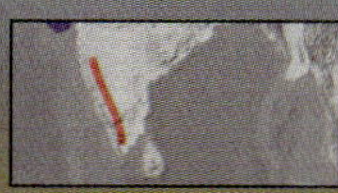

Size 20 cm

Voice Call a deep *chup*. Rather slow song

Range Common breeding resident and summer visitor in N hills from W Pakistan east to W Nepal

Habitat Breeds in dry, rocky, grassy uplands. Winters in dry grasslands, open scrub, woodlands and fallow cultivation

Largest pipit. Greyish-brown with rufous edges to wings, dark lores. Northern races greyest and plainest with barely streaked, whitish-buff or rufous-buff underparts. Southern races more heavily streaked above and more lightly streaked on breast with rufous-buff underparts. Powerful thrush-like bill, short legs and upright stance. Bounding flight; pumps and fans tail upwards.

RICHARD'S PIPIT

Anthus richardi Motacillidae

Size 18 cm

Voice Call a loud, grating *shreep*

Range Fairly common winter visitor to E lowlands including Bangladesh and Sri Lanka

Habitat Often wet grasslands and cultivation

Streaked pipit with strong thrush-like bill. Sandy or greyish-buff upperparts streaked dark brown. Well-streaked breast. Warm buff flanks contrast with white belly. Pale lores, dark moustache bordering white throat. Long hind claws, legs and tail; has upright stance.

TREE PIPIT

Anthus trivialis Motacillidae

Size 15 cm

Voice Call a sibilant, piercing *beeze*, usually louder than Olive-backed's. Loud trilling song

Range Local breeding summer visitor to N mountains from Pakistan to Himachal Pradesh. Winters widely in lowlands except extreme S and E India. Commonest in N and C areas. Vagrant to Bangladesh. Unknown in Sri Lanka

Habitat Breeds on grassy mountain slopes. Winters in open wooded areas, cultivation and village margins with trees

Small, brown pipit, heavily streaked above, especially crown, though rump plain. Buffish edgings to wing feathers and buff-washed breast and flanks, white belly. Indistinct whitish lores and supercilium. Sometimes shows white spots on ear-coverts. Pink legs and bill base. Horizontal stance.

haringtoni

trivialis

OLIVE-BACKED PIPIT

Anthus hodgsoni Motacillidae

Size 15 cm

Voice Call a faint *tseep*. . . . Lark-like song of breeding male

Range Breeds in the Himalayas, east from W Himachal Pradesh; above 2,700 m, to timberline; winters in foothills and almost across India, except arid NW, Kutch

Habitat Forests, grassy slopes

Sexes alike. Olive-brown above, streaked dark brown; dull white supercilium, two wing-bars; pale buff-white below, profusely streaked dark brown on entire breast and flanks. Gregarious in winter; spends considerable time on ground, runs briskly; if disturbed, flies with *tseep*... calls into trees; descends in few minutes.

RED-THROATED PIPIT

Anthus cervinus Motacillidae

Size 15 cm

Voice Call a characteristic *psii*

Range Winter visitor to N subcontinent

Habitat Mountains, marshland and tundra

Small pipit. Adult easily identified in breeding season by brick-red face and throat. Difficult to identify in non-breeding plumage. Heavily streaked brown upperparts with whitish mantle-stripes. Strong flight.

non-breeding

NILGIRI PIPIT

Anthus nilghiriensis Motacillidae

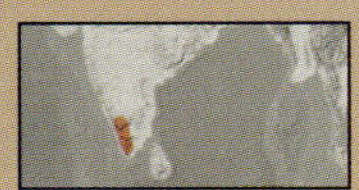

Size 15 cm

Voice Calls see…see

Range Hills of SW India

Habitat Short, montane grasslands

Distinctive species of pipit, endemic to high-altitude hills of southern India. Richer brown than other pipits in the region; non-migratory; tends to fly into low trees when disturbed.

COMMON ROSEFINCH

Carpodacus erythrinus Fringillidae

Size 15 cm

Voice Call a double-noted, questioning, *twee…ee*. Rather quiet in winter. Pleasant song of upto 8 notes; may sing before departure from wintering grounds

Range Breeds in the Himalayas, 2,700-4,000 m; winters over most of India

Habitat Cultivation, open forests, gardens, bushes

Grey-brown finch streaked red. Bright red head and breast; dark eye-stripe; brown wing panel washed crimson; rump and underbody crimson, fading into dull rose-white belly; brown, notched tail. Female buff-brown above, streaked dark; two pale wing-bars; dull buff below, streaked, except on belly. In small flocks; feeds on bushes and crops; often descends to ground; associates with other birds.

♀

non-breeding

breeding

CRESTED BUNTING

Melophus lathami Emberizidae

Size 15 cm

Voice Call a faint *chip*. . . . Pleasant, though somewhat monotonous song of breeding male

Range Resident in India, from the outer Himalayas to about 1,800 m

Habitat Open, bush and rock-covered mountainsides, open country; sometimes also cultivation

Glossy black bunting with long, pointed crest and chestnut wings and tail. Female also crested; olive-brown above, streaked darker; rufous in wings; buffy-yellow below, darkly streaked on breast; darkish moustachial stripe. Juvenile overall duller with streaked upperparts. In small flocks, often spread wide over an area; feeds on ground, paths, meadows and tar roads, especially along mountainsides; perches on ruins, walls, stones and low bushes.

juvenile

GREY-NECKED BUNTING

Emberiza buchanani Emberizidae

Size 15 cm

Voice Call a faint, single note

Range Winter visitor; quite common

Habitat Open, rocky grassy country, scrubs

Bunting of drier regions. Male has bluish-grey head with white eye-ring; buffish sub-moustachial stripe; pale grey nape and head sides; sandy-brown mantle with diffused streaking; brown back with faint rufous wash and dark streaks; white edges to dark tail; not easily visible; pale rufous-chestnut below. Female somewhat duller than male; has more prominent moustachial stripe. Seen in small flocks; feeds mostly on ground, sometimes along with other birds; quite active.

STRIOLATED BUNTING

Emberiza striolata Emberizidae

Size 14 cm

Voice Calls include nasal *chwer* and *tzwee*. Song a *witch… witch weech…witchy…witch*

Range Locally common breeding resident in lowland Pakistan, W Rajasthan and Gujarat

Habitat Scrubby hillsides, semi-desert and ruins, but not usually near human habitation

Nondescript-looking bird with fine, darkly streaked crown. Upperparts sandy-brown, narrowly streaked with rufous-washed wings. Pale grey cheeks; dark eye and moustachial stripes; pale supercilium and diagnostic darkly streaked, grey throat. Female lighter. Yellow lower mandible. Similar to Rock but with paler mantle streaked grey and rufous in wings. Nests in crevices or on ground.

♀

RED-HEADED BUNTING

Emberiza bruniceps Emberizidae

Size 17 cm

Voice Call a high-pitched *tzeett*...

Range Common winter visitor over most of the country, south of the Himalayas; absent in extreme south and along E coastal regions

Habitat Open cultivated areas

Male has rufous-chestnut crown, throat, breast; olive-yellow back streaked blackish; unmarked yellow underparts and rump; whitish wing-bars; yellow neck sides, underbody below breast. Female pale-brown above, has yellowish rump. Highly gregarious winter visitor; appears in huge numbers, frequently along with Black-headed; causes considerable damage to crops.

breeding

non-breeding

BLACK-HEADED BUNTING

Emberiza melanocephala Emberizidae

Size 18 cm

Voice Call note a musical *tzeett...*; faint chip occasionally

Range Common in winter over wide parts in W and C India; Gujarat, Rajasthan, W and C Madhya Pradesh, Maharashtra, parts of Karnataka

Habitat Open cultivation

Male has black head; thin, yellow collar and rufous-chestnut back. Bright yellow underparts with some rufous on breast sides and wing-bars. Female has brown upperparts, streaked; yellowish rump; pale buff-yellow below; very similar to female Red-Headed. Often seen in large flocks with other buntings, notably the Red-headed; feeds on crops and ground; bold, not easily driven away from croplands; in most areas, yellow males seen in greater numbers.

ACKNOWLEDGEMENTS

The authors and Om Books International would like to thank the following photographers for so generously contributing their photographs. If any names have inadvertently been omitted, please contact us at biks.grewal@gmail.com and we will rectify it in the next edition.

A D Wilson CC
A P Zaibin
A V Prassana
Aameesh Patel
Abhay Kewat
Abhilash Arjunan
Abhinash Dhal
Abhishek Das
Abhishek Varma
Abrar Ahmed
Adesh Shivkar
Adrain Pingstone CC
Agnij Sur
Akshay Charegaonkar
Aleksey Levashkin
Alka Vaidya
Amano Samarpan
Amar Jyoti Saikia
Ameya Joshi
Amish Patel
Amit Gupta
Amit Thakurta
Anand Arya
Anand Israel
Ananda Bannerjee
Ananta Singh
Anantha Murthy
Andre Karwath CC
Andrea Trepte CC
Anirban Chatterjee
Ankur Patel
Antony Grossy
Anuj Gande
Anup Dutt
Anushree Bhattacharya
Arka Sarkar
Arpit Bansal
Arpit Deomurari
Ashish Imamdar
Ashok Chaudhary
Atanu Mondal
Ateeb Hussain
Atul Jain
Avinash Adappa
Avinash Khemka
Barsha Gogoi
Bhanu Singh
Bharat Rughani
Bhaskar Das
Bhavita Toliya
Bhilhotra Dips
Bijoy KI
Biju P B
Bikram Grewal
Bishan Monappa
Biswapriya Rahut
Bjorn Johansson
Brian Patteson
Chandima Jayaweera
Charles J Sharp CC
Charles Lam CC
Chewang Bonpo
Phempu Lhasung
Chinmay Rahane
Clement M Francis
Dant Mante CC
Dave Curtis CC
David Iliff CC
Debapratim Saha
Deboshree Gogoi
Deepak Sahu
Devashish Deb
Devindra Dadhwal
Devojit Deb
Devon Pike CC
Dhananjay Joshi
Dhanu Paran
Dhanushka Senadheera
Dharuman Nanjan
Dhritiman Hore
Dhritiman Mukkerjee
Dibyendu Ash
Dileep Kumar Pushpangadhan
Dipaknkar Ghosh
Dolly L Bhardwaj
Donna Dewhurst CC
Dr Tanmoy Das
Dr Vaibhav
Dr. Nagraj
Duncan Wright CC
Dushyant Prashar
Eash Hoskote
Esha Munshi
Falguna Shah
Francis C Franklin CC
Francis Yap CC
Frank Schulenburg CC
Frankie Chu CC
Franky Boy CC
Ganesh Adhikari
Garima Bhatia
Gaurav Bhatnagar
Gaurav Deshmukh
Gaurav Kataria
Gaurika Wijeratne
Gayathri and Mansoor
Gertrud and Helmut Denzau
Girish Ketkar
Gopal Chandra Rao
Gopi Sundar
Gopinath Kollur
Gunjan Arora
Gurum Eklaya
Guruprasad Kambar
Gururaj Moorching
Hardik Pala
Harish Narasimhamurty
Harmenn Ningthoucha
Harshvardhan
HB Varun
Hilary Chambers CC
Hiyashi Haka CC
Igor Karyakin

Ingo Waschkies
J M Garg CC
Jainy Maria Kurikose
James Eaton
James Merrill
James Perdue CC
Jan W van Besten
Jason L Buberal CC
Jaysukh Parekh
Jerry Strzelecki CC
Jignesh
Jitendra Bhatia
JJ Harrison CC
Joanna Van Gruisen
John and Jemi Holmes
Jugul Tiwari
Jyotendra Thakuri
Jyotimoy Dev,
K Ramesh
K Uschel Gurung
Kallol Mukkerjee
Kalyan Varma
Karthik R
Kartik Patel
Kedar Potnis
Kim Rogers CC
Kim Yip Ho CC
Koshy Koshy
Kshounish Shankar Ray
Kulashekara Chakravarthy
Kuldeep Shukla
Kunan Naik
L J Tim CC
Lieven De Temmerman
M Savitha Ravi
Mahesh Reddy
Maitreyee Das
Manjeet Jadeja
Manjula Mathur
Manoj Sharma
Marjolein De Weirdt
Masood Hussain
Maurice van Bruggen CC
MC Sajin
MD Imran
Meg Roy Choudhury
Megna Bannerjee
Michael J Braid CC
Misha Desai
Mital Patel
Mitash Biswas
Mohamed Mothi
Mohan Munivenkatapa
Mohanram Kemparaju
Mousumi Datta
MV Shreeram
N Shiva Kumar
Nandhini Raveendaran
Narbir Singh Kalhon
Natalia Parlina and Christan Orden
Navendu Lad
Nayan Khanolkar
Nikhil Bhopale
Nikhil Devasar
Nilay Desai
Ninaad Kulkarni
Niraj Mistry
Niranjan Sant
Nirmala Sridhar
Nitin Bhardwaj
Nitin Srinivasamurthy
Olivier Klein CC
Otto Pfister
Panchami Manoo Ukil
Paramanand Chikane
Parashuram Lad
Partha Sen
Parvinder S Anand
Pema Bhutia
Peter Kaestner
Porag Jyoti Phukan
Prabhakar Manjunath
Prakash Ramakrishnan
Pranesh Kodancha
Pranjal J Saikia
Prasad Basavaraj
Prashant Kotian
Prashant Poojary
Prassana Parab
Prosenjit Singa Deo
Puja Sharma
Pushpal Goswami
R K Pai
R Kartik
Raghavendra M
Rahul Sachdeva
Raj Kamal Phukan
Raj Phukan
Rajeev Kumar
Rajesh Dhareshwar
Rajesh Panwar
Rajneesh Suvarna
Rakesh Kalra
Ramakrishna Prakash
Ramanan RR
Ramesh Anantharaman
Ramki Sreenivasan
Ranand Israel
Ranjan Barthakur
Ranjan K Das
Rathika Ramasami
Ratna Ghosh
Ravi Chand
Ravindar Musalcol
Rayees Rahman
Remi Bigonneau CC
Rohit Naniwadekar
Rohit Sant
Ron Knight CC
Ronald Haldar
Roon Bhuyan
Roshan Kamath
Rosy Chaudhary
S Krishnamurthy
S N Ragavendra
S Rajeshkumar
Saandip Nandagudi
Saandip Nandangudi
Sachin Rai
Salim Ali
Sameer Khan
Saminathan Babu
Saminathan Babu
Samyak Kaninde
Samyak Kaninde
Sangameshwar Ghattargi
Sanjay Dutt Tiwari
Santosh Gujjar
Sarthak Awhad
SarwanDeep Singh
Satish Chettri Kutwal
Satisha Sarakki
Satyendra Sharma

Savio Fonseca
Savitha Ravi
Sayan U Choudhury
Shahnawaz Khan
Sharad Agrawal
Sharad Sridhar
Shashank Dalvi
Shiva Shankar
Shiva Shankar
Shreya Singha Roy
Shyam Ghate
Sidharth Bramhankar
Sidharth Damle
Simon Cook CC
Sitara Kartikeyan
Solomon Sampath Kumar
Soma Jha
Sonu Anand
Sonu Arora
Soumayjit Nandy
Steve Ryan CC
Subharanjan Sen
Subharghaya Das
Subhasis Roy
Suboranjan Sen
Subramaniam Mani
Subranangshu Ghosh
Subroto Sanyal
Sudeep Dhatre
Sudhir Garg
Sudhir Shivaraman
Sudipto Roy
Sugata Goswami
Sujan Chatterjee
Sumit Das
Sumit K Sen
Supriya Dam
Supriya Das
Supriyo Samanta
Surendra Chouhan
Suresh K Rathod
Suresh Kamath
Suru Nair
Susan Myers
Sushmita
Swethadri Doraiswamy
T Saburaj
Tapas Misra
Tejinder Singh Rawal
Tejus Naik
Tim Loseby
Udayan Borthakur
Udayan Rao Pawar,
Umesh Srinivasan
Urmil Jhaveri
Uttan Mahata
Vaibhav Dalal
Vaibhav Deshmukh
Vaibhav Mishra
Vaidehi Gunjal
Venu Gopal
Vijay Anand Ishmavel
Vijay Cavale
Vijay Sachan
Vijay Sethi
Vishvatej Nair
Vishwatej Pawar
Vitraag Shah
Vivek Tiwari
VK Gupta
Waler Siegmund CC
Yoav Perelmen
Yograj Jadeja

Hundreds of birdwatchers, photographers and friends helped in the creation of this book. We are specially grateful to the following for providing advice and friendship: Aasheesh Pittie, Ajay Mago, Alpa Sheth, Arijit Banerjee, Arjun Sen, Bhavita Toliya, Bill Harvey, Bishan Monappa, Bittu Sahgal, Caesar Sen, Hemlata Pradhan , Krishna Kumari, Lavanya Khare, Meena Subramaniam, Nigel Redman, Om Mago, Prakash Muduli, Pritam Barua, Priyasha Ukil, Prosenjit Singa Deo, Raghuvir Khare, Ramki Sreenivasan, Ranjan K Das, Ranjeet Ranade, Ravi Singh, Rayika Sen, Rohan Chakravarty, Rohit Chakravarty, Samiha Grewal, Sanjay Mago, Sudhir Vyas, Sushama Durve, Tanaji Chakravorty and TV Prabhakar.

Special thanks to Tim and Carol Inskipp for helping in all departments.

Above all, we would like to thank Alpana Khare and her team—Neeraj Aggarwal, Ajmal Nayab Siddiqui and Raj Kishore Beck—for designing this book; and Ipshita Mitra and Dipa Chaudhuri for treating *Birds of South India* as their own.

BIBLIOGRAPHY

Ali, S. (1941) *The Book of Indian Birds*. Bombay: BNHS.

Ali, S. (1953) *The Birds of Travancore and Cochin.* Bombay: OUP.

Ali, S. & Ripley, D. (1964-74) *Handbook of the Birds of India & Pakistan* (Vols. 1-10). Bombay: OUP.

Ali, S. & Futehally, L. (1967) Common Birds. New Delhi: NBT.

Ali, S. (1968) *Common Indian Birds*, A Picture Album. New Delhi: NBT.

Ali, S. (1969) *Birds of Kerala*. Madras: OUP.

Ali, S. & Ripley, D. (1983) *A Pictorial Guide to the Birds of the Indian Subcontinent*. Bombay: OUP.

Ali, S. (1985) *Fall of a Sparrow*. Bombay: OUP.

Ali, S. (1996) *The Book of Indian Birds*. (12th ed.) New Delhi: BNHS & OUP.

Bannerjee, A. (2008) *Common Birds of the Indian Subcontinent*. New Delhi, Rupa.

Besten, J, W den. (2008) *Birds of India*, New Delhi: Mosaic Books.

BirdLife International (2001): *Threatened Birds of Asia: BirdLife International Red Data Book*. Cambridge: BirdLife International.

Daniels, R. (1992). *Birds of Urban South India. Bangalore*: Indian Institute of Science.

Daniels, R. (1996) *Fieldguide to the Birds of Southwest India*. New Delhi: OUP.

EHA Introduction by Ali, S. (1947) *The Common Birds of India*. Bombay: Thacker & Co. Ltd.

Finn, F. (1901) *How to Know the Indian Ducks*. Calcutta: Thacker, Spinks & Co.

Finn, F. (1916) *Game Birds of India & Asia*. Calcutta: Thacker, Spink & Co.

Finn, F. (1920) *How to Know the Indian Waders*. Calcutta: Thacker, Spink & Co.

Finn, F. (1920) *Indian Sporting Birds*. London: F. Edwards.

Finn, F. (1921) *The Water Fowl of India & Asia*. Calcutta & Simla: Thacker, Spink & Co.

Futehally, Z. (ed) (2006) *India Through Its Birds*, Bangalore, Dronequill Publishers Pvt. Ltd.

Grewal, B., Pfister, O. & Harvey, B. (2002) *A Photographic Guide to the Birds of India, and the Indian Subcontinent including Pakistan, Nepal, Bhutan, Bangladesh, Sri Lanka and the Maldives*, Singapore: Periplus.

Grimmet, R. Inskipp, T., & Inskipp, C. (1998) *Birds of the Indian Subcontinent*. UK: A&C Black.

Grimmet, R. & Inskipp, T. (2005) *Birds of Southern India New Delhi*, OUP: (Available also in Kannada, Malayalam, Telugu & Tamil).

Islam, MZ ur and Rahmani, A. (eds) (2004) *A Important Bird Areas in India: Priority Sites for Conservation* Mumbai: BNHS.

Islam, MZ ur and Rahmani, A. (2005) *Threatened Birds of India*, Mumbai, BNHS.

Jerdon, T.C. (1845-1847) *Illustrations of Indian Ornithology*. Madras.

Jerdon, T.C. (1862-64) *The Birds of India: A Natural History*. Vols. I-3. Calcutta: The Military Orphan Press.

Kazmierczak, K. & van Perlo, B. (2000) A *Field-Guide to the Birds of the Indian Subcontinent*. UK: Pica Press.

Naoroji, R (2006) *Birds of Prey of the Indian Subcontinent*, London: Christopher Helm

Neelakantan, K.K., Sashikumar & Venugopalan (1993) *A Book of Kerala Birds*. Trivandrum: WWF.

Pittie, A. (1995) *A Bibliographic Index to the Ornithology of the Indian Region*. Part 1. Hyderabad: Published by the author.

Pittie, A. (2010) *Birds in Books*. New Delhi: Permanent Black.

Rangaswami, S. & Sridhar, S. (1993) *Birds of Rishi Valley*. Andhra Pradesh.

Rasmussen, P. & Anderton, J. (2005) *Birds of South Asia: The Ripley Guide*, Barcelona: Lynx Editions.

Ripley, D. (1982) *A Synopsis of the Birds of India and Pakistan*. Bombay: BNHS.

Sinclair, I., & Langard, O (1998) *Birds of the Indian Ocean*, Struik.

Sonobe, K. (ed) (1993) *A Field Guide to the Waterbirds of Asia*. Tokyo.

Whistler, Hugh. (1928) *Popular Handbook of Indian Birds*. London: Gurney and Jackson.

DESCRIPTIVE PARTS OF A BIRD

A GLOSSARY OF ORNITHOLOGICAL TERMS

Aberrant Abnormal or unusual
Accidental Vagrant
Adult Mature, Capable of breeding
Aerial Making use of the open sky
Allopatric Relating to two or more related species whose range do not overlap
Altitudinal migrant Moving between high mountains and lower foothills
Altricial Blind and helpless when hatched
Apical Outer extremities, particularly of the tail
Aquatic Living on or in water
Arboreal Living in trees
Ashy Greyish Colour
Axillaries Underwing feathers at the base of the wings, forming 'armpits'
Back Loosely applied to the mantle scapulars and rump
Banyan Type of fig tree
Barring 'Sideway' lines such as on tail or breast
Basal Innermost extremities, particularly of the tail or bill
Bheel Shallow lake or wetland
Biosphere The part of earth that is inhabited by life
Biotope Area of uniform environment, flora and fauna
Bristles Sensory feathers near beak
Brood Young hatched from a single clutch
Brood Parasitism Depositing of eggs by one species in the nest of an another
Buff Yellowish white with a hint of pale brown
Bund Man-made mud embankment
Canopy Leafy foliage of treetops
Cap Upper part of head
Carpal Bend of a closed wing, sometimes called shoulder
Casque Growth above bill of hornbills
Cere Patch of bare skin on upper base of bill of raptors
Cheek Term loosely applied to sides of head, below the eye or on ear-coverts
Chevrons V-shaped contrasting marks on wings or bands across breast
Cinnamon Light yellowish-brown colour
Clutch Complete set of eggs laid by a single female
Collar Distinctive band of colour that encircles or partly encircles the neck
Colonial Roosting or nesting in groups
Confiding Not shy
Commensal Living together with man for mutual benefit
Coverts Small feathers on wings and base of tail
Covey Small group of partridges and allied species
Crepuscular Active at dusk (twilight) and dawn
Crest Extended feathers on head
Crop Pouch-like enlargement of gullet in some birds where food is partially digested
Crown Upper part of head
Crown-stripe Distinct line from forehead along centre of crown
Cryptic Hidden - having protective colouring and/ or behaviour
Culmen Ridge on upper mandible of bill
Cursorial Ground running
Deciduous Trees that shed their leaves annually
Decurved Curving downwards
Diagnostic Sufficient to identify a species or sub-species
Dimorphic Having two forms of plumage
Distal Terminal or the outer end
Diurnal Active during daytime
Down Small soft feathers close to body of chicks
Drake Male duck
Drumming Rhythmic territorial hammering on trees by woodpeckers
Duars Forested areas south of eastern Himalayas
Ear-coverts Feathers covering the ear opening. Often distinctly coloured
Ear tufts Feathers protruding near ears
Echolocate Navigate by sound
Eclipse Plumage New dull plumage after breeding season, especially in ducks
Endemic Indigenous and confined to a place
Endangered Species facing high risk of extinction
Eurasian Of both Europe and Asia
Evergreen Forests that always have leaves
Eye-ring Contrasting ring around the eye
Eye-stripe Stripe through eye
Extinct No longer in existence
Extirpated Locally extinct
Extralimital Not existing in the region
Facial Disc Heart-shaped arrangement of feathers as in some owls and harriers
Fallow Cultivated land after cultivation and before ploughing
Family Specified group of genera
Forage Search for food
Ferruginous Rusty-brown colour
Feral Escaped, and living and breeding in the wild
Filoplume Hair-like feathers like in breeding egrets
Flank Side of body
Fledged Having just acquired feathers and ready to leave nest
Fledglings Young birds which have just acquired feathers
Flight feathers Primary and secondary wing feathers
Flushed When disturbed into flight at close quarters
Foreneck The lower throat
Form Sub-species
Frons Forehead
Frugivorous Fruit-eating

Fulvous Brownish-yellow
Game birds Pheasants, partridges and allied species
Gape Basal part of the beak (mainly for young birds and raptors)
Genera Plural of genus
Genus Group of related species
Ghats Hills parallel to the east and west coast of India
Gorget Band across upper chest
Granivorous Grain-eating
Gregarious Sociable living in communities or flocks
Gular pouch Loose area of skin extending from throat as in pelicans and hornbills
Gular stripe Narrow and often dark stripe running down from the centre of throat
Guttural From the throat
Hackles Long and pointed neck feathers
Hawking Capturing insects in flight
Hepatic Rust or liver coloured plumage phase, mainly in female cuckoos
Hood Dark-coloured head and throat
Hunting party Group of birds usually of different species, seeking food
Hybridisation Cross-breeding between two different species
Immature Plumage phases prior to adult
Incubate Giving warmth for eggs to hatch
Iris Coloured eye membrane surrounding pupil
Irruption Mass movement of a population from one place to another
Jheel Shallow lake or wetland
Jizz Essence or striking characteristics of a species;
Juvenile Immature bird immediately after leaving nest
Lamellae Small stiff comb-like membrane on inner edge of bill used for sieving food
Lanceolate Lance-shaped. Slim and pointed
Lantana Invasive aggressive shrub introduced to the region
Leading edge Front edge of wing
Lek Sociable courtship gatherings
Lobe Fleshy extensions to side-edges of toes of some birds
Local Unevenly distributed with a region
Loranthus Parasitical bush that grows on tress and frequented by flowerpeckers
Lores Area between eye and bill base
Lump Treatment of one or more forms previously treated as distinct species as race of a single species
Malar Stripe on side of throat
Mandible Each of the two parts of bill
Mangrove Coastal salt-resistant trees or bushes
Mantle Back, between wings
Mask Dark plumage round eye and ear-coverts
Mesial Stripe Central throat stripe
Migration Seasonal movement between distant places
Mirror White spots in wing-tips, mainly of gulls
Monotypic Of a single form with no subspecies
Montane Pertaining to mountains
Monsoon Rainy season in India
Morph One of several distinct types of plumage in the same species
Moult Seasonal shedding of plumage
Nail Hook on tip of upper mandible
Nape Back of neck
Nares Nostril openings
Necklace Narrow line round neck
Nictitating Membrane Transparent fold of skin forming a third eyelid
Nidicolous Chicks that remain in nests for a long duration after hatching
Nidifugous Chicks that leave the nests soon after hatching
Nidification Relating to nests or nesting
Nocturnal Active at night
Nomadic Species without specific territory except when breeding
Nominate First sub-species to be formally named
Non-passerine All order of birds except for Passerines
Notch Indentations in outline of feathers, wing or tail
Nuchal Crest Crest along back of neck
Nullah Dry or wet stream bed or ditch
Nuptial Plumage Breeding plumage
Ocelli Brightly-coloured 'eye-like' spots as on peacocks
Occipital Back of head
Oology Study of bird's eggs
Orbital ring Narrow ring of skin or feathers round the eye
Order Group of related families
Paddy-fields Rice fields often flooded
Paleartic Old world and arctic zone
Parasitic Deriving sustenance or taking advantage of others, like cuckoos laying eggs in other bird's nest
Passerines Perching and song birds
Pectoral Breast area
Pelagic Ocean-going
Pellet Indigested material regurgitated by owls
Phase Colour form of a species
Pied Black and white
Plumage Feathers of a bird
Plumes Long, showy feathers, acquired during the breeding season
Polyandrous Female having more than one mate
Polygamous Male with more than one mate
Polymorphic Taking several forms
Postocular Area behind the eye
Precocial Young hatched sighted and down-covered, e.g. ducklings
Predator Who feeds on other birds or animals
Primaries Outer flight feathers in wing
Race Sub-species

Rachis Central shaft of a feather
Range Geographical area or areas inhabited by a species
Raptors Birds of prey and Vultures, excluding owls
Record Published, or otherwise broadcast, occurrence
Rectrices Tail feathers
Remiges The primaries and secondaries combined
Rictal Around the bill
Resident Non-migratory and breeding in same place
Riparian Along creeks, streams, rivers and waterways
Roost Resting or sleeping space
Rufescent Inclining to redness
Rufous Reddish brown
Rump Lower back
Sal Dominant tree of North Indian forests
Sallies Short flights and returning to perch as in bee-eaters and flycatchers
Salt pans Shallow reservoirs for drying out salt
Savanna Open flat land with grass and scattered bushes
Sedentary Staying in the same area throughout the year
Scalloped Curved markings on edges of feathers
Scapulars Feathers along edge of mantle
Scrape Shallow depression made by birds to serve as nest
Secondaries Inner wing feathers
Sedentary Confined with a particular area
Shaft Central stem of a feather, often hidden
Shank Bare parts of a leg
Sholas Small forests in SW Indian valleys
Shoulder Where the wing meets the body
Shorebird Long-legged bird living near water
Skins Bird specimens prepared for scientific studies
Skulker Bird that mostly remains within vegetation cover
Slaty Dull bluish-grey
Soar Rising flight on still extending wings using thermals
Speculum Area of colour on secondary feathers of wings
Streamers Long extensions to feathers, usually of tail
Spangles Distinctive white or shimmering spots in plumage
Species Groups of birds reproductively isolated from other such groups
Speculum Shiny, colourful patch on secondary feathers of the wing of some ducks
Storey Level of the tree or forest
Spur Sharp horny growth on legs of some birds
Straw Pale yellow colour
Streaks 'Lengthwise' lines on breasts or tail
Streamers Long extension of tail feathers
Striated Marked with fine streaks
Sooty Blackish Colour
Sub-adult Immature moulting into adult plumage
Sub-montane Hills below highest mountains
Sub-song Subdued version of normal territorial song
Sub-species Distinct form that does not have specific status
Sub-terminal Band Broad band on outer part of feather
Supercilia Plural of supercilium
Supercilium Streak above eye
Symbiotic Interdependence between different species
Tail Streamers Elongated ribbon-like tail feathers
Talons Strong sharp claws used to seize or kill prey
Tank Water reservoir
Tarsus Lower part of a bird's legs
Taxonomy Science of classifying organisms
Teak Dominant tree of South Indian forests
Terai Alluvial strech of land south of the Himalayas
Terminal band Broad band on tip of feather or tail
Terrestrial Living on the ground
Tertials Innermost wing coverts, often covering secondaries
Totipalmate All four toes connected to a single web
Trailing edge Rear edge of wing
Underparts Under surface of a bird from throat to vent
Underwing Undersurface of a wing including the linings and flight feathers
Upperparts Upper surface of a bird including wings, back and tail
Upperstorey Canopy of a tree
Vagrant Accidental, irregular
Vent Undertail area
Ventral Undersurface of body
Vermiculations Wavy (worm-like) markings
Vinaceous Red wine coloured warm pink
Vocal mimicry Imitating the sounds of other birds
Waders Shorebirds. Usually, the smaller, long-legged waterbirds
Washed Suffused with a particular colour
Wattle Bare skin, often coloured, on part of head
Web Skin stretched between toes
Wildfowl Ducks and geese
Wing-bar visible line of colour at tip on wing-coverts
Wing-coverts Small feathers on wing at base of primaries and secondaries
Wing-span Length from one wing tip to the other when fully extended
Winter plumage Plumage seen during the non-breeding winter months
Zygodactylous Having two toes directed forward and two backwards

Rain Quail

CHECKLIST: BIRDS OF SOUTH INDIA

English Name	Scientific Name	Alternative Name(s)
Anseriformes (Anatidae)		
Fulvous Whistling Duck	*Dendrocygna bicolor*	Large Whistling Teal
Lesser Whistling Duck	*Dendrocygna javanica*	Lesser Whistling Teal, Tree Duck
Bar-headed Goose	*Anser indicus*	
Common Shelduck	*Tadorna tadorna*	
Ruddy Shelduck	*Tadorna ferruginea*	Brahminy Duck
Red-crested Pochard	*Netta rufina*	
Common Pochard	*Aythya ferina*	
Ferruginous Duck	*Aythya nyroca*	White-eyed Pochard
Tufted Duck	*Aythya fuligula*	Tufted Pochard
Garganey	*Spatula querquedula*	
Northern Shoveler	*Spatula clypeata*	
Gadwall	*Mareca strepera*	
Eurasian Wigeon	*Mareca penelope*	
Indian Spot-billed Duck	*Anas poecilorhyncha*	Spotbill Duck (incl. A. zonorhyncha)
Mallard	*Anas platyrhynchos*	
Northern Pintail	*Anas acuta*	
Common Teal	*Anas crecca*	Green-winged Teal, Eurasian Teal
Comb Duck	*Sarkidiornis melanotos*	Knob-billed Duck, African Comb Duck
Cotton Teal	*Nettapus coromandelianus*	Cotton Pygmy Goose
Galliformes (Phasianidae)		
Chestnut-breasted Hill Partridge	*Arborophila mandellii*	Chestnut-breasted Partridge
Indian Peafowl	*Pavo cristatus*	Blue Peafowl, Common Peafowl
Common Quail	*Coturnix coturnix*	Grey Quail
Rain Quail	*Coturnix coromandelica*	Black-breasted Quail
Blue-breasted Quail	*Synoicus chinensis*	King Quail, Asian Blue Quail
Jungle Bush Quail	*Perdicula asiatica*	
Rock Bush Quail	*Perdicula argoondah*	
Painted Bush Quail	*Perdicula erythrorhyncha*	
Painted Francolin	*Francolinus pictus*	Painted Partridge
Grey Francolin	*Francolinus pondicerianus*	Grey Partridge
Red Junglefowl	*Gallus gallus*	
Grey Junglefowl	*Gallus sonneratii*	
Red Spurfowl	*Galloperdix spadicea*	
Painted Spurfowl	*Galloperdix lunulata*	
Phoenicopteriformes (Phoenicopteridae)		
Greater Flamingo	*Phoenicopterus roseus*	
Lesser Flamingo	*Phoeniconaias minor*	
Phoenicopteriformes (Podicipedidae)		
Little Grebe	*Tachybaptus ruficollis*	Dabchick
Columbiformes (Columbidae)		
Rock Pigeon	*Columba livia*	Rock Dove, Blue Rock Pigeon
Nilgiri Wood Pigeon	*Columba elphinstonii*	Nilgiri Pigeon
Pale-capped Pigeon	*Columba punicea*	Purple Wood Pigeon
Oriental Turtle Dove	*Streptopelia orientalis*	Rufous Turtle Dove
Eurasian Collared Dove	*Streptopelia decaocto*	Indian Ring Dove
Red Collared Dove	*Streptopelia tranquebarica*	Red Turtle Dove
Spotted Dove	*Streptopelia chinensis*	[Western Spotted Dove, Eastern Spotted Dove]
Laughing Dove	*Streptopelia senegalensis*	Little Brown Dove, Senegal Dove
Orange-breasted Green Pigeon	*Treron bicinctus*	
Pompadour Green Pigeon	*Treron pompadora*	[Grey-fronted Green Pigeon, Andaman Green Pigeon, Ashy-headed Green Pigeon]
Yellow-legged Green Pigeon	*Treron phoenicopterus*	Yellow-footed Green Pigeon
Emerald Dove	*Chalcophaps indica*	
Green Imperial Pigeon	*Ducula aenea*	[Nicobar Imperial Pigeon]
Mountain Imperial Pigeon	*Ducula badia*	Maroon-backed Imperial Pigeon D. b. cuprea & D. b. insignis, Grey-headed Imperial Pigeon D. b. griseicapilla; [Nilgiri Imperial Pigeon]

English Name	Scientific Name	Alternative Name(s)
Pterocliformes (Pteroclidae)		
Chestnut-bellied Sandgrouse	*Pterocles exustus*	Common Indian Sandgrouse, Indian Sandgrouse
Painted Sandgrouse	*Pterocles indicus*	Close-barred Sandgrouse (incl. P. lichtensteinii)
Phaethontiformes (Phaethontidae)		
Red-billed Tropicbird	*Phaethon aethereus*	Short-tailed Tropicbird
White-tailed Tropicbird	*Phaethon lepturus*	White Tropicbird
Caprimulgiformes (Podargidae)		
Sri Lanka Frogmouth	*Batrachostomus moniliger*	
Caprimulgiformes (Caprimulgidae)		
Great Eared Nightjar	*Lyncornis macrotis*	
Grey Nightjar	*Caprimulgus indicus*	[Jungle Nightjar/Indian Jungle Nightjar]
Jerdon's Nightjar	*Caprimulgus atripennis*	
Large-tailed Nightjar	*Caprimulgus macrurus*	Long-tailed Nightjar (incl. C. atripennis & C. andamanicus)
Indian Nightjar	*Caprimulgus asiaticus*	Common Indian Nightjar, Indian Little Nightjar
Savanna Nightjar	*Caprimulgus affinis*	Franklin's Nightjar, Allied Nightjar
Caprimulgiformes (Apodidae)		
Crested Treeswift	*Hemiprocne coronata*	
White-rumped Spinetail	*Zoonavena sylvatica*	White-rumped Needletail, White-rumped Spinetail Swift
Brown-backed Needletail	*Hirundapus giganteus*	Brown-throated Needletail, Large Brown-throated Spinetail Swift
Indian Swiftlet	*Aerodramus unicolor*	Indian Edible-nest Swiftlet
Asian Palm Swift	*Cypsiurus balasiensis*	
Alpine Swift	*Tachymarptis melba*	
Indian House Swift	*Apus affinis*	Little Swift, House Swift (incl. A. nipalensis)
Common Swift	*Apus apus*	Swift
Cuculiformes (Cuculidae)		
Greater Coucal	*Centropus sinensis*	Crow-pheasant; [Andaman Coucal]
Lesser Coucal	*Centropus bengalensis*	
Sirkeer Malkoha	*Taccocua leschenaultii*	Sirkeer Cuckoo
Blue-faced Malkoha	*Phaenicophaeus viridirostris*	Small Green-billed Malkoha
Green-billed Malkoha	*Phaenicophaeus tristis*	Large Green-billed Malkoha
Pied Cuckoo	*Clamator jacobinus*	Pied Crested Cuckoo, Jacobin Cuckoo
Chestnut-winged Cuckoo	*Clamator coromandus*	Red-winged Crested Cuckoo
Asian Koel	*Eudynamys scolopaceus*	Common Koel
Banded Bay Cuckoo	*Cacomantis sonneratii*	Bay-banded Cuckoo
Grey-bellied Cuckoo	*Cacomantis passerinus*	Indian Plaintive Cuckoo
Drongo Cuckoo	*Surniculus lugubris*	[Fork-tailed Drongo Cuckoo, Square-tailed Drongo Cuckoo]
Large Hawk Cuckoo	*Hierococcyx sparverioides*	
Common Hawk Cuckoo	*Hierococcyx varius*	Brainfever Bird
Indian Cuckoo	*Cuculus micropterus*	
Common Cuckoo	*Cuculus canorus*	Eurasian Cuckoo
Lesser Cuckoo	*Cuculus poliocephalus*	Small Cuckoo
Gruiformes (Rallidae)		
Slaty-legged Crake	*Rallina eurizonoides*	Slaty-legged Banded Crake
Western Water Rail	*Rallus aquaticus*	Water Rail (incl. R. indicus)
Slaty-breasted Rail	*Lewinia striata*	Blue-breasted Banded Rail
Spotted Crake	*Porzana porzana*	
Ruddy-breasted Crake	*Zapornia fusca*	Ruddy Crake
Brown Crake	*Zapornia akool*	
Baillon's Crake	*Zapornia pusilla*	
White-breasted Waterhen	*Amaurornis phoenicurus*	
Watercock	*Gallicrex cinerea*	Kora
Purple Swamphen	*Porphyrio porphyrio*	Purple Moorhen, Grey-headed Swamphen P. [p.] poliocephalus
Common Moorhen	*Gallinula chloropus*	Eurasian Moorhen, Indian Moorhen
Common Coot	*Fulica atra*	Eurasian Coot
Gruiformes (Gruidae)		
Sarus Crane	*Antigone antigone*	
Demoiselle Crane	*Grus virgo*	

English Name	Scientific Name	Alternative Name(s)
Common Crane	*Grus grus*	
Otidiformes (Otididae)		
Great Indian Bustard	*Ardeotis nigriceps*	Indian Bustard
Lesser Florican	*Sypheotides indicus*	Leekh, Likh
Procellariiformes (Oceanitidae)		
Wilson's Storm-petrel	*Oceanites oceanicus*	
Procellariiformes (Hydrobatidae)		
Swinhoe's Storm-petrel	*Hydrobates monorhis*	Fork-tailed Storm-petrel
Procellariiformes (Procellariidae)		
Wedge-tailed Shearwater	*Ardenna pacifica*	
Flesh-footed Shearwater	*Ardenna carneipes*	Pink-footed Shearwater (incl. A. creatopus)
Pelecaniformes (Ciconiidae)		
Greater Adjutant	*Leptoptilos dubius*	Adjutant Stork
Lesser Adjutant	*Leptoptilos javanicus*	
Painted Stork	*Mycteria leucocephala*	
Asian Openbill	*Anastomus oscitans*	Openbill Stork, Open-billed Stork
Black Stork	*Ciconia nigra*	
Woolly-necked Stork	*Ciconia episcopus*	Asian Woollyneck C. e. episcopus, White-necked Stork
European White Stork	*Ciconia ciconia*	
Black-necked Stork	*Ephippiorhynchus asiaticus*	
Pelecaniformes (Pelecanidae)		
Great White Pelican	*Pelecanus onocrotalus*	Rosy Pelican
Spot-billed Pelican	*Pelecanus philippensis*	Grey Pelican
Pelecaniformes (Ardeidae)		
Eurasian Bittern	*Botaurus stellaris*	Great Bittern
Yellow Bittern	*Ixobrychus sinensis*	
Cinnamon Bittern	*Ixobrychus cinnamomeus*	Chestnut Bittern
Black Bittern	*Ixobrychus flavicollis*	
Malayan Night Heron	*Gorsachius melanolophus*	Malay Bittern, Tiger Bittern
Black-crowned Night Heron	*Nycticorax nycticorax*	
Striated Heron	*Butorides striata*	Little Green Heron
Indian Pond Heron	*Ardeola grayii*	Paddybird
Cattle Egret	*Bubulcus ibis*	
Grey Heron	*Ardea cinerea*	
Purple Heron	*Ardea purpurea*	
Great Egret	*Ardea alba*	Large Egret
Intermediate Egret	*Ardea intermedia*	Median Egret, Smaller Egret
Little Egret	*Egretta garzetta*	
Western Reef Egret	*Egretta gularis*	Western Reef Heron, Indian Reef Heron
Pelecaniformes (Threskiornithidae)		
Black-headed Ibis	*Threskiornis melanocephalus*	White Ibis, Oriental White Ibis
Eurasian Spoonbill	*Platalea leucorodia*	
Indian Black Ibis	*Pseudibis papillosa*	Red-naped Ibis
Glossy Ibis	*Plegadis falcinellus*	
Pelecaniformes (Fregatidae)		
Lesser Frigatebird	*Fregata ariel*	Least Frigatebird
Great Frigatebird	*Fregata minor*	Lesser Frigatebird (vide HBK)
Pelecaniformes (Sulidae)		
Red-footed Booby	*Sula sula*	
Brown Booby	*Sula leucogaster*	
Masked Booby	*Sula dactylatra*	
Pelecaniformes (Phalacrocoracidae)		
Little Cormorant	*Microcarbo niger*	
Great Cormorant	*Phalacrocorax carbo*	Large Cormorant
Indian Cormorant	*Phalacrocorax fuscicollis*	Indian Shag
Pelecaniformes (Anhingidae)		
Oriental Darter	*Anhinga melanogaster*	Snake-bird
Charadriiformes (Burhinidae)		
Eurasian Thick-knee	*Burhinus oedicnemus*	Eurasian Stone-curlew; [Indian Thick-knee]
Great Thick-knee	*Esacus recurvirostris*	Great Stone-curlew, Great Stone Plover

English Name	Scientific Name	Alternative Name(s)
Charadriiformes (Recurvirostridae)		
Pied Avocet	*Recurvirostra avosetta*	Avocet
Black-winged Stilt	*Himantopus himantopus*	[White-headed Stilt, Pied Stilt]
Charadriiformes (Charadriidae)		
Grey Plover	*Pluvialis squatarola*	Black-bellied Plover
Pacific Golden Plover	*Pluvialis fulva*	Eastern Golden Plover
Common Ringed Plover	*Charadrius hiaticula*	Eastern Ringed Plover
Little Ringed Plover	*Charadrius dubius*	
Kentish Plover	*Charadrius alexandrinus*	[White-faced Plover]
Lesser Sand Plover	*Charadrius mongolus*	Mongolian Plover
Greater Sand Plover	*Charadrius leschenaultii*	Large Sand Plover
River Lapwing	*Vanellus duvaucelii*	Spur-winged Lapwing/Spur-winged Plover (with V. spinosus)
Yellow-wattled Lapwing	*Vanellus malabaricus*	
Red-wattled Lapwing	*Vanellus indicus*	
Sociable Lapwing	*Vanellus gregarius*	Sociable Plover
White-tailed Lapwing	*Vanellus leucurus*	
Charadriiformes (Rostratulidae)		
Greater Painted-snipe	*Rostratula benghalensis*	
Charadriiformes (Jacanidae)		
Pheasant-tailed Jacana	*Hydrophasianus chirurgus*	
Bronze-winged Jacana	*Metopidius indicus*	
Charadriiformes (Scolopacidae)		
Whimbrel	*Numenius phaeopus*	
Eurasian Curlew	*Numenius arquata*	
Bar-tailed Godwit	*Limosa lapponica*	
Black-tailed Godwit	*Limosa limosa*	
Ruddy Turnstone	*Arenaria interpres*	Turnstone
Red Knot	*Calidris canutus*	Knot
Ruff	*Calidris pugnax*	
Broad-billed Sandpiper	*Calidris falcinellus*	
Curlew Sandpiper	*Calidris ferruginea*	
Temminck's Stint	*Calidris temminckii*	
Long-toed Stint	*Calidris subminuta*	
Spoon-billed Sandpiper	*Calidris pygmaea*	
Red-necked Stint	*Calidris ruficollis*	Rufous-necked Stint, Eastern Little Stint
Sanderling	*Calidris alba*	
Dunlin	*Calidris alpina*	
Little Stint	*Calidris minuta*	
Asian Dowitcher	*Limnodromus semipalmatus*	Snipe-billed Godwit
Eurasian Woodcock	*Scolopax rusticola*	
Wood Snipe	*Gallinago nemoricola*	
Pintail Snipe	*Gallinago stenura*	
Swinhoe's Snipe	*Gallinago megala*	
Common Snipe	*Gallinago gallinago*	Fantail Snipe
Jack Snipe	*Lymnocryptes minimus*	
Terek Sandpiper	*Xenus cinereus*	
Common Sandpiper	*Actitis hypoleucos*	
Green Sandpiper	*Tringa ochropus*	
Spotted Redshank	*Tringa erythropus*	Dusky Redshank
Common Greenshank	*Tringa nebularia*	Greenshank
Common Redshank	*Tringa totanus*	
Wood Sandpiper	*Tringa glareola*	Spotted Sandpiper
Marsh Sandpiper	*Tringa stagnatilis*	
Red-necked Phalarope	*Phalaropus lobatus*	
Charadriiformes (Turnicidae)		
Small Buttonquail	*Turnix sylvaticus*	Common Buttonquail, Little Bustard-quail
Yellow-legged Buttonquail	*Turnix tanki*	Yellow-legged Bustard-quail
Barred Buttonquail	*Turnix suscitator*	Common Bustard-quail
Charadriiformes (Dromadidae)		
Crab-plover	*Dromas ardeola*	

English Name	Scientific Name	Alternative Name(s)
Charadriiformes (Glareolidae)		
Jerdon's Courser	*Rhinoptilus bitorquatus*	Double-banded Courser
Indian Courser	*Cursorius coromandelicus*	
Oriental Pratincole	*Glareola maldivarum*	Large Indian Swallow-plover, Large Indian Pratincole
Little Pratincole	*Glareola lactea*	Small Pratincole, Small Indian Pratincole, Small Indian Swallow-plover
Charadriiformes (Stercorariidae)		
Long-tailed Skua	*Stercorarius longicaudus*	Long-tailed Jaeger
Arctic Skua	*Stercorarius parasiticus*	Parasitic Jaeger
Pomarine Skua	*Stercorarius pomarinus*	Pomarine Jaeger
South Polar Skua	*Stercorarius maccormicki*	
Brown Skua	*Stercorarius antarcticus*	Antarctic Skua, Southern Skua
Charadriiformes (Laridae)		
Brown Noddy	*Anous stolidus*	Noddy Tern
Lesser Noddy	*Anous tenuirostris*	
White Tern	*Gygis alba*	Fairy Tern
Indian Skimmer	*Rynchops albicollis*	
Slender-billed Gull	*Chroicocephalus genei*	
Brown-headed Gull	*Chroicocephalus brunnicephalus*	
Black-headed Gull	*Chroicocephalus ridibundus*	Common Black-headed Gull
Sooty Gull	*Ichthyaetus hemprichii*	
Pallas's Gull	*Ichthyaetus ichthyaetus*	Great Black-headed Gull
Caspian Gull	*Larus cachinnans*	
Sooty Tern	*Onychoprion fuscatus*	
Bridled Tern	*Onychoprion anaethetus*	Brown-winged Tern
Little Tern	*Sternula albifrons*	White-shafted Ternlet S. a. pusilla
Gull-billed Tern	*Gelochelidon nilotica*	
Caspian Tern	*Hydroprogne caspia*	
Whiskered Tern	*Chlidonias hybrida*	
White-winged Tern	*Chlidonias leucopterus*	White-winged Black Tern
River Tern	*Sterna aurantia*	
Roseate Tern	*Sterna dougallii*	Rosy Tern
Black-naped Tern	*Sterna sumatrana*	
Common Tern	*Sterna hirundo*	
White-cheeked Tern	*Sterna repressa*	
Black-bellied Tern	*Sterna acuticauda*	
Lesser Crested Tern	*Thalasseus bengalensis*	
Sandwich Tern	*Thalasseus sandvicensis*	
Greater Crested Tern	*Thalasseus bergii*	Large Crested Tern
Accipitriformes (Pandionidae)		
Osprey	*Pandion haliaetus*	
Black-winged Kite	*Elanus caeruleus*	Black-shouldered Kite
Oriental Honey Buzzard	*Pernis ptilorhynchus*	Crested Honey Buzzard
Jerdon's Baza	*Aviceda jerdoni*	Brown Lizard Hawk
Black Baza	*Aviceda leuphotes*	Black-crested Baza, Black-crested Lizard Hawk
Egyptian Vulture	*Neophron percnopterus*	Scavenger Vulture, White Scavenger Vulture
Crested Serpent Eagle	*Spilornis cheela*	[Central Nicobar Serpent Eagle]
Short-toed Snake Eagle	*Circaetus gallicus*	Short-toed Eagle
Red-headed Vulture	*Sarcogyps calvus*	King Vulture, Black Vulture, Pondicherry Vulture
White-rumped Vulture	*Gyps bengalensis*	White-backed Vulture
Indian Vulture	*Gyps indicus*	Long-billed Vulture (incl. G. tenuirostris)
Griffon Vulture	*Gyps fulvus*	Eurasian Griffon
Mountain Hawk Eagle	*Nisaetus nipalensis*	[Legge's Hawk Eagle, Hodgson's Hawk Eagle]
Changeable Hawk Eagle	*Nisaetus cirrhatus*	[Crested Hawk Eagle]
Rufous-bellied Eagle	*Lophotriorchis kienerii*	Rufous-bellied Hawk Eagle
Black Eagle	*Ictinaetus malaiensis*	
Indian Spotted Eagle	*Clanga hastata*	Lesser Spotted Eagle (with C. pomarina)
Greater Spotted Eagle	*Clanga clanga*	
Tawny Eagle	*Aquila rapax*	
Steppe Eagle	*Aquila nipalensis*	
Bonelli's Eagle	*Aquila fasciata*	Bonelli's Hawk Eagle

English Name	Scientific Name	Alternative Name(s)
Booted Eagle	*Hieraaetus pennatus*	Booted Hawk Eagle
Western Marsh Harrier	*Circus aeruginosus*	Eurasian Marsh Harrier (incl. C. spilonotus)
Hen Harrier	*Circus cyaneus*	Northern Harrier
Pallid Harrier	*Circus macrourus*	Pale Harrier
Pied Harrier	*Circus melanoleucos*	
Montagu's Harrier	*Circus pygargus*	
Crested Goshawk	*Accipiter trivirgatus*	
Shikra	*Accipiter badius*	
Besra	*Accipiter virgatus*	
Eurasian Sparrowhawk	*Accipiter nisus*	
White-bellied Sea Eagle	*Haliaeetus leucogaster*	
Pallas's Fish Eagle	*Haliaeetus leucoryphus*	Ring-tailed Fishing Eagle
Grey-headed Fish Eagle	*Icthyophaga ichthyaetus*	Grey-headed Fishing Eagle
Brahminy Kite	*Haliastur indus*	
Black Kite	*Milvus migrans*	Pariah Kite, Black-eared Kite M. m. lineatus
White-eyed Buzzard	*Butastur teesa*	White-eyed Buzzard Eagle
Common Buzzard	*Buteo buteo*	Eurasian Buzzard, Steppe Buzzard/Desert Buzzard B. b. vulpinus
Long-legged Buzzard	*Buteo rufinus*	
Strigiformes (Tytonidae)		
Bay Owl	*Phodilus badius*	[Oriental Bay Owl, Sri Lanka/Ceylon Bay Owl]
Eastern Grass Owl	*Tyto longimembris*	Australasian Grass Owl
Common Barn Owl	*Tyto alba*	Barn Owl, Western Barn Owl
Strigiformes (Strigidae)		
Brown Hawk Owl	*Ninox scutulata*	Brown Boobook; [Hume's Hawk Owl]
Jungle Owlet	*Glaucidium radiatum*	Barred Jungle Owlet
Spotted Owlet	*Athene brama*	
Forest Owlet	*Heteroglaux blewitti*	Forest Spotted Owlet, Blewitt's Owl
Pallid Scops Owl	*Otus brucei*	Striated Scops Owl
Oriental Scops Owl	*Otus sunia*	Scops Owl; [Walden's Scops Owl]
Collared Scops Owl	*Otus bakkamoena*	[Indian Scops Owl]
Short-eared Owl	*Asio flammeus*	
Mottled Wood Owl	*Strix ocellata*	
Brown Wood Owl	*Strix leptogrammica*	
Eurasian Eagle Owl	*Bubo bubo*	Great Horned Owl (incl. B. bengalensis)
Spot-bellied Eagle Owl	*Bubo nipalensis*	Forest Eagle Owl
Dusky Eagle Owl	*Bubo coromandus*	Dusky Horned Owl
Brown Fish Owl	*Ketupa zeylonensis*	
Trogoniformes (Trogonidae)		
Malabar Trogon	*Harpactes fasciatus*	
Bucerotiformes (Bucerotidae)		
Great Hornbill	*Buceros bicornis*	Great Pied Hornbill, Great Indian Hornbill
Malabar Pied Hornbill	*Anthracoceros coronatus*	
Oriental Pied Hornbill	*Anthracoceros albirostris*	Indian Pied Hornbill
Malabar Grey Hornbill	*Ocyceros griseus*	
Indian Grey Hornbill	*Ocyceros birostris*	Common Grey Hornbill
Bucerotiformes (Upupidae)		
Common Hoopoe	*Upupa epops*	Eurasian Hoopoe
Piciformes (Picidae)		
Eurasian Wryneck	*Jynx torquilla*	Wryneck, Northern Wryneck
Speckled Piculet	*Picumnus innominatus*	
Heart-spotted Woodpecker	*Hemicircus canente*	
Common Golden-backed Woodpecker	*Dinopium javanense*	Common Flameback, Indian Golden-backed Three-toed Woodpecker
Lesser Golden-backed Woodpecker	*Dinopium benghalense*	Black-rumped Flameback
Pale-headed Woodpecker	*Gecinulus grantia*	
Greater Yellow-naped Woodpecker	*Chrysophlegma flavinucha*	Greater Yellownape, Yellow-naped Woodpecker
Lesser Yellow-naped Woodpecker	*Picus chlorolophus*	Lesser Yellownape, Small Yellow-naped Woodpecker
Streak-throated Woodpecker	*Picus xanthopygaeus*	Little Scaly-bellied Green Woodpecker
White-bellied Woodpecker	*Dryocopus javensis*	Great Black Woodpecker

English Name	Scientific Name	Alternative Name(s)
Greater Golden-backed Woodpecker	*Chrysocolaptes lucidus*	[Greater Flameback, Large Golden-backed Woodpecker, Malabar Flameback]
White-naped Woodpecker	*Chrysocolaptes festivus*	Black-backed Woodpecker
Brown-capped Pygmy Woodpecker	*Dendrocopos moluccensis*	Indian Pygmy Woodpecker D. [m.] nanus
Fulvous-breasted Pied Woodpecker	*Dendrocopos macei*	Fulvous-breasted Woodpecker; [Spot-breasted Woodpecker, Freckle-breasted Woodpecker]
Yellow-fronted Pied Woodpecker	*Dendrocopos mahrattensis*	Yellow-crowned Woodpecker, Mahratta Woodpecker
Piciformes (Ramphastidae)		
Brown-headed Barbet	*Psilopogon zeylanicus*	Large Green Barbet
White-cheeked Barbet	*Psilopogon viridis*	Small Green Barbet
Malabar Barbet	*Psilopogon malabaricus*	Crimson-throated Barbet (with P. rubricapillus)
Coppersmith Barbet	*Psilopogon haemacephalus*	Crimson-breasted Barbet
Coraciiformes (Meropidae)		
Blue-bearded Bee-eater	*Nyctyornis athertoni*	
Green Bee-eater	*Merops orientalis*	Small Green Bee-eater, Little Green Bee-eater
Chestnut-headed Bee-eater	*Merops leschenaulti*	
Blue-tailed Bee-eater	*Merops philippinus*	
Blue-cheeked Bee-eater	*Merops persicus*	
European Bee-eater	*Merops apiaster*	
Coraciiformes (Coraciidae)		
Indian Roller	*Coracias benghalensis*	[Indochinese Roller]
European Roller	*Coracias garrulus*	Kashmir Roller
Dollarbird	*Eurystomus orientalis*	Broad-billed Roller
Coraciiformes (Alcedinidae)		
Oriental Dwarf Kingfisher	*Ceyx erithaca*	[Rufous-backed Dwarf Kingfisher, Black-backed Dwarf Kingfisher]
Blue-eared Kingfisher	*Alcedo meninting*	
Common Kingfisher	*Alcedo atthis*	Small Blue Kingfisher
Pied Kingfisher	*Ceryle rudis*	Lesser Pied Kingfisher
Stork-billed Kingfisher	*Pelargopsis capensis*	Brown-headed Stork-billed Kingfisher
Brown-winged Kingfisher	*Pelargopsis amauroptera*	Brown-winged Stork-billed Kingfisher
White-throated Kingfisher	*Halcyon smyrnensis*	White-breasted Kingfisher
Black-capped Kingfisher	*Halcyon pileata*	
Collared Kingfisher	*Todiramphus chloris*	White-collared Kingfisher
Falconiformes (Falconidae)		
Lesser Kestrel	*Falco naumanni*	
Common Kestrel	*Falco tinnunculus*	Eurasian Kestrel
Red-necked Falcon	*Falco chicquera*	Red-headed Falcon, Red-headed Merlin
Amur Falcon	*Falco amurensis*	
Oriental Hobby	*Falco severus*	
Laggar Falcon	*Falco jugger*	
Peregrine Falcon	*Falco peregrinus*	Shaheen Falcon F. p. peregrinator; [Barbary Falcon]
Psittaciformes (Psittaculidae)		
Plum-headed Parakeet	*Psittacula cyanocephala*	Blossom-headed Parakeet
Malabar Parakeet	*Psittacula columboides*	Blue-winged Parakeet
Alexandrine Parakeet	*Psittacula eupatria*	Large Indian Parakeet
Rose-ringed Parakeet	*Psittacula krameri*	
Vernal Hanging Parrot	*Loriculus vernalis*	Indian Lorikeet
Passeriformes (Pittidae)		
Indian Pitta	*Pitta brachyura*	
Passeriformes (Campephagidae)		
White-bellied Minivet	*Pericrocotus erythropygius*	
Small Minivet	*Pericrocotus cinnamomeus*	
Scarlet Minivet	*Pericrocotus flammeus*	[Orange Minivet]
Ashy Minivet	*Pericrocotus divaricatus*	
Rosy Minivet	*Pericrocotus roseus*	
Large Cuckooshrike	*Coracina javensis*	
Black-winged Cuckooshrike	*Lalage melaschistos*	Dark Grey Cuckooshrike
Black-headed Cuckooshrike	*Lalage melanoptera*	

English Name	Scientific Name	Alternative Name(s)
Passeriformes (Oriolidae)		
Black-hooded Oriole	*Oriolus xanthornus*	Black-headed Oriole
Indian Golden Oriole	*Oriolus kundoo*	
Black-naped Oriole	*Oriolus chinensis*	
Passeriformes (Artamidae)		
Ashy Woodswallow	*Artamus fuscus*	Ashy Swallow-shrike
Passeriformes (Vangidae)		
Bar-winged Flycatcher-shrike	*Hemipus picatus*	Pied Flycatcher-shrike
Large Woodshrike	*Tephrodornis virgatus*	[Malabar Woodshrike]
Common Woodshrike	*Tephrodornis pondicerianus*	
Passeriformes (Aegithinidae)		
Common Iora	*Aegithina tiphia*	
Marshall's Iora	*Aegithina nigrolutea*	White-tailed Iora
Passeriformes (Dicruridae)		
Black Drongo	*Dicrurus macrocercus*	
Ashy Drongo	*Dicrurus leucophaeus*	Grey Drongo
White-bellied Drongo	*Dicrurus caerulescens*	
Bronzed Drongo	*Dicrurus aeneus*	
Hair-crested Drongo	*Dicrurus hottentottus*	Spangled Drongo
Greater Racket-tailed Drongo	*Dicrurus paradiseus*	
Passeriformes (Rhipiduridae)		
White-browed Fantail	*Rhipidura aureola*	White-browed Fantail-flycatcher
White-throated Fantail	*Rhipidura albicollis*	White-throated Fantail-flycatcher; [White-spotted Fantail, Spot-breasted Fantail]
Passeriformes (Laniidae)		
Brown Shrike	*Lanius cristatus*	Philippine Shrike L. c. lucionensis, Japanese Shrike L. c. superciliosus
Red-backed Shrike	*Lanius collurio*	
Burmese Shrike	*Lanius collurioides*	Chestnut-rumped Shrike
Long-tailed Shrike	*Lanius schach*	Rufous-backed Shrike
Lesser Grey Shrike	*Lanius minor*	
Passeriformes (Corvidae)		
Rufous Treepie	*Dendrocitta vagabunda*	Indian Treepie
Grey Treepie	*Dendrocitta formosae*	Himalayan Treepie
White-bellied Treepie	*Dendrocitta leucogastra*	Southern Treepie
House Crow	*Corvus splendens*	
Large-billed Crow	*Corvus macrorhynchos*	[Jungle Crow, Indian Jungle Crow, Eastern Jungle Crow]
Passeriformes (Monarchidae)		
Black-naped Monarch	*Hypothymis azurea*	Black-naped Monarch Flycatcher, Black-naped Flycatcher
Indian Paradise-flycatcher	*Terpsiphone paradisi*	Asian Paradise-flycatcher (incl. T. affinis)
Passeriformes (Dicaeidae)		
Thick-billed Flowerpecker	*Dicaeum agile*	[Modest Flowerpecker]
Pale-billed Flowerpecker	*Dicaeum erythrorhynchos*	Tickell's Flowerpecker
Passeriformes (Nectariniidae)		
Little Spiderhunter	*Arachnothera longirostra*	
Ruby-cheeked Sunbird	*Chalcoparia singalensis*	Rubycheek
Purple-rumped Sunbird	*Leptocoma zeylonica*	
Crimson-backed Sunbird	*Leptocoma minima*	Small Sunbird
Purple Sunbird	*Cinnyris asiaticus*	
Loten's Sunbird	*Cinnyris lotenius*	Long-billed Sunbird, Maroon-breasted Sunbird
Crimson Sunbird	*Aethopyga siparaja*	Yellow-backed Sunbird (incl. A. vigorsii)
Passeriformes (Irenidae)		
Asian Fairy-bluebird	*Irena puella*	
Golden-fronted Leafbird	*Chloropsis aurifrons*	Gold-fronted Chloropsis, Golden-fronted Chloropsis
Blue-winged Leafbird	*Chloropsis cochinchinensis*	Gold-mantled Chloropsis
Passeriformes (Ploceidae)		
Black-breasted Weaver	*Ploceus benghalensis*	Bengal Weaver, Black-throated Weaver
Streaked Weaver	*Ploceus manyar*	
Baya Weaver	*Ploceus philippinus*	Indian Baya

English Name	Scientific Name	Alternative Name(s)
Passeriformes (Estrildidae)		
Red Munia	*Amandava amandava*	Red Avadavat
Green Munia	*Amandava formosa*	Green Avadavat
Indian Silverbill	*Euodice malabarica*	White-throated Munia
White-rumped Munia	*Lonchura striata*	White-backed Munia
Scaly-breasted Munia	*Lonchura punctulata*	Spotted Munia
Black-throated Munia	*Lonchura kelaarti*	Rufous-bellied Munia
Passeriformes (Passeridae)		
House Sparrow	*Passer domesticus*	
Eurasian Tree Sparrow	*Passer montanus*	Tree Sparrow
Yellow-throated Sparrow	*Gymnoris xanthocollis*	Chestnut-shouldered Petronia
Passeriformes (Motacillidae)		
Forest Wagtail	*Dendronanthus indicus*	
Tree Pipit	*Anthus trivialis*	Eurasian Tree Pipit
Olive-backed Pipit	*Anthus hodgsoni*	Indian Tree Pipit
Red-throated Pipit	*Anthus cervinus*	
Nilgiri Pipit	*Anthus nilghiriensis*	
Richard's Pipit	*Anthus richardi*	
Paddyfield Pipit	*Anthus rufulus*	
Tawny Pipit	*Anthus campestris*	
Long-billed Pipit	*Anthus similis*	Brown Rock Pipit
Western Yellow Wagtail	*Motacilla flava*	
Grey Wagtail	*Motacilla cinerea*	
Citrine Wagtail	*Motacilla citreola*	Yellow-headed Wagtail
White-browed Wagtail	*Motacilla maderaspatensis*	Large Pied Wagtail
White Wagtail	*Motacilla alba*	Pied Wagtail
Passeriformes (Fringillidae)		
Common Rosefinch	*Erythrina erythrina*	
Passeriformes (Emberizidae)		
Striolated Bunting	*Fringillaria striolata*	House Bunting
Crested Bunting	*Melophus lathami*	
Red-headed Bunting	*Granativora bruniceps*	
Black-headed Bunting	*Granativora melanocephala*	
Grey-necked Bunting	*Emberiza buchanani*	Grey-hooded Bunting
Passeriformes (Paridae)		
Rufous-naped Tit	*Periparus rufonuchalis*	Black-breasted Tit, Dark-grey Tit, Simla Black Tit
Cinereous Tit	*Parus cinereus*	Grey Tit/Great Tit (with P. major)
White-naped Tit	*Machlolophus nuchalis*	White-winged Black Tit
Black-lored Tit	*Machlolophus xanthogenys*	Yellow-cheeked Tit (incl. M. spilonotus); [Indian Tit, Indian Black-lored Tit, Himalayan Black-lored Tit, Black-lored Yellow Tit]
Passeriformes (Alaudidae)		
Rufous-tailed Lark	*Ammomanes phoenicura*	Rufous-tailed Finch Lark
Ashy-crowned Sparrow Lark	*Eremopterix griseus*	Ashy-crowned Finch Lark
Singing Bushlark	*Mirafra cantillans*	
Indian Bushlark	*Mirafra erythroptera*	Red-winged Bushlark
Jerdon's Bushlark	*Mirafra affinis*	
Greater Short-toed Lark	*Calandrella brachydactyla*	
Oriental Skylark	*Alauda gulgula*	Small Skylark
Crested Lark	*Galerida cristata*	
Malabar Lark	*Galerida malabarica*	Malabar Crested Lark
Sykes's Lark	*Galerida deva*	Tawny Lark, Deccan Crested Lark, Sykes's Crested Lark
Passeriformes (Cisticolidae)		
Zitting Cisticola	*Cisticola juncidis*	Streaked Fantail Warbler
Golden-headed Cisticola	*Cisticola exilis*	Bright-capped Cisticola, Red-headed Cisticola C. e. erythrocephalus, Yellow-headed Cisticola C. e. tytleri
Rufous-fronted Prinia	*Prinia buchanani*	Rufous-fronted Wren Warbler
Rufescent Prinia	*Prinia rufescens*	Rufous Wren Warbler

English Name	Scientific Name	Alternative Name(s)
Grey-breasted Prinia	*Prinia hodgsonii*	Franklin's Wren Warbler, Ashy-grey Wren Warbler
Jungle Prinia	*Prinia sylvatica*	Jungle Wren Warbler
Ashy Prinia	*Prinia socialis*	Ashy Wren Warbler
Plain Prinia	*Prinia inornata*	Plain Wren Warbler
Common Tailorbird	*Orthotomus sutorius*	
Passeriformes (Locustellidae)		
Grasshopper Warbler	*Locustella naevia*	
Striated Grassbird	*Megalurus palustris*	Striated Marsh Warbler
Broad-tailed Grassbird	*Schoenicola platyurus*	Broad-tailed Grass Warbler
Bristled Grassbird	*Chaetornis striata*	Bristled Grass Warbler
Passeriformes (Acrocephalidae)		
Thick-billed Warbler	*Arundinax aedon*	
Blyth's Reed Warbler	*Acrocephalus dumetorum*	
Paddyfield Warbler	*Acrocephalus agricola*	
Clamorous Reed Warbler	*Acrocephalus stentoreus*	Indian Reed Warbler / Indian Great Reed Warbler A. s. brunnescens
Passeriformes (Hirundinidae)		
Northern House Martin	*Delichon urbicum*	Common House Martin, European House Martin
Nepal House Martin	*Delichon nipalense*	
Streak-throated Swallow	*Petrochelidon fluvicola*	Indian Cliff Swallow
Pacific Swallow	*Hirundo tahitica*	[Hill Swallow, House Swallow]
Wire-tailed Swallow	*Hirundo smithii*	
Barn Swallow	*Hirundo rustica*	Common Swallow
Eurasian Crag Martin	*Ptyonoprogne rupestris*	Crag Martin
Dusky Crag Martin	*Ptyonoprogne concolor*	
Plain Martin	*Riparia paludicola*	Grey-throated Sand Martin/Grey-throated Martin R. [p.] chinensis
Sand Martin	*Riparia riparia*	Collared Sand Martin (incl. R. diluta), Bank Swallow, Common Sand Martin
Pale Martin	*Riparia diluta*	Pale Sand Martin
Passeriformes (Pycnonotidae)		
Black Bulbul	*Hypsipetes leucocephalus*	[Square-tailed Bulbul, Himalayan Black Bulbul]
Black-crested Bulbul	*Pycnonotus melanicterus*	[Flame-throated Bulbul, Ruby-throated Bulbul]
Red-whiskered Bulbul	*Pycnonotus jocosus*	
Red-vented Bulbul	*Pycnonotus cafer*	
Yellow-throated Bulbul	*Pycnonotus xantholaemus*	
White-browed Bulbul	*Pycnonotus luteolus*	
Grey-headed Bulbul	*Brachypodius priocephalus*	
Yellow-browed Bulbul	*Acritillas indica*	
Passeriformes (Phylloscopidae)		
Hume's Leaf Warbler	*Abrornis humei*	Hume's Warbler, Mandelli's Leaf Warbler A. [h.] mandellii
Dusky Warbler	*Phylloscopus fuscatus*	Dusky Leaf Warbler
Common Chiffchaff	*Phylloscopus collybita*	Siberian Chiffchaff P. [c.] tristis
Tytler's Leaf Warbler	*Phylloscopus tytleri*	
Sulphur-bellied Warbler	*Phylloscopus griseolus*	Olivaceous Leaf warbler
Tickell's Leaf Warbler	*Phylloscopus affinis*	
Green Leaf Warbler	*Seicercus nitidus*	Bright-green Leaf Warbler
Greenish Leaf Warbler	*Seicercus trochiloides*	
Large-billed Leaf Warbler	*Seicercus magnirostris*	
Blyth's Leaf Warbler	*Seicercus reguloides*	
Western Crowned Leaf Warbler	*Seicercus occipitalis*	Large Crowned Leaf Warbler
Passeriformes (Scotocercidae)		
Pale-footed Bush Warbler	*Hemitesia pallidipes*	
Passeriformes (Sylviidae)		
Eastern Orphean Warbler	*Curruca crassirostris*	
Lesser Whitethroat	*Curruca curruca*	[Hume's Whitethroat, Desert Whitethroat, Small Whitethroat]
Yellow-eyed Babbler	*Chrysomma sinense*	

English Name	Scientific Name	Alternative Name(s)
Passeriformes (Zosteropidae)		
Oriental White-eye	*Zosterops palpebrosus*	
Passeriformes (Timaliidae)		
Rufous-throated Wren Babbler	*Spelaeornis caudatus*	Tailed Wren Babbler
Mishmi Wren Babbler	*Spelaeornis badeigularis*	Rusty-throated Wren Babbler
Bar-winged Wren Babbler	*Spelaeornis troglodytoides*	Spotted Long-tailed Wren Babbler
Naga Wren Babbler	*Spelaeornis chocolatinus*	Streaked Long-tailed Wren Babbler
Chin Hills Wren Babbler	*Spelaeornis oatesi*	Chin Hills Long-tailed Wren Babbler
Grey-bellied Wren Babbler	*Spelaeornis reptatus*	
Tawny-breasted Wren Babbler	*Spelaeornis longicaudatus*	Long-tailed Wren Babbler
Spotted Wren Babbler	*Elachura formosa*	Spotted Elachura, Spotted Short-tailed Wren Babbler
Red-billed Scimitar Babbler	*Pomatorhinus ochraceiceps*	Long-billed Scimitar Babbler
Coral-billed Scimitar Babbler	*Pomatorhinus ferruginosus*	[Phayre's Scimitar Babbler, Black-crowned Scimitar Babbler]
Slender-billed Scimitar Babbler	*Pomatorhinus superciliaris*	
Indian Scimitar Babbler	*Pomatorhinus horsfieldii*	
Tawny-bellied Babbler	*Dumetia hyperythra*	Rufous-bellied Babbler D. h. hyperythra, White-throated Babbler D. h. albogularis & D. h. abuensis
Dark-fronted Babbler	*Rhopocichla atriceps*	Black-headed Babbler
Striped Tit Babbler	*Mixornis gularis*	Yellow-breasted Babbler, Pin-striped Tit Babbler
Buff-chested Babbler	*Cyanoderma ambiguum*	Rufous-fronted Babbler/Red-fronted Babbler (with C. rufifrons)
Passeriformes (Pellorneidae)		
Puff-throated Babbler	*Pellorneum ruficeps*	Spotted Babbler
Abbott's Babbler	*Malacocincla abbotti*	
Passeriformes (Leiothrichidae)		
Quaker Tit Babbler	*Alcippe poioicephala*	Brown-cheeked Fulvetta, Quaker Babbler
Large Grey Babbler	*Argya malcolmi*	
Rufous Babbler	*Argya subrufa*	Indian Rufous Babbler
Common Babbler	*Argya caudata*	Scrub Babbler
Jungle Babbler	*Turdoides striata*	
Yellow-billed Babbler	*Turdoides affinis*	White-headed Babbler
Wynaad Laughingthrush	*Garrulax delesserti*	
Kerala Laughingthrush	*Trochalopteron fairbanki*	Grey-breasted Laughingthrush, White-breasted Laughingthrush, Palani Laughingthrush T. [f.] fairbanki, Travancore Laughingthrush T. [f.] meridionale
Black-chinned Laughingthrush	*Trochalopteron cachinnans*	Nilgiri Laughingthrush / Rufous-breasted Laughingthrush T. [c.] cachinnans, Banasura Laughingthrush / Coorg White-breasted Laughingthrush T. [c.] jerdoni
Passeriformes (Sittidae)		
Chestnut-bellied Nuthatch	*Sitta castanea*	[Indian Nuthatch]
Velvet-fronted Nuthatch	*Sitta frontalis*	
Beautiful Nuthatch	*Sitta formosa*	
Passeriformes (Sturnidae)		
Common Starling	*Sturnus vulgaris*	European Starling
Rosy Starling	*Pastor roseus*	Rosy Pastor
Asian Pied Starling	*Gracupica contra*	Pied Myna
Brahminy Starling	*Sturnia pagodarum*	Black-headed Myna, Brahminy Myna
Chestnut-tailed Starling	*Sturnia malabarica*	Grey-headed Myna; [Malabar Starling, Malabar White-headed Starling]
Common Myna	*Acridotheres tristis*	Indian Myna
Bank Myna	*Acridotheres ginginianus*	
Jungle Myna	*Acridotheres fuscus*	
Hill Myna	*Gracula religiosa*	[Southern Hill Myna, Lesser Hill Myna, Common Hill Myna]

English Name	Scientific Name	Alternative Name(s)
Passeriformes (Muscicapidae)		
Oriental Magpie Robin	*Copsychus saularis*	
White-rumped Shama	*Kittacincla malabarica*	[Andaman Shama]
Asian Brown Flycatcher	*Muscicapa dauurica*	
Brown-breasted Flycatcher	*Muscicapa muttui*	
Rusty-tailed Flycatcher	*Muscicapa ruficauda*	Rufous-tailed Flycatcher
White-bellied Shortwing	*Brachypteryx major*	[Rufous-bellied Shortwing, Nilgiri Shortwing, White-bellied Blue Robin, Nilgiri Blue Robin]
Indian Blue Robin	*Larvivora brunnea*	Indian Blue Chat
Bluethroat	*Luscinia svecica*	
Malabar Whistling Thrush	*Myophonus horsfieldii*	
Siberian Rubythroat	*Calliope calliope*	Rubythroat
Kashmir Flycatcher	*Ficedula subrubra*	Kashmir Red-breasted Flycatcher
Red-breasted Flycatcher	*Ficedula parva*	
Taiga Flycatcher	*Ficedula albicilla*	Red-throated Flycatcher
Ultramarine Flycatcher	*Ficedula superciliaris*	White-browed Blue Flycatcher F. s. superciliaris, Little Blue-and-white Flycatcher F. s. aestigma
Yellow-rumped Flycatcher	*Ficedula zanthopygia*	Korean Flycatcher
Black-and-orange Flycatcher	*Ficedula nigrorufa*	Black-and-rufous Flycatcher
Blue-capped Rock Thrush	*Monticola cinclorhyncha*	Blue-headed Rock Thrush
Blue Rock Thrush	*Monticola solitarius*	[Asian Rock Thrush]
Brown Rock Chat	*Oenanthe fusca*	Indian Chat
Passeriformes (Turdidae)		
Scaly Thrush	*Zoothera dauma*	Scaly Mountain Thrush, Small-billed Mountain Thrush/Small-billed Scaly Thrush Z. d. dauma; [Nilgiri Thrush]
Pied Thrush	*Geokichla wardii*	Pied Ground Thrush
Orange-headed Thrush	*Geokichla citrina*	Orange-headed Ground Thrush, White-throated Ground Thrush G. c. cyanota
Grey-winged Blackbird	*Turdus boulboul*	
Tickell's Thrush	*Turdus unicolor*	

INDEX